The Flying Machine and Modern Literature

The Flying Machine and Modern Literature

Laurence Goldstein

Indiana University Press
Bloomington

Manufactured in Great Britain

Library of Congress Cataloging-in-Publication Data
Goldstein, Laurence, 1943–
  The flying machine and modern literature

  Bibliography: p.
  1. American literature—20th century—History and
criticism. 2. Airplanes in literature. 3. Flying-
machines in literature. 4. Aeronautics in literature.
5. Flight in literature. 6. English literature—20th
century—History and criticism. I. Title.
PS228.A57G65   1986   810'.9'356   84–48043
ISBN 0–253–32218–9
  1 2 3 4 5   89 88 87 86

For
Andrew Goldstein
Jonathan Goldstein
junior birdmen of America

Contents

Preface

"Now the earth has been elevated symbolically into the heavens ... The old dichotomy between spirit and matter, God and man, is finished." Joseph Campbell's vatic pronouncement on the recent moon landings, in the July 1971 issue of *Psychology Today*, cannot help but provoke a smile in the less hubristic period of the 1980s. And yet his remark, steeped as it is in the ancient and modern mythologies of humankind, remains an essential part of the Apollo missions, just as the excited rhetoric permeating the earlier history of aviation tells us more accurately than statistics precisely what that history *meant* for those whose minds and lives were touched by a seemingly miraculous machine. My chief debt, I believe, after years of studying such texts, is to those critics like Campbell, Sacvan Bercovitch, Mircea Eliade, Michel Foucault, Northrop Frye, and Lewis Mumford who have enabled me to apprehend myths, texts, and machines as the interlocking parts of a dynamic cultural system.

My colleagues on the faculty and my students at the University of Michigan have listened to my discourses on the subject of flight for many years; I am grateful for their patience and advice. Of special assistance to me were the lively discussions in my graduate seminars on "Literature and Technology" during 1981–82.

For close and sympathetic readings of the manuscript my special thanks goes to Charles Baxter, Clive Hart, Scott Shuger, Barton St. Armand, Alan Wald and Robert Wohl – all of whom will see instances of their useful suggestions in this final version. I am also indebted for help in revision of individual chapters to Diane Ackerman, Rudolf Arnheim, Gorman Beauchamp, Donald L. Hill, Marjorie Perloff, Howard Segal, Jon Silkin, and Steven Zwicker.

A grant from the Horace Rackham School of Graduate Studies at the University of Michigan came at a crucial time in my researches, and financial aid from the College of Literature,

Science and the Arts helped me to prepare the manuscript for publication.

Earlier versions of three sections in this book appeared in journals: chapter 6 in *Prospects: An Annual of American Studies* (Vol. v), the portion of chapter 10 devoted to Robert Frost in *The Iowa Review*, and chapter 11 in the *Michigan Quarterly Review*. For permission to reprint in a revised form my thanks go to Jack Salzman and David Hamilton.

Finally, I want to acknowledge my chief debt, to Nancy Goldstein, whose years as an airline stewardess kept this subject tantalizingly alive in my imagination, and whose years as a one-person ground crew made possible the speculative flights and technical applications that produced this book.

Acknowledgments

Dick Allen, excerpt from "The Coming of the First Aeroplanes," from *Regions with No Proper Names*. Copyright © 1975 by Dick Allen. Reprinted by permission of the author.

William Rose Benét, excerpt from "The Ballad of Louis Blériot," from *With Wings as Eagles*. Copyright © 1940 by William Rose Benét. Reprinted by permission of Dodd, Mead & Company.

Paul Bewsher, excerpts from *The Bombing of Bruges*. Reprinted by permission of Hodder & Stoughton Limited.

Robert Bly, excerpts from "The Teeth Mother Naked at Last," from *Sleepers Joining Hands*. Copyright © 1970 by Robert Bly. Reprinted by permission of the author.

Hart Crane, excerpts from "Cape Hatteras," from *The Complete Poems and Selected Letters and Prose of Hart Crane*, edited by Brom Weber. Copyright © 1933, 1958, 1966 by Liveright Publishing Corporation. Reprinted by permission of Liveright Publishing Corporation.

James Dickey, excerpts from "The Firebombing," *Poems 1957–1967*. Copyright © 1964 by James Dickey. Reprinted by permission of Wesleyan University Press.

T. S. Eliot, excerpt from "Little Gidding" in *Four Quartets*. Copyright © 1943 by T. S. Eliot; renewed 1971 by Esme Valerie Eliot. Reprinted by permission of Harcourt Brace Jovanovich, Inc., and Faber and Faber Ltd.

Robert Frost, excerpts from "Kitty Hawk" and "For John F. Kennedy His Inauguration," from *The Poetry of Robert Frost*, edited by Edward Connery Lathem. Copyright © 1956, 1961, 1962 by Robert Frost. Copyright © 1969 by Holt, Rinehart and Winston. Reprinted by permission of Holt, Rinehart and Winston, Publishers.

Robinson Jeffers, excerpt from "Pelicans" from *Roan Stallion, Tamar and Other Poems*. Copyright © 1925 by Horace Liveright, Inc.; renewed 1953 by Robinson Jeffers. Reprinted by permission of Random House, Inc. "Shiva" from *The Selected*

Poetry of Robinson Jeffers. Copyright © 1938 by Robinson Jeffers; copyright renewed 1959 by Robinson Jeffers. Reprinted by permission of Random House, Inc.

Philip Levine, excerpt from "The Poem of Flight" from *One for the Rose*. Copyright © 1981 by Philip Levine. Reprinted by permission of Atheneum Publishers and the author.

C. Day Lewis, excerpts from "A Time to Dance" from *Collected Poems 1954*. Reprinted by permission of the Executors of the Estate of C. Day Lewis, The Hogarth Press, and Jonathan Cape Limited.

Robert Lowell, excerpt from "Moon Landings" from *History*. Copyright © 1973 by Robert Lowell. Reprinted by permission of Farrar, Straus & Giroux, Inc.

Louis MacNeice, excerpt from "Brother Fire" from *The Collected Poems of Louis MacNeice*. Reprinted by permission of Faber and Faber Publishers.

Selden Rodman, excerpt from *The Airmen: A Poem in Four Parts*. Copyright © 1941 by Selden Rodman. Reprinted by permission of the author.

Muriel Rukeyser, excerpts from "Theory of Flight" from *Collected Poems*. Copyright © 1935 and 1963 by Muriel Rukeyser. Reprinted by permission of International Creative Management, Inc.

Stephen Spender, "Air Raid Across the Bay at Plymouth" from *Collected Poems*. Copyright © 1955 by Stephen Spender. Reprinted by permission of Random House, Inc.

Allen Tate, excerpts from "Ode to Our Young Pro-Consuls of the Air" from *Collected Poems 1919–1976*. Copyright © 1959, 1960, 1965 by Allen Tate. Reprinted by permission of Farrar, Straus & Giroux.

W. B. Yeats, excerpt from "In Memory of Major Robert Gregory," "An Irish Airman Foresees His Death," from *The Poems of W. B. Yeats*, edited by Richard J. Finneran. Copyright © 1919 by Macmillan Publishing Co., Inc; renewed 1947 by Bertha Georgie Yeats. Reprinted by permission of Macmillan Publishing Company, Michael B. Yeats, and Macmillan London, Ltd.

List of Illustrations

The promoters of utility . . . follow the
footsteps of poets, and copy the sketches
of their creations in the book of common
life.
—Percy Bysshe Shelley, *A Defence of Poetry*

Real flight and dreams of flight go together.
Both are part of the same movement. Not A
before B, but all together.
—Thomas Pynchon, *Gravity's Rainbow*

1. Introduction

This book had its modest origin in an essay, projected but never written, on the similarities in rhetorical style of the Romantic poem addressed to a bird and the modern poem on the airplane. As I studied the matter, I found that the first aeronautical mechanics, from Leonardo da Vinci to Otto Lilienthal and Louis Mouillard, responded no less admiringly than poets to the bird's mysterious aura. Inspired as they were by the same natural object, poets and inventors sought, like the fabulous artificer Daedalus, to alter human nature by craft toward the common goal of privileging air over earth. The relations proved to be dialectical, one enthusiast prompting another toward an ultimate destiny in the heavens. It became clear to me that what needed description, then, was not only a species of literary influence but the complex transactions between the dreamers, makers, and landmark events of human flight. By a reading of texts that both document and contribute to the emergence of air-craft as a potent historical force, I have tried to define the cultural implications of the technological capture in this century of an oneiric creation.

Emerson's epithet for the bird – "Reality most like to dreams"[1] – effectively condenses most Romantic statements on the subject. Such dreams, though they initiated an experimental tradition culminating in the events at Kitty Hawk, have no datable beginning in human consciousness. The research of anthropologists and folklorists has uncovered no historical period – not even in the most archaic cultures – in which the desire for flight did not exist. Such a desire may be coeval with the category we call "human." "The longing to break the ties that hold him in bondage to the earth," Mircea Eliade writes, "is not a result of cosmic pressures or of economic insecurity – it is constitutive of man, in that he is a being who enjoys a mode of existence unique in the world. Such a desire to free himself from his limitations, which he feels to be a kind of degradation,

1

and to regain spontaneity and freedom . . . must be ranked among the specific marks of man."[2] The Romantic attention to birds, then, can be interpreted as a recent expression of a primordial envy. As *Homo signifex* observed the mysterious creatures in the sky, he could not resist the desire to impersonate them – and this mental action comprised his dawning consciousness of his distinct, and in some sense inferior, place in the Creation. The act of imitation carried forward by *Homo faber* of constructing the machinery of that desire was, by this definition, a later and inevitable development.

Such at least is the line of evolution proposed by Shelley in the first epigraph to this book. Wondering which came first, the reality or the dream, the bird or the yearning for flight which recognized the bird as an appropriate example, may seem an idle controversy. But the precise significance of aviation as a phenomenon depends on establishing precedence. If the bird is considered primary, the artifacts shaped in imitation of its perfection will have no more than a secondary mimetic value. Many of the earliest inventors expressed a deference toward their models that diminished the prestige of human ingenuity. Alberto Santos-Dumont declared in 1904, "Does man fly? No. Does the bird fly? Yes. Then, if man would fly, let him imitate the bird. Nature has made the bird. Nature never goes wrong."[3] Likewise Louis Mouillard set down his awed response to the flight of large vultures in Egypt: "When I saw these uncommon birds," he wrote Octave Chanute in 1891, "I was rendered immobile by this spectacle. I studied then that mode of flight which is the non plus ultra an aviator may dream of." These early mechanics exchanged practical suggestions for achieving parity with the prototype that inspired them, but the awesome, inimitable powers of their muse measured down their "making" capacity. "This bird," Mouillard wrote of the vulture, "not I, is the real author of my two books [on flight]. I am only a plain copyist, a poor photographer. This bird is much more explicit and more affirmative than I have ever been, despite my style as a prophet. This bird alone demonstrates; all I can do is to say: I have seen." When Mouillard finally hammered out his effective form of speech, "the greatest pair of articulated wings that ever existed on the globe," it proved a failure.[4]

That way lay despair and self-loathing, the appropriate emotions for technical incapacity. But as air-craft improved, and achieved the transformation at Kitty Hawk, the second kind of mimetic theory came into favor: inventors are no mere copiers of the superior attributes of the bird, but creators who draw principally upon the laws of physics they themselves have formulated. The Wright brothers, who acknowledged in early writings that they learned their wing-warping techniques from buzzards, insisted later on the uniqueness of their creation as a thing in its own right, obeying its own ontological laws. Orville wrote a correspondent:

> I cannot think of any part bird flight had in the development of human flight excepting as an inspiration. Although we intently watched birds fly in a hope of learning something from them I cannot think of anything that was first learned in that way. *After we had thought out certain principles, we then watched the bird* to see whether it used the same principles. In a few cases we did detect the same thing in the bird's flight.[5]

The primacy of human conception in this art – the word the Wrights consistently gave to their making – resembles the emphasis given to non-mimetic or abstract forms in the new century's aesthetics. The Romantic bird poem certainly must be called non-mimetic. Shelley's address to the skylark, "Bird thou never wert," has the force of a manifesto. The flying machine likewise desacralized the bird as a privileged member of the Creation. Once human beings accomplished heavier-than-air flight a new order of religious feeling evolved in which elect members of the community who participated in the mysteries of the winged life experienced the ecstasy resulting from an immediate apprehension of the infinite. Inevitably, the new forms of magical flight began to challenge the icons which preceded them – the Romantic bird, the risen Christ – for cultural dominance.

That aviation history would become a sacred history informed by the vocabulary and canonical shape of Scripture, was more apparent to the inventors than to the poets, who were slow to observe what Orville and Wilbur Wright, sons of a bishop in the United Brethren Church, saw at once. The Wrights and their admirers propagated what might be called an ecclesiastical view of the cause advanced so dramatically at Kitty Hawk. Such advocates conceived of aeronautics as part of the Creator's divine plan for mankind in the twentieth century. The recent success of another technological creation, the train, provided a useful precedent. Walt Whitman, who would have hailed the airplane if he had lived to see it, celebrated the locomotive as "Type of the modern – emblem of motion and power – pulse of the continent," and in one sense he was right.[6] A machine that could so diminish the sway of time and space seemed to inaugurate a millennium of happiness and prosperity for the commonwealth. In America, especially, the train, as later the airplane, absorbed into its complex symbolic meaning the native myth of manifest destiny, derived from the conception of America as a New Israel. Each new type of the modern before 1900 enhanced that myth, which benefited as well from two influential nineteenth-century articles of faith, the Idea of Progress and the Theory of Evolution. When Samuel Langley – himself an inventor of the flying machine – showed Henry Adams the Gallery of Machines at the Trocadero Exposition of 1900 in Paris, Adams recognized at once that the dynamo was another, and perhaps the ultimate, symbol of divinity for the power it possessed to transform matter into the unlimited forms of human desire.

Nothing better reveals the congruence of evangelical and Romantic modes than the zeal with which writers like Whitman and Adams brought tidings of irresistible technological energies. Whitman in "Song of the Exposition" can celebrate the new machines with the same fervor that Blake and Wordsworth greeted the apocalyptic promise of the French Revolution, but where those writers principally celebrated a demolition, symbolized by the fall of the Bastille, Whitman erects a superstructure upon the ruins of time:

> Mightier than Egypt's tombs,
> Fairer than Grecia's, Roma's temples,
> Prouder than Milan's statued, spired cathedral,
> More picturesque than Rhenish castle-keeps,
> We plan even now to raise, beyond them all,
> Thy great cathedral sacred industry, no tomb,
> A keep for life for practical invention.

In "Years of the Modern," Whitman prophesies something "unperform'd, more gigantic than ever" advancing to further the transfiguration of the world performed in his time by "the steamship, the electric telegraph, the newspaper, the wholesale engines of war." Similarly, Whitman's contemporary in France, Victor Hugo, foresaw in his so-called "Bible of Progress," *Légende des Siècles*, a flying machine, or "*aéroscaphe*," that would preside over a "future divine and pure" as it carried humanity's thoughts higher into the atmosphere, and finally to the stars.[7]

There is a less optimistic way of formulating the "technological sublime" succeeding upon the sublime of nature in the Romantic era. In historical surveys like Leo Marx's *The Machine in the Garden* (1964) and Herbert L. Sussman's *Victorians and the Machine* (1968), we see that most of the classic writers of the nineteenth century accommodated themselves to new inventions like the railroad with considerable wariness and distrust. Because these writers felt alienated from the forces of industrial change, they looked upon new phenomena intruding on a pastoral or genteel society as monstrous and inhumane, less a "great cathedral" than a version of Pandemonium, the sublime erection of the fallen angels in *Paradise Lost*. The aerial navies raining "ghastly dew" upon nations in Tennyson's "Locksley Hall"; the train in Dickens's *Dombey and Son*; the factories in *The Old Curiosity Shop* and *Hard Times*; the Pequod in Melville's *Moby Dick*, and the steamboat in Twain's *Huckleberry Finn* – these and kindred images symbolize the threatening power of the environment man had recently created. Like Victor Frankenstein in Mary Shelley's seminal version of the new Prometheanism, nineteenth-century man boldly dissolved the boundary of dream and reality in order to shape a dangerous destiny expressive of his science.

"Myth-history men must have; and if Christian myth-history fails them, they will find it elsewhere," Lynn White, Jr. remarks.[8] He makes the point that Darwin's *Descent of Man* (1871) obliterated the keystone of Christian myth-history, Adam and the Garden, sending a whole generation in search of new images to replace those in Genesis. As the title of White's book suggests, *Machina ex Deo*, he finds the universe of technology the place to seek such a sacred history. Technology, in this view, is the enabling mode of human salvation. Through his tools man constructs the great collective story of his evolution as God presumably intended. My own readings in modern literature have persuaded me that no area of technics embodies the new religious attitude so intensely for so long as aviation. The airplane was perceived immediately as a material counterpart of the aspiring spirit, with the enviable ability to fly clear of a creaturely realm characterized by confinement and decay. As a semi-magical instrument of ascent the flying machine offered to its apostles a form of *transport* in both familiar senses of that word. It provided a mobile and beatific vision of a new heaven and a new earth. It was inevitable that typology became a popular hermeneutical mode after Kitty Hawk offered the public a new beginning in its own time.

In conflating Genesis and the Nativity I have followed the interpretive practice of authors I study in this book. The orthodox theory of typology requires a *type* like Adam or Moses who prefigures the *antitype* Christ in the sacred history of the Christian church. The earliest inventors and writers had a model – the bird – but no historical figure whose ascent into the heavens could be cited as a useful precedent. The closest to a type for aviation was Daedalus, and to a degree he did serve as an exemplar for enthusiasts of the flying machine. One of the first important works on mechanical flight is Bishop John Wilkins's *Daedalus*, the second book of *Mathematical Magick* (1648), in which the author urged his readers to study the *volant automata* of legend and to experiment at making machines capable of carrying a human being. In 1742 Jean-Jacques Rousseau called attention to the wizard of Crete in his essay *Le Nouveau Dédale*, and praised "the ingenious men" who "have tried at different times and in diverse ways to open up a new route in the air."[9] In 1886, on the eve of aviation's nativity, Andrew Lang has his aeronautical inventor in *The Mark of Cain* invoke Daedalus for the same purpose:

> As soon as we get a whisper of civilisation in Greece, we find Daedalus successful in flying. . . . In Daedalus I see either a record of a successful attempt at artificial flight, or, at the very least, the expression of an aspiration as old as culture.[10]

The dramatic escape by Daedalus from the imprisoning labyrinth of Minos recalls the escape to freedom by Moses from bondage in Egypt and its New Testament parallel, the Resurrection of Christ. As a mythic figure, Daedalus promises deliverance from whatever characterizes the gravity-bound condition of man.

The myth had a secondary aspect that made it popular with those who were tempted to use it typologically. The death of his son Icarus overshadowed the father's creative success, rendering the use of wings a conventional symbol of vain mechanics. The fall of Icarus became a cautionary tale used against inventors to preach resignation to one's terrestrial lot. If a "tower-jumper" was tempted to invoke Daedalus before leaping into the air on homemade wings, his invariable humiliation deepened the association of flight and Icarus. As the Wright brothers and other inventors pursued their dream of wings they were no doubt haunted and taunted by the popular ballad of John Townsend Trowbridge, "Darius Green and His Flying Machine" (1880), with its comic lapse:

> he's goin' to fly!
> Away he goes! Jiminy! what a jump!
> Flop-flop – an plump
> To the ground with a thump!
> Flutt'rin' an' flound'rin', all'n a lump!

Precisely because the Wright brothers and their *Flyer* succeeded where every Icarus figure had failed, they achieved Christic identity. They were routinely praised – as Lindbergh was later – for "redeeming" Icarus as Christ redeemed the fallen Adam.

The brothers made no such claims for themselves, content to wait upon others to fashion the myth-history in which their invention would take its place as a nativity. But if it were ever to be a type of the modern, the "bird" they displaced into history had to possess a legitimate claim to its unique position. Without agreement on a comprehensive definition of what a flying machine was, it would be impossible to disqualify the many predecessors of the Wrights, including the balloonists, whose inventions fell short of the *Flyer*'s unique authority. The unremitting patent suits in which the Wrights defended their authorship of the first airplane must be seen not just as a means of protecting their financial investment, but as an assertion of what Wilbur called "the real truth" of origins. "The world owed the invention to us, and to no one else," he remarks of the crucial system of control, and elsewhere, "It must always be remembered that today [1911] when everyone knows the Wright invention, *and the world has assigned certain words to describe it*, those words now produce a mental picture which they did not and could not produce when men knew nothing of this method of

control."[11] The sacred history of flight in this century begins
with those testamentary words. As Northrop Frye has pointed
out in regard to the Book of Genesis, new forms of life are *spoken*
into existence by God as a model for the naming and narrativizing
that constitute the communal myth thereafter.[12] Nobody before
Kitty Hawk had formulated so precisely and successfully the
new being upon which this belated "great cathedral sacred
industry" had taken form. That aviation established a fixed
origin for its ceremonial calendar so close to the beginning of
the century seemed providential in retrospect. Henry Adams
had noted the appropriate emergence of the dynamo at the Paris
Exposition of 1900, but within a few years others would claim
that God's revelation had more significantly appeared in
paradigmatic aerial events – the ritual "firsts" of aviation
history – as a sign of His unfolding design for the epoch to come.

It is common to speak of technological history as autotelic:
an invention generates its own future forms and its cultural
imperatives, realizing its evolutionary potential *qua* machine.
The society into which the new invention intrudes must simply
adapt to its powers for good or ill. But closer examination of the
evidence suggests that historical circumstances play a more vital
role than is usually acknowledged. Certainly this is true of the
flying machine, which might have languished for decades as a
personal plaything had it not been for the infusion of financial
support directed toward the goal of military implementation.
The earliest writers on the flying machine deserve some credit
for insuring that – in the words of Thomas Pynchon I have used
as the second epigraph to this book – real flight and dreams of
flight went together. Two writers, especially, imagined a military
destiny for the airplane that history lost little time in fulfilling.
The first was H. G. Wells, whose scientific romances from *The
War of the Worlds* (1898) to *The War in the Air* (1908) popularized
the image of the flying machine as an agent of universal holocaust.
The second was F. T. Marinetti, founder of Futurism, who
described the airplane as a "cruel razor of speed" in his manifesto
War, the World's Only Hygiene (1911–15). Because Marinetti's
aesthetics of force and mechanics corresponds so closely to
Leonardo da Vinci's Daedalean efforts to construct a *volo
strumentale*, and because Leonardo was universally regarded in
the early decades of the century as a model of the technological
imagination, it seemed essential to begin my study with an

investigation of this supremely air-minded personality. As Freud recognized in his monograph of 1910, Leonardo's obsession with the flying machine informs twentieth century fantasies of ultimate power in the most significant way.

Leonardo's example illuminates the meditations on ascent surveyed in the second chapter, "Birds with a Human Face." Romantic literature carries forward in surprising ways the Christian and scientific views of the flying machine popular in the Renaissance, as well as the neurotic yearnings to be a "birdman" that have their fullest expression in the Futurist idolatry of the flier. Set against this background, as it must be, the scenario of Wells's *The War in the Air*, to which I devote my third chapter, assumes the dimensions of higher prophecy than the merely predictive. From this point I trace the landmark events of aerial progress as each is incorporated into an increasingly coherent typological structure. First there is the Great War, which Wells's fiction and the fulminations of Futurism anticipated in so many ways. Though the airplane acquired a certain glamor during The Great Crusade it could not avoid associations with the victims of its bombs. The "Knights of the Air" who became celebrities for their daring exploits nevertheless required a greater paladin to redeem their violent deeds in order for the airplane to reenter the historical record as a legitimate part of the romance of progress.

It would have given this book, and the history it interprets, a perfect symmetry if this redemptive figure had been the admiral named Byrd – he did in fact help to win public support for aviation. There is no question, however, that Charles A. Lindbergh's transatlantic flight of 1927 was universally regarded as the fulfillment of the events at Kitty Hawk. The rainbow arc sculpted in the upper air by his flight to the City of Lights represented a revival of the covenant violated by the demonic events of the Great War. The first interpreters of Lindbergh's flight associated his solo exploit with almost every myth in Western culture. They glorified him as a modern hero and his flight as a synthesis of older religions of heaven and modernist faith in the new order of machinery. Lindbergh's success made possible the creation of a coherent myth-history in which origins were finally canonized and a renaissance of the spirit triumphantly announced.

In the foreshortened history of aviation, however, it is a small step from resurrection to Armageddon. The bombings of the Spanish Civil War and World War II, the onset of rocket technology, and the events at Hiroshima and Nagasaki, diverted writers from the happier literary models of panegyric, romance, sacramental history, and epic, which thrived during the 1930s, and sent them to the only text they could find that accounts for the afflictions of midcentury, The Book of Revelation. For Americans, especially, who inherited the powers alchemized during the war, the manifest destiny of their native myth took on an increasingly oneiric or visionary character. Science fiction seemed the only response appropriate to a historical moment when, as Norman Mailer writes in the context of the Apollo project, "the real had become more fantastic than the imagined." [13] The content of science fiction is usually space travel, an apparent revival of the paradigmatic magical flight signified earlier by Kitty Hawk and Lindbergh's crossing. But the romance of interplanetary travel, as it was commonly called, reminded many writers of the craving for new wildernesses that had spoiled successive Edens in Western history. The moon landing of 1969 raised anew the essential questions of the flying machine's nature and destiny. Had it been an exterminating angel all along, as Wells prophesied? Or could it still be imagined as a benign form of transport that insured our salvation in the body by carrying human presence and human purpose not only from terrestrial place to place but further into the cosmos?

This synopsis of the study that follows will suggest the diachronic model that emerged from my first investigations into the links between Romantic and modern expressions of awe for the act of flight. Given the obvious, indeed overwhelming importance of the flying machine in the twentieth century, a period shaped in no small part by air power, it was inevitable that those writers who self-consciously constructed a canon appropriate to contemporary signs and wonders would have recourse to typology and allegory as interpretive modes. My reading of masterpieces in the field, with a selection of minor texts from popular culture, persuades me that the myth-history described above provides the most accurate framework for an understanding of this tradition. Though the literature of every nation is richly endowed with commentaries on the flying machine, I have confined myself almost entirely to English and American works because it seems essential to illustrate how the conventions within a single linguistic family so often determine the shape and voice of individual texts. Especially in America, site of crucial events from Kitty Hawk to the Apollo 11 mission, the self-referential character of this tradition demands a clear focus. When the impact of non-English works has been significant, however, as in the case of Leonardo da Vinci, Jules Verne, and Antoine de Saint-Exupéry, I have made such texts welcome in my own. The privileged place given to literary analysis throughout is intended to feature the history of aviation *as myth*. The multiplication of examples, for which I ask the reader's patience, better guarantees that ideological distortions will not follow upon a too-limited choice of texts or events.

However complex the interrelationships, there is a sense in which I have been faithful to my original intention to compare and contrast Romantic bird poems with modern airplane poems. The chief similarity between those two modes is a binary opposition between earth and sky, mortality and immortality, body and spirit, by which an earthly observer expresses an envious desire to leap into the aerial form he apprehends above him. When men become as birds they look down upon the earth with the kind of cruel condescension appropriate to a "scorner of the ground," as Shelley calls the skylark. In modern literature, at last, the Romantic bird is given an intelligible song – and it is rarely the "sweet thoughts" of Shelley's melodist that flow into print. Cecil Lewis captures a typical sentiment when he remarks from the cockpit:

Men! Standing, walking, talking, fighting, there beneath me! I saw them for the first time with detachment, dispassionately: a strange, pitiable, crawling race, to us who strode the sky. Why, God might take the air and come within a mile of earth and never know there were such things as men. Vain the heroic gesture, puny the great thought! Poor little maggoty men![14]

The magnification of self when aloft – Lewis clearly identifies his elevated position with God's – corresponds to the self-depreciation produced by the pathology of envy. For this reason modern writers on aviation provide us with some of the most intriguing commentary on Romantic psychology, both when they indulge in aerial perspective and when they keep their feet on the ground.

The airplane is one form of what Frank Kermode defines as a Romantic Image, a figure of determinable presence which also participates in a timeless order of existence. By achieving magical flight the airplane retains its identity with the "immortal bird" (Keats) of Romantic myth, yet at the same time its adaptability in a society that makes routine use of its powers historicizes it as an image. Like the icons in Melville's *Typee* which the natives pray to, and then beat with a stick when their prayers go unanswered, the flying machine has always been the object of double vision. As technological improvements made it more viable, social units like the airmail service, the airline industry, the Air Force, and NASA proliferated, each adding an earth-centered component to the "blithe Spirit" (Shelley). The utilitarian associations did not pull the Romantic Image from the sky, however, but paradoxically intensified and renewed the need for transcendent visions afforded by some new form of the same machine: real flight stimulated a responsive dream of flight equal in power.

These dynamics are worth emphasis in a period when the use of technological materials in serious literature, and especially the airplane, tends more often than not to the negative. Theodore Roszak's lament for the demystification of flight in *Where the Wasteland Ends* insists that no positive usage is possible. Likewise, in Wylie Sypher's *Literature and Technology: The Alien Vision* the rage for order represented by most technology is revealed as a sickness of our time. In a recent essay Robert Beum casts a cold eye back on the claims of *machinisme* earlier in the century, and editorializes: "Modern technics and its products refuse to symbolize anything except negation on the one hand and [the] march of science and commerce, of materialization and materialism on the other. The march has much to do with politics and rhetoric but nothing to do with the instinctive ends of great literature: the strengthening of personal consciousness and the wakening of spiritual desire."[15] I too believe that negation, the annihilation of life as we know it, is one meaning of the flying machine in modern history, but I take exception to the categorical denial of worth to the entire tradition. Beum's collapse of all technological metaphors into the single one of "cancer" suggests that he, like most technophobes, has his own political motives. In an era when rocket technology has endangered the planet's survival, such hostility is understandable. But the literature Beum and others neglect or misrepresent, and certainly the literature of flight, may yield precisely the light they demand from authentic and sacred texts. I have proceeded on this assumption, in any case. Without consenting to the shibboleths of either the advocates or enemies of *machinisme* I have tried in this book to represent the full range of responses to the most fascinating of modern inventions.

2. Leonardo da Vinci and the Modern Century

> He was cruel, as God is.
> —Rachel Annand Taylor[1]

By the time Rachel Annand Taylor published *Leonardo the Florentine* in 1928 her subject was universally considered the peerless forerunner of "the modern," however that term was defined. In the twentieth century Leonardo had become a strategic redoubt which opposing world views struggled to claim as conquest. Taylor, a mystical poet, rightly believed that her own party of aestheticism and spiritual idealism had first occupied the field, but in the postwar period she had watched the reputation of Leonardo's notebooks, published in full only recently, almost overshadow that of his paintings. The massive accumulation of empirical observation and technological designs in the *Codice Atlantico* persuaded a growing majority that Leonardo had been primarily a latter-day Daedalus who could serve modern engineers as a type of their profession. "What kind of man was Leonardo?" asked Elbert Hubbard in a widely read pamphlet of 1902. "Why he was the same kind of man as Edison. ... Both are classics and therefore essentially modern."[2] This perspective on Leonardo received broad distribution thanks to H. G. Wells's *The Outline of History* (1920), which dwells exclusively on Leonardo's scientific accomplishments. By 1927, when Emil Ludwig's *Genius and Character* was translated into English, a majority of readers probably would have agreed with Ludwig's conclusion that it was Leonardo's practice of the experimental method, not his art, that made him "the greatest pathfinder of the new Occident."[3] If the positivist view prevailed, then the renaissance of spirit that Taylor looked for in the ferment of the 1920s might be corrupted further by the mechanistic thinking she deplored and which till then had lacked a champion of Leonardo's luster.

Drawing upon Walter Pater's chapter on Leonardo in *The Renaissance* (1873), the most influential of the many studies published during the half-century before World War I, Taylor portrays Leonardo as a "sheer aesthete" (p. 499), who, as the title of her book suggests, never escaped the formative influences of Lorenzo de Medici's glittering court and the Florentine Academy of Marsilio Ficino. She acknowledges the appeal of mechanics to Leonardo in his later years but insists that he designed only on paper fantastic conceptions that satisfied his "ruthless curiosity" (p. 31), never condescending to actually build machines for civic improvement. Leonardo's saving grace, Taylor asserts, was a contempt for public opinion which the common mind judges "cruel" but which higher minds understand as a divine prerogative. Taylor interprets the recent praise of Leonardo's inventions as a revenge of the masses upon his genius, for how better to domesticate him than to publicize him as a fabricator of crude versions of newly achieved industrial products?

Taylor's counterattack takes the form of biographical recreation, a cataloguing of the historical particulars that nourished Leonardo's artistic sensibility. (By contrast, Paul Valéry disdains historicism in his essays of 1894 and 1929 on Leonardo, the better to criticize a vocabulary like Pater's and establish Leonardo's credentials as "an authentic and immediate ancestor of science as it exists today."[4]) Like others in the aesthetic movement Taylor argues for renewed appreciation of the centrality of Renaissance Florence as a rationale for prolonged attention to milieu. Situated midway between the Near East and Western Europe, with sea and land routes to the whole world, the Italian city-states believed that the density of Occidental culture depended on their *invenzioni*, but Florence more than any was the nucleus of the new Hellenistic civilization. Of special relevance to Taylor's Rosicrucian sympathies, Florence was the center for astronomical studies. She emphasizes the habitual conversations about superlunary realms that Leonardo must have enjoyed with astronomers like Paolo del Pozzo Toscanelli and Carlo Marmocchio.

Here Taylor may have been influenced by Oswald Spengler's conception of the Faustian character of the Italian Renaissance, its essentially Gothic expression of "infinity-wistfulness" of which Leonardo is called the chief practitioner. In Spengler's schema the decline of the West can be perceived as a devolution from the stage of self-contained *culture* to a *civilization* characterized by expansive tendencies of a demonic kind. Taylor seems to adapt this schema when she describes Leonardo's emigration from Florence to Milan, at the age of thirty, as a descent into a worldly society diseased by ambition. It was to the Duke of Milan, Lodovico Sforza, whom Taylor compares to Macbeth, that Leonardo addressed his notorious letter seeking employment as a military technician, bragging of his ability to construct machines of mass destruction. Taylor sees Leonardo's settlement in a city that valued mechanics above all things as a fall into time which obscured his transcendent vision, until his return to Florence in the early 1500s when he regathered his powers in the service of divine conceptions like the Mona Lisa and Leda.

Taylor's book could not have appeared at a worse time for her message to take effect. Even as she deprecated the significance of Leonardo's engineering designs their realization in the form of airplanes was being hailed as the fulfillment of Renaissance aspirations. The accomplishments of Richard Byrd and Charles Lindbergh, especially, had directed renewed attention to Leonardo's efforts to construct a flying machine that would elevate man above his limited nature. One captures the synchronism of historical periods in Edward MacCurdy's *The Mind of Leonardo da Vinci* (also 1928), when the author breaks off his discussion of Leonardo's experiments to announce that "the air is still ringing with the news of Lindbergh's achievement," an event MacCurdy describes as a consummation of Leonardo's prophecy in 1505 that when his "great bird" takes flight it will fill "the whole world with amazement" and "all records with its fame; and it will bring eternal glory to the nest where it was born."[5] As Spengler fixed upon the discovery of the telescope as the moment when the vault of heaven opened to reveal the infinity that Western man must henceforth seek to fill with his presence and passion for order, so MacCurdy seizes upon a mechanical triumph to characterize the legitimacy of Leonardo's claim upon the twentieth century.

Taylor's biography, by contrast, treats Leonardo's engineering designs with scathing contempt. Citing his definition of mechanics as "the paradise of mathematics," Taylor remarks,

"The fruits he gathered in this peculiar paradise were of the Dead Sea, for, all unconscious, this love of beauty helped to prepare the Mechanical Age" (p. 538). Taylor's previous book, *The End of Fiametta* (1923), comprises 243 poems without a single reference to an artifact unique to the nineteenth or twentieth century. With the same programmatic fervor she carries into her biography an ideology that owes less to Pater than to Savonarola, who had perpetuated in Leonardo's time the medieval belief that the mechanical arts had no dignity. This prejudice brought her book much criticism, but, as we shall see, her single-mindedness yields an interpretation of Leonardo's career that illuminates all other responses in this century to the flying machine as a fact and symbol.

THE ANNUNCIATION

There are two originating impulses which lie behind Leonardo's fascination with aerodynamics, and I hope to show that they are inextricably linked in his imagination. The first is a conventional identification of the celestial sphere and its inhabitants as a place of infinite power; the second is an obsession with artifacts that allow mankind to overcome the limitations of time and space. It is because in his career the two interests cohere into one that he achieved the reputation of being, in Michelet's phrase, "the Italian brother of Faust," a title that Leonardo would not have disavowed in its positive aspect. "Man is subject to heaven," he wrote, a gesture of piety reflecting orthodox belief, then added, "but heaven is subject to reason."[6] A sacred order can be made to serve human designs.

Leonardo inherited his appreciation of the celestial from the various religious and philosophical traditions actively studied in Florence during his apprenticeship in Verrocchio's *bottega* from age sixteen to age thirty. Florence remained a principal European center for Platonic and Neoplatonic studies, and though Ernst Cassirer calls Leonardo a Platonist *despite* the influence of the Florentine Academy, he acknowledges the probable impact of ideas popularized by the Academy, especially the doctrine of Eros, based upon the *Symposium*, which honored artists for their ability to reveal correspondences of higher and lower realms of being.[7] The Aristotelian tradition impressed Leonardo even more forcibly. MacCurdy points out that in Leonardo's manuscripts there are more references to Aristotle than to any other writer.

It is useful to perceive Aristotle's presence and influence through the medium of Dante, the one poet Leonardo seems to have studied carefully. In Dante the journey of life is dramatized as an ascent from appetitive desires toward the fulfillment of intellectual – that is, more spiritual – yearnings. The ascent occurs not by chronological progress through the stages of life, but by a heightening or broadening of perception. Natural phenomena belong to a living system which it is man's obligation to understand as a whole even as he perceives it moment by moment in discrete parts. Leonardo writes, "The eye, which is called the window of the soul, is the chief means whereby the understanding may most fully and abundantly appreciate the infinite works of nature" (p. 852). The model for the eye's (the soul's) gradual expansion of power is given in *The Divine Comedy*, in which Dante is first shown, in *The Inferno*, the dark forms of earthly desires and then is guided by figures of higher reason – Virgil and Beatrice – upward into realms of light, ultimately to the Empyrean Paradise which lies beyond the stars and the outermost crystalline sphere or primum mobile.

Dante's example is crucial because as an artist he necessarily rendered his vision in concrete form. Of Dante one must say, as Karl Jaspers does of Leonardo, "For him, to *know* is to *reproduce*."[8] Expansion of understanding must be made manifest by visionary depiction of the secondary creation, which formally expresses the dynamic "reason" of the divine I AM. In his treatise on painting Leonardo asserts that "the divinity which is the science of painting transmutes the painter's mind into a resemblance of the divine mind."[9] The artistic work which aspires to a perfection of seeing must make the infinite a part of its visible design. Just as Dante converted the physical presence of Beatrice, a Florentine girl, into a figure of divine mercy, so Leonardo the painter undertook to render created forms in their spiritual glory. The viewer must be willing to participate in this enterprise, as Dante the literary character must follow his wiser guides step by step to the contemplation of God.

Certainly this is true of Leonardo's first important painting. In the Uffizi *Annunciation* the viewer must actively appreciate the dynamic significance of the familiar scene. First, there is the madonna at right, a carnal being, a figure of the phenomenal world of generation and decay that is secular time. But a viewer does not so much see Mary, a beautiful woman resembling the portraits of Florentine ladies, as see *within her* the ultimate divinity, descended from heaven, which she incorporates. The archangel Gabriel's function in the scene is to awaken the viewer's soul to a fundamental mystery of Christian philosophy: that spirit participates in the life of matter as a formal influence, and by doing so redeems time and gives it a sacred meaning. That divine spirit is "perceptible" only by the understanding which sees through the eye, the window of the soul, in order to apprehend the holy power of which it is suddenly conscious of being a part. As in natural philosophy so in mystical philosophy, the respondent must move, in meditation, from smaller evidences to capacious conceptions. *The Annunciation* contains the Resurrection and the Last Judgment; these scenes are no less latent in the painting than the impending birth of the divine child.

The depicted scene, then, increases in intensity as the viewer's eye receives support from the understanding. Cues are present in the painting for this spiritual ascent. An invisible line connects the angel's upraised hand with the Virgin's womb. The terrace setting reveals in the background not only trees and mountains, which lift the eye upward, but the harbor town as well, with its tall towers, sharp conical roofs and pointed gables. The horizontal line of the trees is blocked in part by the angel's wing, which serves the same significatory function as an emblem of heaven. The wing is overpainted, obscuring Leonardo's more birdlike wing, for he wished to draw attention to the natural creature most firmly linked in the human imagination with the motion of ascent. Gabriel is iconographically related to the dove or holy spirit descending from heaven in so many medieval and Renaissance paintings, including Verrocchio's *Baptism of Christ*, to which Leonardo contributed an angelic figure. The absence of the dove in *The Annunciation* reveals that Mary has already conceived; in pictorial terms its absence removes the apex of the conventional triangle in paintings of the Annunciation, and thus focuses attention more directly upon the winged human figure. Raymond S. Stites has pointed out that Gabriel's face is a copy of Leonardo's earliest self-portrait.[10] This suggestion of narcissism may give us a clue as to Leonardo's persistence later in constructing a flying machine on the angelic model, a large wing on each arm.

The rigidity of perspective construction in *The Annunciation* recalls *The Last Supper*, but as with that later work the viewer feels the formal elements as a containment of tremendous forces embodied in the dramatic situation. In effect the Annunciation as a motif can be viewed as a supremely challenging problem in the science of physics. Notice, for example, how Leonardo's definition of force applies to the subject of the painting:

> Force I define as a spiritual power, incorporeal and invisible, which with brief life is produced in those bodies which as the result of accidental violence are brought out of their natural state and condition. [p. 68]

This definition must be juxtaposed with a famous passage from elsewhere in the notebooks:

> Behold now the hope and desire of going back to one's own country or returning to primal chaos, like that of the moth to the light, of the man who with perpetual longing always looks forward with joy to each new spring and each new summer, and to the new months and the new years, deeming that the things he longs for are too slow in coming; and who does not perceive that he is longing for his own destruction. But this longing is in its quintessence the spirit of the elements, which finding itself imprisoned within the life of the human body desires continually to return to its source.
>
> And I would have you to know that this same longing is in its quintessence inherent in nature, and that man is a type of the world. [p. 75]

Life, obedient to the laws of physics, is only perceptible as a moment's organization of universal energies proceeding at greater or lesser speed toward extinction. Force or energy compels everything it engages to change shape and lose its original freedom in the act of accommodation. The Christian story of the Incarnation, then, is a special case of a familiar physical principle. Christ becomes a man, a "type of the world," by entering the generational process symbolized by the carnal Mary. At the end of his metamorphosis, having made of his infinite being "the spirit of the elements," he returns to the heavenly source of motive power. Though they are commonly opposed as philosophies, the

Christian myth, interpreted by someone as uninterested in eschatology as Leonardo, is a version of Aristotelian *physis*, a closed historical cycle of birth, growth, and death. The "accidental violence" done to Mary by the agency of a dove constrains her in an inescapable natural cycle. Leonardo's distance from her is measured by his self-portraiture as the angel; she is Humanity in need of salvation from imprisonment in time and space. The mechanism of that salvation is knowledge of the spirit rendered or reproduced in paintings such as this one. Another kind of release is implied, however. A counterforce to entropy in the form of a birdlike instrument of ascent would transform Humanity, including the painter Leonardo da Vinci, into a figure mediating between divine and human conditions.

Edward MacCurdy hypothesized in 1928 that Leonardo drew his inspiration for the angel in *The Annunciation* from a bas-relief designed by Giotto and executed by Andrea Pisano at the base of the campanile of the Church of Santa Maria del Fiore in Florence. The relief represents Daedalus in the act of trying his artificial wings. MacCurdy, intoxicated by the recent history of aviation, did not hesistate to proclaim that Leonardo's first view of this artwork was the precise origin of his conception of a mechanism of flight. The identification is so unlikely as to be almost preposterous, but MacCurdy's naive connection reveals something very important about twentieth-century interest in Leonardo and the flying machine: that Leonardo's commitment to a view of life in terms of physics and mechanics, so intense that he could assimilate Christian beliefs into it, made him a superb representative of the modern century.

MacCurdy credits his discovery of the relation between Leonardo's angelic imagination and the flying machine to his attendance at the aviation meeting at Brescia in 1909. (Franz Kafka's "The Aeroplanes at Brescia" is still the best account.) On that occasion Luca Beltrami published a groundbreaking article on Leonardo and the airplane, reprinted the next year in *Leonardo da Vinci, Conferenze Fiorentine*, a volume of papers dealing with Leonardo's seminal influence on modern culture. The air show was a visible exhibition of what Leonardo knew to be true of aeronautics but failed to achieve in viable form. Left unmentioned by MacCurdy is another event of that year not unconnected to the excitement of the air show: the publication of the first manifestos of the Futurist movement. Italian Futurism, the first significant aesthetic to make a religion of physics and mechanics, employed the airplane as a new organ of perception on the model of Leonardo's innovative use of aerial perspective. From Giovanni Papini's proto-Futurist proclamations in the boisterous journal *Leonardo* (1903–7) to the 1913 sequence of drawings by Giacomo Balla of swifts in imitation of Leonardo's studies, the Renaissance master haunted the new movement.

The ecstasy of forceful release from limits is the supreme ideal that underlies the Futurist adoration of the machine – an homage manifest most strikingly in the postwar "aeropainting" of Gerardo Dottori, among others, and in the many poems – like F. T. Marinetti's "To the Automobile" and Liber Altomare's "To an Aviator" – which apotheosize new inventions. "We cooperate with Mechanics," Marinetti wrote in 1911, "in destroying the old poetry of distances and wild solitudes ... for which we substitute the tragic lyricism of ubiquity and omnipresent speed." Mechanics can render human longings as even art cannot, for the machine performs what the represented image only depicts. The machine is "the spirit of the elements" set in motion by an act of will and, in the case of the automobile and the airplane, capable of attaining that ubiquity and acceleration for which man has always envied the birds ... and the angels. Writers influenced by Futurism – Guillaume Apollinaire, D. H. Lawrence, Hart Crane – soon began comparing either the pilot or the flying machine itself to the figure of Christ. "We already live in the absolute," Marinetti wrote, "because we have discovered speed."[11]

Here then is the nightmare from which Rachel Annand Taylor tried to awaken her audience: a vision of Mechanics as Paradise in which Daedalus – and by association Leonardo – becomes a type of the modern religion of machinery. It is essential to notice, however, that Leonardo himself steps back from such a philosophy of dynamism. In his parables – the most emphatic of his moral sayings – he tends to counsel against overreaching. He describes how the arrogant ivy branching across the high road is broken by passersby; the hawk chasing the duck into the water is drowned; the eagle by descending too low gets its wings smeared with birdlime and is captured and killed. Or consider his depiction of ambitious water:

The water on finding itself in the proud sea, its element, was seized with a desire to rise above the air; and aided by the element of fire having mounted up in thin vapour, it seemed almost as thin as the air itself; and after it had risen to a great height it came to where the air was more rarefied and colder, and there it was abandoned by the fire; and the small particles being pressed together were united and became heavy; and dropping from thence its pride was put to rout, and it fell from the sky, and was then drunk up by the parched earth, where for a long time it lay imprisoned and did penance for its sin. [p. 1072]

In this allegory the "pride" which causes "a desire to rise above the air" leads to self-destruction in the form of an imprisonment. One thinks of Satan at the conclusion of *The Inferno*. When Leonardo is in this mood he is an ardent anti-technologist. "The knife, an artificial weapon, deprives man of his nails – his natural weapon," he writes (p. 1073). Mechanics diminishes man's actual capabilities and makes him dependent on prosthesis and invention for well-being. The *vita activa*, in other words, constantly exposes creatures to the experience of the Fall within the hierarchy of natural kinds and types. The *vita contemplativa*, of which painting is a kindred pacific expression, has the best chance of preserving the spirit from corruption by the accidents of worldly fortune.

If this description may be said to apply to the "medieval" Leonardo, the immaterialist and mystic whom Taylor praises as the essential Florentine, then how can we account for the designer of flying machines, the inventor who yearns to steal the principles of flight from the birds he envies? Taylor took this to be the central question of Leonardo's career, and one with enormous implications for the modern world. "The dream of Icarus," she writes, "is Leonardo's most passionate dream; it is the supreme fantasy where emotional desires and intellectual powers are at one; it is his unique image, his symbolic vision of himself as a god in that unprecedented ascendancy" (p. 265). It is also, she writes, an example of his "serene inhumanity" and a precedent which the ironics of history had caused to threaten civilization itself in her own time. As her comparison to Icarus suggests, Leonardo's fall into the watery chaos of the material world, into the *vita activa*, can be read as a premonitory fable of the decline of the West.

THE NECROMANCER

There are various theories about the derivation of Leonardo's interest in flight. I have cited MacCurdy's hypothesis that Giotto's design of a Daedalus figure inspired the youthful Leonardo, and there have been source studies tracing the possible influence of Eilmer of Malmesbury, Roger Bacon, Albertus Magnus, and especially Regiomantanus, as well as craftsmen from the near-legendary Archytas who in 400 B.C. launched a wooden pigeon in southern Italy, to G. B. Danti who is credited with the first attempt to fly with moving wings, in 1498, in Perugia. More recently, Clive Hart has drawn attention to Giovanni da Fontana's aerodynamical speculations in a treatise of 1420 which influenced scientists and military strategists.[12]

What seems the clearest immediate cause of Leonardo's researches has been neglected by scholars, with the exception of Rachel Annand Taylor, whose interest in Leonardo's "cruelty" led her to insist on the connection between the artist's first enthusiastic projects in mechanical engineering at Lodovico Sforza's court in Milan and the drawings of flying machines of the same period. It seems undeniable that in Milan Leonardo encountered a philosophy of the *vita activa* that directed his constructivist talents into channels of military invention. Milan was a city where the view of statecraft later made famous by Machiavelli flourished in its first strength. The cornerstone of this secular ideal was the necessity of educating the Prince of a nation-state in the arts of war. "A Prince should ... have no other aim or thought, nor take up any other things for his study, but war and its organization and discipline," Machiavelli wrote in *The Prince*, "for that is the only art that is necessary to one who commands."[13] Milan's major industry was the manufacture of arms, and its leaders encouraged the study of warfare as an exact science. Leonardo's letter of application to Lodovico suggests that he envisioned his work in Milan to be a series of inventions that would perpetuate the Duke's power by defensive and offensive military means.

The art of war during the Renaissance demanded an acute knowledge of aerodynamical and ballistic principles. In Leonardo's time, a century after the invention of the cannon, the high-walled castle was rendered obsolete by the growing strength of siege artillery. As a way of opening more distance between deadly cannon fire and vulnerable fortresses, the science of warfare began to stress the importance of outflanking buildings from which crossfires and pincer attacks could be mounted. For the attacker – Milan at this time had recently overwhelmed neighboring towns – the chief requirement was the penetration of a defense curtain by well-aimed firepower. Catapults and cannons had to have a longer range than usual, and we can see in Leonardo's designs during this period how the element of sheer size and velocity became paramount, as in his machines for projectiles and his giant crossbow. But the strategic problem remained that an opposing army could maneuver secretly behind a curtain of fortifications (primitive forms of the bastion) and ditches. The situation, in fact, recalls the standoff in trench warfare during World War I, and it is no accident that Leonardo's military designs first attracted attention after the war, for in machines like his "armored vehicle" he anticipated engines of destruction that had been developed to overcome a common tactical problem. Similarly, his interest in machines to aid underwater hostilities was fulfilled in the submarines and diving outfits of the Great War. It seems unlikely that Leonardo did not also conceive that other machine of tactical support used in the Great War, the airplane, for the same purposes. In an era that saw the ascendancy of the infantry, reconaissance would be of major importance, as well as the capacity to drop firebombs of some sort on exposed positions. If Leonardo could conceive formulas for poison gas, what he called "deadly smoke," then he would certainly want to provide a machine to carry it over walls or across a field to drop it – or any bomb – in the midst of a surprised army. To a Renaissance imagination all such inventions would naturally cluster together in a single purpose. We see their conjunction in Francis Bacon's catalogue of projects in Salomon's House, in *The New Atlantis* (1624):

> We represent also ordnance and instruments of war, and engines of all kinds: and likewise new mixtures and compositions of gun-powder, wildfires burning in water, and unquenchable. Also fireworks of all variety both for pleasure and use. We imitate also flights of birds; we have some degrees of flying in the air.[14]

Though the construction is paratactic, the common function is clearly implied.

The connection between aerodynamical researches and warfare is even more obvious in the second phase of Leonardo's studies of flight, during the period of 1504–5, when he wrote his treatise *On the Flight of Birds*, returned to his designs for a flying machine, and, in Clive Hart's opinion, very possibly constructed a full-scale model of one or more of his ornithopters. Previous to this renewed interest in the subject, he had done the following: (1) Reported in March 1500 on military matters and fortifications for the city of Venice. He made notes for a pet invention, a diving dress and small, submergible vessel, for use against the Turkish fleet. (2) Put himself in service in 1502 to Cesare Borgia, who had recently defeated the Duchy of Urbino and was threatening Bologna – and seems to have been contemplating an invasion of Florence as well. Borgia sent Leonardo to Arezzo, where troops were fighting, to prepare maps and make recommendations for military tactics. (3) In July of 1503 advised the Florentine military leaders as to the feasibility of diverting the Arno River to cut off supplies to the Pisan armies. (4) Met Machiavelli, in Florence, and no doubt discussed military matters, for in 1504 Machiavelli recommended Leonardo for a program of fortifications projects requested by the Lord of Piombino, an ally of the Florentines at the time of the Pisan War. (5) Made preliminary sketches for his wall painting *The Battle of Anghiari*. According to Carlo Pedretti, there is "indisputable evidence" that Machiavelli wrote the account of the battle which Leonardo used as a source for his scenes of conflict.[15]

The coincidence at two different periods of researches into military weaponry and researches into the construction of a flying machine suggests very strongly that Leonardo had in mind, though he nowhere makes the connection in his notebooks, the use of such a machine in actual warfare. Warfare is not the final cause but the efficient cause of obsession; it provides the occasion for Leonardo to satisfy his envy of avian and angelic forms. And, as always with Leonardo, his instinct to reproduce follows his scrutinizing eye. He required a sense of destiny to work at both strategy and machinery, and it must have become a habit of mind for one to suggest the other in his studio. In an early manuscript page circa 1496, for example, he has speculated on the flying machine, and then broken off to draw a map of Europe with places in Spain, France, and Germany – three rivals of the Italian city-states in the period just after Charles VIII of France crushed Medicean rule in Florence, causing Lodovico to correctly foresee the same fate for his dynasty. The drawing is, as Ritchie Calder says, an "aviator's map" similar to aerial views of strategic locations that Leonardo commonly drew for princes on the battlefield.[16]

This is not to say that Leonardo was warlike or aggressive in temperament. His description of war as "the most bestial of follies" is certainly sincere, and everything in his work supports a generous interpretation of his statement, "To preserve nature's chiefest boon, that is, freedom, I can find means of offense and defense, when it is assailed by ambitious tyrants."[17] One must imagine him smiling as he wrote those words, knowing as he did the ambitions of princes he served, but he is not being ingenuous when he summons the specter of tyranny. He knew better than most the perilous dangers of living in his time and place. Foremost, of course, was the fear of invasion from without, an inescapable anxiety to humanists whose chosen task was the preservation of a secure environment on the model of Athens and ancient Rome. Milan especially, as the northern "Gate of Italy," had become a fortress-city armed against France and the tribes beyond the Alps. What makes Leonardo seem warlike is his vision of the state as subject to the laws of physics, so that radical improvement of "the means of offense and defense" became equivalent to an act of self-destruction. Here is a definition of force from the notebooks somewhat different from the one quoted earlier:

> [Force] is born in violence and dies in liberty; and the greater it is the more quickly it is consumed. It drives away in fury whatever opposes its destruction. It desires to conquer and slay the cause of opposition, and in conquering destroys itself. It waxes more powerful where it finds the greater obstacle. Everything instinctively flees from death. Everything when under constraint itself constrains other things. [p. 520]

Man is a constrained creature, subject to the teleology that governs all of nature. So constrained he constrains other things in his role as *Homo faber*, the maker. In the political realm the opposition he overcomes necessarily alters the state's destiny by transforming the community into an engine of destruction and (by the logic of physics) self-destruction. The state is destroyed if it does not resist violence, and destroyed if it does. Leonardo had witnessed both fates overwhelm great city-states during the later period of the Quattrocento.

A flourishing center of culture like Florence or Milan is a moment's successful organization of elements in the flow of history, but in that ephemeral rest from violence the artist can fashion works that outlive the changes that destroy artist and state alike. The Prince is the preserver of such order; he delivers the community from its mere creatureliness, its humiliation before the laws of generation and decay, by allowing it to become a City of Art. The instrument of deliverance is military force, and the desirable effect the Prince seeks is often the annihilation for a generation or more of enemies who would overwhelm the city. To this end the artist is obligated to work, in Leonardo's view, as a craftsman. Those who sentimentally opposed such duties were the object of contempt among Leonardo's aristocratic contemporaries. As Sir Frederick explains in Castiglione's *The Courtier*: "It is lawful for a man sometime in his Lords service, to kill not one man alone, but ten thousand, and to doe many other thinges, which if a man waigh them not as he ought, wil appeare ill, and yet are not so in deede."[18] Machiavelli likewise emphasized that the Prince is often obliged "in order to maintain the state, to act against faith, against charity, against humanity, and against religion" (p. 65). He must, in Machiavelli's crucial phrase, "be able to do evil if constrained." According to Leonardo's definition above, force inevitably exhausts itself in the act of conquering opposition, but what choice is there? The Prince must be able to summon force to break the constraints threatened by foreign armies, if only to delay the moment of metamorphosis. And as for the artist, he is able to adopt new Princes in succession, as Leonardo did when he carried his work from state to state during years of cataclysmic civil war and foreign invasion.

Leonardo's supreme fantasy, then, is not the dream of Icarus, as Taylor suggests, but the dream of Daedalus. He desires to invent engines of titanic force that will assist the Prince, as Daedalus assisted Minos, to maintain and extend his power. How else explain the unusually abundant depictions in his notebooks of arsenals, cannons, gun castings (including a primitive pistol and machine-gun), enormous crossbow, scythed car, catapults, pocket battleship, ammunition (including the first shrapnel shell), bombs of all kinds, scaling devices, gunpowder, and much else? These are not inventions that were requisitioned, but products of free fancy trying to duplicate the powers of nature. Leonardo was not the only Renaissance engineer who filled notebooks with sketches of this sort, but none of his contemporaries matched his genius or enthusiasm for constructing instruments of violence. "This is the most deadly machine that exists," he declares in his notebooks, in a mixed tone of cruel pride and scientific detachment, "when the ball in the centre [of a firebomb] drops it sets fire to the edges of the other balls, and the ball in the centre bursts and scatters the others which catch fire in such time as is needed to say an Ave Maria" (p. 826). Gabriel's greeting to Mary is an apt literary touch here, for as we have seen Leonardo's mind characteristically links the Annunciation with an imagery of constrained force awaiting release.

Leonardo recognized that envy is the human emotion that provides the mechanism of release. Though he wrote that man should not enviously aspire to a superior element, like the ambitious water in his parable, yet he returned to the flying machine with ardor. In one caption for a series of drawings depicting Invidia, he wrote, "Envy is represented making a contemptuous motion toward heaven, because if she could she would use her strength against God" (p. 1096). It is said that man cannot envy God, because divinity and humanity are not proximate conditions. Leonardo knew otherwise, and set down a narrative, "Of Necromancy," which demonstrates the triumph of the envious mortal who has discovered the secret of unlimited movement in the heavens.

Though his necromancer is nominally the magus of superstition, the Faust of legend who achieves power by magical (unscientific) means, the actions of this sorcerer resemble many of the aims of Leonardo's inventions. One sees this as Leonardo proceeds from routine condemnation of Satanic tricks to his fantasy of the necromancer's power:

And undoubtedly, if this necromancy did exist, as it is believed by shallow minds, there is nothing on earth that would have so much power either *to harm or to benefit* man. [p. 81]

The phrase I have italicized reveals Leonardo's identification with the necromancer, for he is about to describe the cataclysms that this magus could inflict upon humanity. But the hope that such a person might benefit man represents his self-justification for proceeding in projects identical to those he will summon with such horror in the fable. Leonardo's imagined Prince is able to survey his domain with the speed and ubiquity of an angel:

> In truth, whoever has control of such irresistible forces will be lord over all nations, and no human skill will be able to resist his destructive power. ... no lock, no fortress, however impregnable, will avail to save anyone against the will of such a necromancer. He will cause himself to be carried through the air from East to West and through all the uttermost parts of the universe. [p. 82]

By flying from place to place the necromancer will guarantee that no resistance constrains his freedom to destroy. In effect, war is abolished by a reign of terror administered by the first magus who unlocks the secrets of aerodynamics and finds the technical means to patrol his kingdom from above.

Clearly, Leonardo, dreamer of benevolent and destructive projects alike, had a complex character. Freud was fascinated by this very complexity and wrote his controversial study, *Leonardo da Vinci and a Memory of His Childhood* (1910). That Leonardo, in Freud's view, often appeared to be indifferent to good and evil and that this indifference anticipated the moral anarchism threatening the Europe of Freud's own time made it imperative that the new century be warned against the kind of personality Leonardo embodied, the more so because of his artistic accomplishments – which Freud genuinely admired. Freud takes as his chief text a memory that Leonardo records in his notebooks, the only recollection of childhood in all of his writings. In Freud's version:

> It seems that it had been destined before that I should occupy myself so thoroughly with the vulture, for it comes to my mind as a very early memory, when I was still in the cradle, a vulture came down to me, opened my mouth with his tail, and struck me many times with his tail against my lips.

Because Freud's reading of the text depended upon an identification of the vulture as a traditional Mediterranean symbol of the mother, his book received much criticism when it was discovered that he had used an incorrect translation of the Italian, and that the bird Leonardo cites is the kite, or hawk. But I think Kurt Eissler is correct in arguing that Freud's analysis of Leonardo's career remains sound in its essentials, grounded as it is in a general theory of instincts and a reliable intuition about the significance of fantasy material.

For our purposes what is most important is Freud's attention to Leonardo's apparently traumatic association of his aerodynamical studies with an indignity forced upon him by a bird. In Freud's description of the Oedipal situation the child's response when so offended is to identify with the power of the aggressor and seek vengeance upon it by adapting its own means of attack. By this theory Freud is led to a view of aviation itself as an expression of infantile erotic desires for supreme control over the external world – the containing figure of the mother. This is so because the mother is the model for all libidinal relationships, especially for a narcissistic and indeed homosexual type like Leonardo. In Freud's view, all love objects become images of the childish self to such a personality, who then plays the sexual role of his own mother. Such autoeroticism tends to the sadistic, for the ego is weakened when the love object is absent. Leonardo is able to recreate the sustaining image of the mother in his portraits – Mary, St. Anne, Leda, Mona Lisa – but never to free himself from his dependence on it, and therefore he remains trapped in the developmental stage of an inquiring child oblivious of the damage his persistent questioning and possessive desires for dominance may cause himself and his community – a type of Oedipus, in other words.

Leonardo has no conscience, which Freud defines elsewhere as dread of the community. Why should he care about the community when his vision is fixed, or fixated, inward and backward upon infantile pleasures? Leonardo's investigations inevitably turn more and more toward the mechanical as an end in itself. Many of his inventions are recognizable as childish play, such as his mechanical toys of astonishing complexity which he created for the amusement of the nobility, but the more urgent need for domination led to artifacts of potential aggression against a species he both loved and detested, for humanity could only be an apparition of the detested father. Freud's account can be supplemented by passages in the notebooks which reveal an extreme hostility to mankind:

> Creatures shall be seen upon the earth who will always be fighting one with another, with very great losses and frequent deaths on either side. These shall set no bounds to their malice ... and when they have crammed themselves with food it shall gratify their desire to deal out death, affliction, labours, terrors and banishment to every living thing. And *by reason of their boundless pride they shall wish to rise towards heaven but the excessive weight of their limbs shall hold them down.* [pp. 1112–3]

Here Leonardo acknowledges, especially in the phrase I have italicized, that his yearning for levitation belongs to the disease of ambition which is so destructive to all humanity. Such ambition deserves punishment from heaven, as in the parable of the aspiring water.

As we have seen in the fable of the necromancer, Leonardo is willing to view himself as the instrument of such punishment, the exterminating angel. The mask of necromancer is the ultimate inflation of the infantile ego, which strikes down the authority of the external world. "There are an infinite number of persons who in order to gratify one of their appetites would destroy God and the whole universe," Leonardo remarks in his fable, and he is surely one of them. Freud does not explicitly state this conclusion, but it seems obvious from his text that it was Leonardo's fate to indulge in flight as a supreme fantasy of mechanical triumph precisely *because* of its destructive potential, for nothing less than mass annihilation of the psychic obstacles represented by the physical limits of mortality, the "excessive weight of ... limbs," could satisfy the immensity of his envy for the powers that constrained and daily offended his lordly (because infantile) conceptions.

Writing this book in 1909–1910, Freud explained in psychoanalytical terms the impulses that were at the same time being celebrated in the burgeoning movement of Futurism. It is as if the Futurists seized upon the historical nexus of flight, cruelty, and mechanics, and enshrined it as the next step of human evolution. At the level of ideology, Futurism too abhorred genital sexuality as an indignity for those who possessed the

Daedalean power to occupy the absolute, the heavenly regions, by means of invention. Marinetti wrote:

> You will certainly have watched the takeoff of a Blériot plane, panting and still held back by its mechanics, amid mighty buffets of air from the propeller's first spins.
>
> Well then: I confess that before so intoxicating a spectacle we strong Futurists have felt ourselves suddenly become too earthly, or, to express it better, have become a symbol of the earth we ought to abandon.
>
> We have even dreamed of one day being able to create a mechanical son, the fruit of pure will, a synthesis of all the laws that science is on the brink of discovering. [p. 75]

To connect Leonardo with the Futurists may seem unjust, but the linkage did not seem preposterous to the Futurists, who declared him as their ancestor. Nor would a statement like the one above have startled Freud, who took some pains to explain the libidinous character of the flying machine. If Freud had known Leonardo's quotation about the infinite number of persons who in order to gratify one of their appetites would destroy God and the whole universe, and apparently he did not know it, he would have connected it to the nihilist tradition of his own time: the iconoclasm of Nietzsche, the ravings of Ivan Karamazov and Kirilov in Dostoevsky's novels, and not least the sadism of Marinetti himself, who called war "the world's only hygiene," and a decade after the Great War would look to the aviator Benito Mussolini as a Prince willing to cleanse the Western world by means of modern weapons such as the airplane.

LEDA AND THE SWAN

Leonardo wrote his treatise *On the Flight of Birds* at a time when the Aristotelian method of deriving knowledge of objects – personal observation, comparison, generalization from research and abundant example – had succeeded a scholastic tradition in which lore rather than evidence was transferred from book to book without empirical verification. Leonardo observed birdflight closely but he was not interested in matters of taxonomy or full organic description so much as in the mechanics of flight. A revealing set of drawings in the *Codex Madrid* shows him gradually disassemble a bird into vectors of thrust. It is *physis*, as always, that fascinates him, and for a purpose: the laws of aerodynamics can aid man in transfiguring his condition. One sees the intention clearly in the following passage:

> A bird is an instrument working according to mathematical law, which instrument it is within the capacity of man to reproduce with all its movements, but not with a corresponding degree of strength, though it is deficient only in the power of maintaining equilibrium. We may therefore say that such an instrument constructed by man is lacking in nothing except the life of the bird, and this life must needs be supplied from that of man. [p. 493]

Here again heaven becomes subject to human reason, in the form of the man's "life" which can occupy the formal instrument of impetus and ascent. Man has the capacity to become the soul or living principle of the bird by stealing the formerly secret laws of flight, as Prometheus stole the secret of fire. One should not sentimentalize Leonardo's intentions by speaking of the unity or community of bird and man; his own fables and parables must guide us in regarding this usurpation of the bird's unique powers as an impious act with perilous implications. "Flying creatures will support men with their feathers" runs one of his riddling prophecies (p. 1105). The product is meant to be seen as a grotesque rival of God's creation – a monster designed by Envy.

Leonardo uses the same word – *uccello* – for bird and flying machine alike. Freud remarks that the word has a long history as a slang term for the penis, an insight which Kurt Eissler develops in his study of Leonardo. Just as birds' darting upward motion toward heaven was used as a symbol of supreme religious ecstasy, so, according to Eissler, Leonardo's special interest in bats and hawks derived from their special capabilities of flight which make them symbols of the penis "free from deficiencies." The building of a machine which repeated such activity would be a triumph of the will over generative nature symbolized by the penis, and therefore a triumph of the spirit over the flesh. An airborne creature is a suitable model of perfected being, one which Leonardo would willingly "reproduce," that is, father, in the identical form it presented to his eye. The invention of a flying machine is essentially an attempt to define man's place in the divine scheme as a constrained creature capable of transforming himself into a potent lord of the air.

Within this context it seems inevitable that the mythological theme of Leda and the Swan should be one of Leonardo's most compelling images, and that he should commit it to canvas during the period (1504–5) of his manuscript *On the Flight of Birds* and his activities as a military advisor already described. The painting has been lost, but it survives in copies made by his students, and though these copies take different forms Kenneth Clark has pointed out that a contemporary description of the work by a visitor to Leonardo's studio allows us to identify the painting by his pupil Césare da Sesto at Wilton House as the most accurate depiction of Leonardo's intentions.[19]

This picture belongs thematically to the tradition of Annunciation paintings, of which it is a pagan version, and to all treatments of the Jupiter myth, including the kindred subject of Jupiter and Danaë, which occupied Leonardo's attention in Milan when he designed scenery of a festival play on that subject in the house of Count Gianfrancisco Sanseverino. Leda, like Mary and Danaë, belongs to the category of celestially visited maidens, and though she is distinguished in myth from Mary by being the victim of physical rape, she displays in this artwork the same calm we find in Leonardo's portraits of Mary. The calm in this case expresses a strong element of erotic satisfaction, but the same element is present in the portraits of Mary as well. More important, the formality of composition conveys the same effect of *amor fati* that links the two mothers-to-be in *The Annunciation* and *Leda*. The crucial difference is that the progeny of Leda and the Swan are visible as the Christ child is not. Where in one painting we find the angel opposite the virgin, in the later one we behold, as does Leda in seductive contrapposto, the generated figures of harmony and discord (Castor and Pollux, Helen and Clytemnestra). Though the issue of Leda's violation is tragic, the subject of so much epic and drama, she looks upon the scene with what Théophile Gautier called "that expression of sarcastic and superior gayety which is the very mark of Leonardo."[20] Her sphinx-like smile is Mona Lisa's and like the Gioconda, in Pater's phrase, she has known "the sins of the Borgias" well in advance.

Leda is a figure who experiences viscerally the interpenetration of heavenly power into the mortal condition. As a carnal being she *is* emblematically the appetitive world whose essence is the act of generation. Leonardo's first drawings of Leda are imitations of the classical Venus Anadyomene. As viewers we are asked to see in Leda the alluring beauty that brought the Trojan War and its grievous aftermath to the Mediterranean states. Leda at least sees this, for in her smiling expression we read plainly not only satisfaction in the success of her seductive charm but also in the issue of her conception. To W. B. Yeats's question, "Did she put on his knowledge with his power / Before the indifferent beak could let her drop?" Leonardo answers, she put on that knowledge even before coitus, for her lascivious beauty represents the natural state of carnal aggression and strife of which the rape and its effects are necessary elements.

As Yeats recognized, the theme of Leda and the Swan is a political one, for it draws spiritual and military realms together in the same legend. In nature and human society the "force" of Leonardo's definitions is experienced as "accidental violence," aggression against an object that constrains its freedom. Leonardo's greatest work before *Leda* was the mural of *The Battle of Anghiari*, which abounds in vignettes of unexampled cruelty in his oeuvre; in fact, the earliest studies for *Leda* are found on some of the *Anghiari* drawings. As in *The Annunciation* the drama of *Leda* lies in what is masked or invisible to the viewer – though here the cues are overt – until his powers of conception make them accessible. What we see, then, is a succession of combats past and present of which Anghiari was the most recent to Italian memory as Troy was most distant. Supernatural or spiritual force, in the Swan-disguise of the King of Heaven, has effects which are transferable only by thanatological imagery, for such "union" with the divine must result in either the perpetuation of the species, and therefore the perpetuation of war – "the coitus of war" as Marinetti would name it longingly in 1909 – or the annihilation of the species, as in the Christian myth of the Last Judgment which begins to obsess Leonardo during the years in Milan and culminates in his Deluge drawings of the 1500s.

The rape of Leda returns us to Leonardo's memory of violation by the fierce hawk pushing its tail feathers into his infant mouth. If in one part of his psyche Leonardo takes vengeance upon the lord of the air by assuming his powers, in the fantasy of the necromancer, in another part he is the helpless victim still, seeking some avenue of escape from the imperial figures of earth and heaven. We must set beside his description of the necromancer the fable he included in a letter to Benedetto Dei of an ogre that threatens mankind with destruction:

> And believe me there is no man so brave but that, when the fiery eyes were turned upon him, *he would willingly have put on wings* in order to escape, for the face of infernal Lucifer would seem angelic by contrast with this. . . .
>
> I do not believe that ever since the world was created there has been witnessed such lamentation and wailing of people, accompanied by so great terror. In truth the human species in such a plight has need to envy every other race of creatures; for though the eagle has strength sufficient to subdue the other birds, they yet remain unconquered through the rapidity of their flight, and so the swallows through their speed escape becoming the prey of the falcon . . . *but for us wretched mortals there avails not any flight*, since this monster when advancing slowly far exceeds the speed of the swiftest courser. [pp. 1054–5, italics added]

If you are a human like Leda how do you escape the power of the Swan but by possessing the speed given by artificial wings? One escapes constraint by constraining one's body to become superhuman, a subordinate part of a machine, and by so doing avoids the generation in coitus of more war. One remains solitary, free, the creator of a mechanical child, as in Marinetti's fantasy, which is stronger and more resourceful than flesh.

If Leonardo's inquiring temperament can be fruitfully derived from cultural circumstances expressed in the legend of Leda and the Swan, the violation of the passive by the active and aggressive principle, then we can appreciate how aptly this mythic scene prefigures historical events which intellectuals in the twentieth century witnessed in their inception. For many of them the desideratum became the celebration of war itself, obviously in Marinetti's case, but also in an England that sought to regain the power by scientific means that it had lost in the Great War. J. B. S. Haldane, in his monograph of 1924, *Daedalus, or Science and the Future*, remarks that "science is yet in its infancy, and we can foretell little of the future save that the thing that has not been is the thing that shall be, that no beliefs, no values, no institutions are safe. So far from being an isolated phenomenon the late war is only an example of the disruptive results that we may constantly expect from the progress of science."[21] Haldane welcomes such war with a Leda-like smile, for at the end of catastrophe he hopes that "the thing that has not been" will triumph, a utopian state fashioned by the elite corps of engineers who have usurped the power of blundering politicians. It is a vision of Daedalus, "the first modern man" (p. 47), become Minos, a more efficient leader fulfilling the plans of Renaissance writers like Machiavelli and Bacon who are Haldane's inspiration. Haldane's program informs the politics of H. G. Wells's *The Shape of Things to Come* (1933), which depicts global rule by aeronautical aristocrats who are pilots and scientists alike, and thus enforce their power by their ubiquity. "There was no other way to the Renaissance," remarks the book's futuristic narrator.[22]

The chief figure of that Renaissance is Ariston Theotocopulos, a "gifted painter and designer" of the twenty-first century, whose Note Books the narrator Philip Raven presents as the best guide to the life of the mind in that period. If we do not recognize Leonardo from this description, we would do so from Raven's enthusiastic praise of him in the book's conclusion. The treatment of Theotocopulos is a tour de force, a hilarious parody of Leonardo's notebooks and the seriousness of scholarship upon them. Wells has no trouble plumbing the depths of Leonardo's obsession with the flying machine:

> "We still dream of air raids and war in the air," he said, and he speaks elsewhere of "the inmates of those fortifications. ... If only I could get hold of an aeroplane and a bomb! Perhaps after all there is some sense in keeping intelligent people like me out of the air, with this sort of stuff about." [p. 369]

All airplanes must be registered in this period, and Theotocopulos has been denied the right to own one, for reasons he and Wells understand. The creative personality can be a cruel one because its rage for order may endanger the community.

W. B. Yeats provides a more apocalyptic reading in *A Vision*, which places Leonardo just at the point of oscillation between the fifteenth and sixteenth phases of his occult scheme, in the seventh gyre when "*primary* curiosity and the *antithetical* dream are for the moment one." The artist at this point desires to realize what he can imagine, and therefore a desire for power succeeds the disinterested pursuit of knowledge. From this point there is a clear progression in his system toward the scientific phase typified, in Phase 21, by Bernard Shaw, H. G. Wells, and others who overtly try to control the destiny of society by the force of will rather than imagination. Yeats of course prefers to place himself among the aristocratic party of Leonardo and Castiglione, courtiers of some all-powerful Prince who rules a city of art such as Florence – or Byzantium – nor does he blink at the implications of such a desire. In all his work Yeats attempts to portray art as a violence-inducing element of the public imagination, an agent of renewal that will sweep away bourgeois hegemony in the interests of a society composed on the model of a perfected artwork. In *A Vision* he remarks, "Love war because of its horror, that belief may be changed, civilization renewed. We desire belief and lack it. Belief comes from shock and is not desired."[23] His poem "Leda and the Swan" is a paradigmatic enactment of this shock, which in political terms would take the form of universal war.

As historical figures analogous to the Swan, the "Aeroplane and Zeppelin" Yeats summons in his poem "Lapis Lazuli" would provoke the same responses of shock and belief in Yeats's contemporaries. The observations and fantasies in Leonardo's notebooks bequeathed to the twentieth century the binary meanings of the flying machine that characterize most literature on the subject. To be a lord in the air / to be the victim of a lord in the air; flight as access to annihilating power / flight as a means of escape from annihilating power – this is the fundamental dichotomy that the modern imagination confronts after Kitty Hawk.

As for the debate over Leonardo, it came to an end in 1939, when two events suspended hostilities by altering the context in which Leonardo had to be understood. The milder event was the publication of Kenneth Clark's *Leonardo da Vinci*, a series of lectures which synthesized the "two cultures" of Leonardo's work in so persuasive an interpretation that later scholarship could not maintain the old quarrel without appearing eccentric. The other event was the outbreak of World War II in Europe, when demonic forms of the Prince sought imperial power with the most sophisticated instruments of destruction that engineers could put into their hands. The war's aftermath proved not to be the renaissance that writers like Marinetti, Haldane, Yeats and Wells had hopefully prophesied. Indeed, even Leonardo's warmest admirers must have felt in 1945 as Paul Valéry did after the Great War, when he depicted Humanity as Hamlet in the graveyard of Europe: "Every skull he picks up is an illustrious skull. *Whose was it?* This one was Lionardo [sic]. He invented the flying man, but the flying man has not exactly served his inventor's purposes."[24] Not exactly, but more than most recent scholars care to acknowledge.

3.   Birds with a Human Face

It is as though we have grown wings, which, thanks to
Providence, we have learnt to control.

—Louis Blériot[1]

In the four centuries after Leonardo's failed attempts to construct
a flying machine no genius of the same order graces the historical
record, or none who left us notebooks and designs. As there are
mute inglorious Miltons in every country churchyard, perhaps
inventors who derived from their observations of flying creatures
the "secret" of human flight lie in obscurity because they were
unwilling to make public their private discoveries. Secondhand
reports of human flight in various countries exist in abundance,
and apparently significant numbers of cranks and geniuses threw
themselves from rooftops and ran down hills with a mechanism
attached to their shoulders. But the theory of flight made little
progress, even in the eighteenth century when the vogue of
ballooning distracted most people from the hopelessness of
heavier-than-air ascent. Had Leonardo's projects become known
at that time, he too would have been lampooned by the likes of
Addison, Swift, and Johnson, all of whom were amused and
appalled by apparatus for imitating the birds.

Technology was an amateur's hobby before the nineteenth
century, which accounts in part for the slow tempo of progress
in the mechanical arts. Especially in the derisive area of flight
the practitioner was by necessity a solitary. One thinks of him
sitting in the open field watching the sudden updarting of the
lark, or by the shore studying the soaring gull, in order to
discover the mystery of aerial capability. He would feel the
longings articulated by the lyric poets who inspired him.

41

O could I fly, I'd fly with thee:
  We'd make, with social wing,
Our annual visit o'er the globe,
  Companions of the Spring.

So speaks Michael Bruce (1746–67) to the cuckoo.[2] Bringing his notes and his envy back to the laboratory, the inventor then had to attempt the impossible: a mechanism that would lift the human body and sustain it above ground. Injury was likely, death possible, and ridicule certain. Actual flight, even if it were consummated, would be clumsy and short-lived compared to the flights of fancy undertaken by poets, who remained the most successful practitioners of ascent. Could any actual flight equal the vicarious sensations aroused by Milton's account of Satan's passage through Chaos in *Paradise Lost?* And then, of what use would flight be to mankind compared to the spinning jennies and steam engines that reconstituted the work of the world? Only one specific use immediately suggested itself, a military one, and inventors might be modest about trumpeting this capacity, like the "artist" in Samuel Johnson's *Rasselas*, who explains to the Prince:

> If men were all virtuous ... I should with great alacrity teach them all to fly. But what would be the security of the good, if the bad could at pleasure invade them from the sky? Against an army sailing through the clouds neither walls, nor mountains, nor seas, could afford any security. A flight of northern savages might hover in the wind, and light at once with irresistible violence upon the capital of a fruitful region that was rolling under them. [chapter VI]

Access to precisely this kind of power tempted the necromancer in Leonardo, as we have seen, but most craftsmen would prefer machines with more benevolent uses.

The dilemma of the artist-inventor can be profitably examined in a short story by Nathaniel Hawthorne, "The Artist of the Beautiful," first published in 1844. Owen Warland, the protagonist, is an unintended version of Leonardo to set beside those surveyed in the last chapter. As a child Owen liked to tinker with wood and metal objects and fashion them into simulations of animate nature. As an adult he continues his

efforts to "spiritualize machinery" by making artifacts from his
inward perception of Beauty – from his soul. The narrator
expresses mixed feelings about this enterprise:

> Alas that the artist, whether in poetry, or whatever other
> material, may not content himself with the inward enjoyment
> of the beautiful, but must chase the flitting mystery beyond
> the verge of his ethereal domain, and crush its frail being in
> seizing it with a material grasp. Owen Warland felt the
> impulse to give external reality to his ideas as irresistibly as
> any of the poets or painters who have arrayed the world in a
> dimmer and fainter beauty, imperfectly copied from the
> richness of their visions.

"The flitting mystery," like Emerson's famous "flying Perfect,"[3]
is an eidolon that obsesses the Romantic artist to whom Warland
is constantly compared. We must be careful not to collapse the
story entirely into a fable of the poet or painter, however; Owen
is a manufacturer, a master of technique comparable in many
ways to his watchmaker employer, Peter Hovenden. Hovenden's
down-to-earth daughter Annie is Owen's beloved muse, for
whom his efforts are bent in the best chivalric manner. After
several years Owen does succeed in making an "ideal butterfly,"
an automaton that flies about the room more gracefully than
Nature's own. It flits from Annie to her blacksmith-husband,
until their infant son crushes it in his strong grasp. The reified
figure has thus succumbed to two injuries in the story: Owen's
"material grasp" mentioned above, and the boy's fatal grip.

There are two principal features or mythemes in this story
useful as touchstones for discussion: (1) the figure of the butterfly,
natural and mechanical, and (2) the fate of the automaton. They
characterize the literature of flight throughout the centuries in
which the flying machine evolved. Indeed, Hawthorne's butterfly
reminds us of Leonardo's *uccello*, not only because the natural
thing is the model for the artificial in both cases, but because
the object is the symbol of nearly identical concepts. The butterfly
since ancient times has been an emblem of the soul and of
spiritual rebirth; the Greek word (*psyche*) for butterfly and soul
is the same. Inspired by the presence of butterflies in his youth,
Owen is saved from dissipation and despair by a butterfly's
timely visitation after Annie accidentally ruins his first model

early in the story. Perhaps the butterfly, the narrator hypothesizes, "was indeed a spirit commissioned to recall him to the pure ideal life that had so etherealized him among men." For Leonardo, the intercession is a stranger one, as he describes it in his memory of being struck in the lips by a hawk's tail. The dream of possessing that aggressive power nourished his inventiveness in art and science, not least his continuing investigation into birdflight and his efforts to emulate it by mechanical means. Leonardo's avian model proved to be the most powerful influence on imaginative writers. A fragile butterfly has little anatomy compared to the bird, and so its symbolic character is definitively fixed. The bird's complexity as a symbol lies in its more substantive force, its greater weight and articulation; it is conceivable as a rapist, as in the myth of Leda and the Swan, and also of being crushed to death as easily as the most delicate of God's creatures.

THE ENVIOUS EYE

The bird has been used by poets as sign and symbol for almost every human or divine attribute, demonic as well as beneficent, but most frequently for the human soul aspiring toward heaven. "Oh that I had wings like a dove! for then I would fly away, and be at rest," says the author of Psalms (55:6). "They that wait upon the Lord shall renew their strength: they shall mount up with wings as eagles," Isaiah proclaims (40:31). Milton borrows such associations for his invocation in *Paradise Lost*:

> Join voices all ye living Souls; ye Birds
> That singing up to Heaven Gate ascend,
> Bear on your wings and in your notes his praise ...
> [V.197–9]

Likewise Plato remarks in the *Phaedrus* that "the wing is the corporeal element which is most akin to the divine, and which by nature tends to soar aloft and carry that which gravitates downwards into the upper region, which is the habitation of the gods."[4] This emblematic identification is simply symbol taking its strength from a larger allegorical structure. Once God's dwelling is located in a superlunary direction, those creatures most "at home" in the air become two-way messengers between the realms of earth and heaven. The symbol partakes of the thing it stands for, as in the miraculous ritual of the Eucharist. A heaven-climbing bird is the inevitable symbol of the divine.

The poetry of birdflight, then, tends to be a sacred poetry, a tradition of the religious sublime. In William Blake's brief epic *Milton*, for example, "The Lark is a mighty Angel" (36:12) that announces the dawn of a new era in history. Blake depicted the lark's human face in a lovely engraving to illustrate Milton's poem "L'Allegro," and in *Milton* he praises its spiritual quality with a tenderness characteristic of that epic, in which the natural world receives more praise than in any other of Blake's works following the *Songs of Innocence*: "His little throat labours with inspiration; every feather on throat & breast & wings vibrates with the effluence Divine" (31:34). Blake charts the movement of the Lark as a *novum* or new imaginative force through the twenty-seven heavens of his historical cycle, and then releases the bird directly into the unrealized heaven; the Lark carries the desire of a fallen Humanity toward a state of redemption. (A century later Blake's successors will imagine the airplane performing the same mission.) The Lark's ascent signals the readiness of nations "To go forth to the Great Harvest & Vintage" promised by the prophetic books of the Bible.

The most celebrated example of the redemptionist mode is Percy Shelley's "To a Skylark," a poem that haunts the literature of the twentieth century as it did that of the nineteenth. Shelley's glorious bird, as he hastens to tell us, is not to be confused with the object of ornithological scrutiny ("Bird thou never wert"), but is a figure of the *prima musica* associated with the original act of Creation, and which Milton claimed was still audible to Adam and Eve. As the perfect type of the poet – to whom the bird is compared explicitly – the bird is a "scorner of the ground," a "Sprite" whose joy is derived from the upper world toward which it aspires in flight. As the poet follows its movement by its ascending sound, the contrast between his condition and the bird's becomes more plangent. He idealizes the bird as a creature insusceptible to mortal pains:

> With thy clear keen joyance
>   Langour cannot be:
> Shadow of annoyance

Never came near thee:
Thou lovest – but ne'er knew love's sad satiety.

The act of idealizing is a recognition of unsatisfied need, a form of envious self-laceration which causes more despondency. Shelley recovers from momentary self-pity by identifying with the lark's escape from the imprisoning world, and by turning that escape to altruistic purposes by rhetorically enacting for others the "rain of melody" which brings relief and release to the poet himself. Shelley's poem offers us an image of the longing for the totality of experience symbolized by the upper air. Like Leonardo, who stripped the bird of its bodily features in order to discover fundamental aerodynamical principles, Shelley allegorizes the nominal bird into non-entity, into a spiritual force moving progressively toward supernatural completion. At the furthest reach of the upward ascent the bird breaks the boundaries set by terrestrial perspective, and inspires the poet to apocalyptic speech in turn.

The lark has performed in this poem what the flying machine did in Hawthorne's tale: "It has absorbed my own being into itself," Owen explains, "And in the secret of that butterfly, and in its beauty – which is not merely outward, but deep as its whole system, – is represented the intellect, the imagination, the sensibility, the soul of an Artist of the Beautiful." Its flight is a perfected form of its creator's spiritual activity, which is not subject to mutability. The bird, then, contains an *occult* identity, in the word's original sense of "hidden from sight, concealed"; as Hawthorne says, this identity is "secret" and "deep" and apprehensible only by the imagination, which realizes and gives form to what is invisible. The inventor and poet alike can overcome their envy of the occult force flying above them by producing a representation (a song, an automaton) that manifests the secret qualities of the flying Perfect.

Like Shelley's ode, John Keats's "Ode to a Nightingale," often called the greatest poem ever written about a bird, depends upon a perceived opposition between ethereal minstrel and earthbound auditor. And here too the poet keeps from despair by his identification with the occult force whose music lures his spirit from his body. Though Keats disowns "envy of thy happy lot" because of his powers of sympathy, even that sympathy, "too happy in thine happiness," causes the species of pain Shelley attributes to the sweetest songs.

In fact, the poem is charged with envy, if we define that emotion as the morbid contemplation of another's superior advantages. The descent into envy occurs in the third stanza of the ode, after Keats has entertained the possibility that if he drinks deeply enough of some intoxicant as steeped in summer glory as the bird's song – "the country green, / Dance, and Provençal song, and sunburnt mirth" – he can "leave the world unseen." But how account for the opposition of summer landscape and "the world"? Keats is driven back by the force of his idealizing imagination to define "the world" as something entirely inferior to the imagined paradise of the bird, who has never known "the weariness, the fever, and the fret" of earthbound existence. In "To the Skylark" Wordsworth will call the bird "Type of the wise, who soar, but never roam – / True to the kindred points of Heaven and Home." But Keats does not describe birdflight as a commutation from higher to lower worlds. The nightingale's situation in the poem remains constantly out of reach, and though Keats in stanza six can perceive the negative implication of his desire to die into the bird's life:

> Still wouldst thou sing, and I have ears in vain –
> To thy high requiem become a sod

he nevertheless continues to will such a death-in-life throughout the next, penultimate stanza, enjoying vicariously the timeless being of the bird until betrayed by the elegiac language ("Forlorn!") that belongs to the envious eye.

Keats loses contact with the *novum* that has entered his sublunary sphere to torment him with its occult power of transcending time and space. Its inevitable disappearance causes Keats to figuratively enact the myth of the nightingale itself, pressing his bosom against the thorns of life which inspire his invidious comparisons:

> Thou wast not born for death, immortal Bird!
> No hungry generations tread thee down.

Keats knows that the model in English literature of vindictive envy is Milton's Satan, whose unbearable consciousness of exile from heaven leads him to plot against the Creator's great artifice, the Garden and Humankind. Keats's task, then, once he exalts the bird and locates himself in a lower order of being, "where but to think is to be full of sorrow," is to work free of postlapsarian attitudes toward the bird. His solution, a repeated one in his work, is to immobilize the forceful presence of the bird (its "anthem") by interpreting it as a "vision or a waking dream." Both terms, though set in opposition, shift the burden of emotion away from the speaker's momentary distress in favor of the process of idealization. Unlike Satan who must assert himself in order to assuage his envy, Keats relapses into the lethargic passivity which opened the poem, emphatically ending the last stanza on the word "sleep." The ego, which would insist on "the envious spoiling of the object," as Melanie Klein puts it,[5] is placed in suspended animation so that no violation occurs. It is at least conceivable that the nightingale, like the Grecian urn, remains a friend to man, though as in all decrescendos in Romantic visionary poetry, the scent of sour grapes lingers with the last affirmation.

"OUR BUSINESS IS WITH MECHANISM"

Why should the bird be privileged and man be exiled forever from the upper world he can imagine with such prolific affection? According to the logic of Romantic philosophy the first step toward realizing aspirations is the imagining of them: making into concrete forms by human technics the fantasies propagated by desire. Thus Shelley's statement that "the promoters of utility ... follow the footsteps of poets, and copy the sketches of their creations into the book of common life."[6] But the order of sequence is not so simply stated. Shelley was writing at a time when the art of ballooning had reached a consummate point, marked in England by the ascent of the first English aeronaut James Sadler on 15 July 1814, to an altitude of five miles. In 1804 George Cayley built a model airplane with a wing area of 154 square inches, arguably the first genuine "airplane" ever constructed. In 1809 Cayley described a system of thrust for an airplane as well as a system of lift. "I feel perfectly confident," he wrote, "... that this noble art will soon be brought home to man's general convenience, and that we shall be able to transport ourselves and families, and their goods and chattels, more securely by air than by water. . . . The air has already been made navigable, and no one . . . can doubt the ultimate accomplishment of this object."[7] Also in 1809 the Swiss clockmaker Jacob Degen designed a *Flugsmaschine* resembling an ornithopter, attached it to a large hydrogen balloon and sailed into the open skies. A part-time English inventor, Thomas Walker, published his own design for an ornithopter in 1810 in *A Treatise on the Art of Flying by Mechanical Means*. (A later work by Walker influenced Blériot's designs.) In 1816–7 Cayley contributed three articles on "navigable balloons" or airships to the *Philosophical Magazine*. These and many other projects form the background to Shelley's flying machines, such as the aerial cars in *Prometheus Unbound* and the aerial boat in "The Witch of Atlas" (st. XLV). Literary sources can be found for Shelley's constructions, of course, but the possibility of actual human ascent they symbolize derives from the engineering achievements of his generation.

The extent to which the natural philosophy of the eighteenth century persuaded the artist-inventor to think of himself as a semi-divine figure has been much studied in recent decades, for its own sake and in connection with those writers like Blake and Wordsworth who were most suspicious of such doctrines. This is not the place to retrace the sequence of rationalistic philosophers who interpreted the Creation as a mechanized system, beginning with Descartes's epoch-making proclamation of the *bête machine* and Newton's discovery of unvarying physical and astronomical laws. For our purposes it will suffice to recall the central assumptions of this philosophy and suggest how they sponsored a climate of experimentation that led to the flying machine.

The most useful text is William Paley's *Natural Theology* (1802), a work which uses a scientific vocabulary throughout in order to discuss natural objects and creatures. "Our business is with mechanism"[8] he emphasizes characteristically at one point when his argument turns abstract, and indeed the book becomes a classic of its kind by its singleminded attempt to familiarize its large audience with birds, beasts (including man) and insects by recourse to the language of industrial manufacture.

Paley's theory of mechanism depends upon his reiterated assertion that the Creation is essentially perfect in its operations; that every part has been wrought or manufactured by God with a dexterity and ingenuity that cannot be bettered. For example, in this passage:

> The *covering of birds* cannot escape the most vulgar observation. Its lightness, its smoothness, its warmth; the disposition of the feathers all inclined backward, the down about their stem, the overlapping of their tips, their different configurations in different parts, not to mention the variety of their colors, constitute a vestment for the body so beautiful, and so appropriate to the life which the animal is to lead, as that, I think, we should have had no conception of any thing equally perfect, if we had never seen it, or can now imagine any thing more so. [p. 132]

A rhetoric of sublimity more often applied to the categories of landscape and human action is here employed to praise the utility of each moving part in the artifice isolated for analysis. As Paley anatomizes objects like the bird-mechanism they come to resemble contrivances within the powers of the scientific method to duplicate. The book's conclusion sounds like a challenge to industry: "Design must have a designer. That designer must have been a person. That person is God" (p. 268). Paley's choice of metaphor is vulnerable to the machinations of human pride. A designer who can construct a working simulation of birdflight, or in Owen Warland's case the flight of a butterfly, is likely to lay claim to the divinity he has usurped by his demiurgic skill.

As Mary Shelley perceived when she wrote *Frankenstein*, a novel influenced by Paley's speculations, the supreme challenge to the authority of the divine person would not be the construction of a mere toy but the renovation of the human person into a mechanism with powers humans have envied in other creatures more "perfect" (in Paley's sense) than their own. The most ambitious attempt to "invent" a flying person, a bird with a human form, in a fictional narrative previous to the nineteenth century, is Robert Paltock's *The Life and Adventures of Peter Wilkins* (1751), a novel which Shelley read as a boy, and which he reread with Mary Shelley in 1815, the year before she wrote *Frankenstein*. The novel has received renewed attention for prophetic qualities more obvious to an aeronautical civilization than they were to an audience which considered Johnson's lampooning of the inventor in *Rasselas* the last word on human aspirations to fly.

Peter Wilkins is a first-person account in the manner of Defoe in which an English fugitive in Africa comes upon a race of winged persons, the Glumms (male) and Gawreys (female), and lives with them for many years. Wilkins has endured fourteen chapters of adventures and reached a resting place in his explorations before the novel takes its significant turn. One night Wilkins dreams of his English wife, Patty, whom he has abandoned in an effort to seek his fortune. He awakens to find a female form before him, whom he tries wilfully to make resemble Patty, but who is clearly a more numinous creature. This celestial person – later called a "Gift of Heaven"[9] – is Youwarkee, a winged Gawrey, who replaces Patty as Wilkins's wife. Once she appears his sufferings come to an end; she is an angelic presence who brings beauty, virtue, and love to her earthbound mate.

Patty is a figure like Hawthorne's Annie – he calls her "the representative of the world." In their positive form they are nurturing figures for the male heroes of home, family, and community. But to the extent they press their claims upon the protagonist they constrain him by obscuring his vision of the more perfect world urged by the "soul," "spirit," or "psyche" as manifested in "dream." The essential imaginative act of a human creature will be one in which an "inferior" reality is usurped by a "superior" or spiritual one. In this novel, because the Glumms and Gawreys "act as they please" (p. 175) – perform their desire unconfined by the force of gravity – Wilkins's discovery of and union with Youwarkee represents an annunciation of a new social order in which man is emancipated from the negative aspects of his condition. Paltock's introduction of a fantastic *novum* allows him to articulate the laws of this transfiguration. In his artful adaptation of Milton's scene in the Garden, when Adam awakens from his dream of Eve to find it true, Wilkins as a type of all humanity awakens to a reality *beyond* his powers of conception, but which he instantly recognizes as the occult form of his desire. He comes to possess the winged life as the reward for his determined quest for improved fortune.

Like so many utopian fantasies beginning in the Renaissance, the novel combines two elements, what Marshall McLuhan calls a pre-technological appetite with a technological fix.[10] Youwarkee is the consummate version of the mechanical bride, for she carries with her at all times a suitable "Machinery" (p. 140) of winged parts. The Graundee, as the mechanism is called, resembles bird- or bat-wings less than an extended ribbed cape running full-length from shoulders to feet when opened from a fan-shaped case at the bottom of the spine. The visual effect is of a person attached to a kite, but text and illustrations stress the flexibility of the mechanism, which can be drawn into itself for an effect of near-invisibility. The encounter with this new biomorphic thing takes on a comic aspect during the wedding-night scene, when Peter tries to determine how best to make love to a creature encumbered with an "Apparatus" (p. 138).

Make love to a winged thing! Wilkins's fascinated curiosity about Youwarkee reminds us of Adam's about the fornication of angels in *Paradise Lost*. Such fascination is part of the pre-technological appetite that humanizes all animate being. Certainly the language of courtship and uxorious affection is common to poems about birds, as in the passage from Michael Bruce already quoted, or the popular evocation in Paltock's other contemporary, James Thomson:

> 'T'is love creates their melody, and all
> This waste of music is the voice of love;
> That even to birds and beasts the tender arts
> Of pleasing teaches. Hence the glossy kind
> Try every winning way inventive love
> Can dictate, and in courtship to their mates
> Pour forth their little souls.
>
> [*Spring*, ll. 614–20]

When Keats borrowed that last line for his ode ("While thou art pouring forth thy soul abroad / In such an ecstasy!"), he called attention to the erotic character of the longing for transcendence; thus the nightingale is first described as a "light-winged Dryad of the trees." Peter Wilkins can "fly" with Youwarkee; he has been permitted into her occult world symbolized by the mystique of her apparatus. Norman O. Brown may exaggerate when in *Love's Body* he argues that the protagonist of every narrative is the penis and the containing world of its movement the vagina, but in this novel one constantly has the sense that Peter's liberation from an English form of servitude and his advance toward some higher destiny in his newfoundland depends upon the new potency endowed by the Graundee. When we learn that the punishment for antisocial activity in this civilization is a "slitting" of the Graundee to render it inoperable, we need no assistance from psychoanalysis to follow the symbolism.

If the flying machine haunts the first part of the novel, "the Terror of the Gun" (p. 340) is the dominant motif of the second. Indeed, one seems to follow upon the other, for Wilkins's increasing sense of power leads him to undertake imperial adventures. Wilkins himself cannot don the Graundee, but he can be flown from place to place in a chair carried by Glumms. The astonishing fact of his rifle causes neighboring tribes to yield to the demands of Youwarkee's tribe, and a colonial system is established – not without resistance and warfare – by the end of the novel. Like Leonardo's necromancer, Wilkins enforces his will by the aerial transportation of irresistible firepower. He makes the obvious connection: "Had my Countrymen but the Graundee to convey their Cannon ... from place to place, the whole world would not stand before us" (p. 293). Paltock devotes so much of the novel to martial skirmishes that the effect of the *novum* is narrowed rather than expanded. Perhaps it is Paltock's purpose, as it was Johnson's in *Rasselas*, to suggest that the flying machine is essentially a military instrument. Like the gun, it becomes an equalizer: first, raising man up to the level of birds and angels, and then, from his need to act upon his new powers, thrusting him back into the structures of political experience from which it had briefly liberated him.

Another text of the Industrial Revolution that seeks to empower the aspiring human spirit is an essay of 1842 by Martin Farquhar Tupper, "A Flight Upon Fancy." More famous as the priggish moralist of *Proverbial Philosophy*, Tupper describes in this essay the compelling need for a flying machine. He is less interested in prophesying than in persuading others to take heed of legitimate prophecy when it appears, a characteristically modest post-Romantic stance. And yet there is genuine longing in his essay, perhaps generated from the shattered futuristic dreams of the French Revolution. His text is the passage of Ecclesiastes that tells us there is nothing new under the sun. "Novelty, – whither hast thou fled?" the essay begins, and the first sentences of the next three paragraphs return to the same plaint.[11] Tupper is not denying that new ideas, new information, and new dispensations – all of what we call "change" – occur in his daily life. His point is that the very quantity of such petty novelties erodes our desire for Mystery. His prescription is a simple one: "Turn we, then, from this obsolete Earth, to the novelty and freshness of the AIR; ... The Air, the Air, is free unto us yet; who will fashion us a song of triumph on the Air?" He goes on to recommend the imitation of birds in the construction of an apparatus for human flight, and to conjure authorities to make this a project for the whole community. Only in this way can the "axiom of modernity" be altered from a despairing to a restorative one. An illustration by George Cruikshank accompanying the article shows men in birdlike guise gliding from a cliff. "Are these things quite impossible?" Tupper queries. "Arise, my grandfather, and mock at steam! Appear, my grandson, and come unto me flying!"

Tupper's essay seems to acknowledge that earth will yield no Eden to human desire as travelers as late as the eighteenth century thought possible. But Eden as a state of being in which one's life can be transformed by the perfect freedom to act one's desire – this dream cannot be surrendered by the imagination. In the generation before Tupper, as we have seen, the bird was the conventional symbol for such aspirations. Tupper's determination to *be* a bird is nourished by a faith that the advances of technology will allow his romance of progress to be realized.

If the AIR becomes a subject of increasing attention in the latter part of the nineteenth century it is in part because of the progress in aerial technology. The improvement in glider techniques, the development of the gas engine and steam power, culminating in the invention of the four-stroke internal combustion engine by N. A. Otto in 1876, the forging of more durable and flexible materials for machines – all enhanced the feasibility of occupying the upper air. How does one estimate the complementary contribution of, say, John Ruskin who directed so much attention to the skies by his worshipful accounts of clouds in *Modern Painters* or his survey of the mythology of the aerial element in *Queen of the Air*? Or of Jules Michelet, whose beautifully illustrated book *The Bird* represents the apotheosis of that creature to the status of divinity? Despite Shelley's ordering, the "promoters of utility" and the artists of the beautiful were engaged in a mutually reinforcing dialogue that would conclude when man did in fact transform himself into an airborne creature. Especially at the end of the century, experiments with the glider had constant reference to the bird as a model, not just honorific reference but as in Leonardo's studies very explicit scientific observation. Otto Lilienthal's *Birdflight as the Basis for Aviation* (1893) outlined in abundant charts and mathematical formulas the best ways of imitating the perfection of soaring achieved by familiar birds. In his more than two thousand flights of 300 to 700 feet he demonstrated the viability of a cambered-winged glider that Paltock and Tupper would have recognized.

The end of the century, then, finds man seizing the Promethean fire and transforming himself into a more "perfect" creature according to the divinizing myths of birds and angels he had held before him for so many centuries as a beacon. The capacity to produce a spiritualized machinery, what Owen Warland called a "new species of life and motion," was in its first stages of realization. The inception of the Wright brothers' interest in flight, so they claimed, was the day their father brought home a flying toy of cork and bamboo covered with paper, called a *hélicoptère*. Though a neighbor vindictively crushed it, the brothers built another and another, until the succession of model planes culminated in the *Flyer*. In this achievement the ruin of Warland's *psyche* was finally redeemed.

THE MURDER OF BIRDS

An optimistic reading of the evolution of the flying machine demands that this chapter conclude here, and the next one, devoted to H. G. Wells's evaluation of its possibilities, begin straightaway. Wells inaugurated his literary career, as it happens, with an unsigned article for the *Pall Mall Gazette* of 8 December 1893 on "The Advent of the Flying Man," which remarks on Lilienthal's experiments and takes them to their seemingly logical conclusion in the manner of Tupper by sketching a scene of London commuters winging to the suburbs. And yet Wells's full-length narratives of aircraft are not optimistic; they assume a cruelty in human nature and public policy that has a tradition in the literature of birdflight as well. In order to account for Wells's dark vision, and the dialectic of positive and negative views of the flying machine that derives from his seminal writings, we must backtrack through nineteenth-century literature to locate and describe a second strain intermixed with the one already documented.

In the nineteenth century the most efficient flying machine was the bird. As we have seen, its upward movement and astonishing agility made it a symbol of the highest achievement a human being could imagine. Wordsworth writes that the wild swans at Grasmere "scarcely seem / Inferior to the angelical" which they so much resemble in their whiteness and propellent force.[12] But nothing is more susceptible to vertiginous downward movement than the angelical, as the myth of Lucifer reminded its believers. Earth and earthliness draw celestial creatures downward; that is a fact of nature and a fancy of the religious imagination alike. H. G. Wells's novel concerning an angel's descent into an English village, *The Wonderful Visit* (1895), like Hawthorne's fable of the marvelous automaton, is a forum for speculation on how human beings might deal with the miraculous presence of a spiritual entity. The angel, unsurprisingly, is pelted with rocks by schoolboys and treated with scarcely less hostility by adults. Likewise, the bird has a nature vulnerable to ruin when engaged by the human creatures whose "invidious proximity" – to cite the essential precondition for envy – threatens at all times to crush its body and spirit by malicious aggression.

The bird's maltreatment proceeds from precisely the same process of idealization described earlier. In its simplest form the mechanism of envious resentment can be seen in a lyric by Mary Howitt (1799–1888) on the sea-gull. "The sea-gull laughs at the pride of man, / And sails in a wild delight / On the torn-up breast of the night-black sea, / Like a foam-cloud calm and white," it runs in part.[13] We don't need an ornithologist to tell us that sea-gulls do not laugh at human pride; in fact they don't laugh at anything. Howitt is exalting the bird to a superhuman dimension of being and projecting upon it her own desire for the ecstasy of release. As a human being she is restrained from expressing "wild delight" and so she transfers it as an ideal to the bird, thereby tormenting herself further by the contrast so created. To the extent one imagines a sea-gull looking down contemptuously upon the earthbound, the environment will correspondingly be darkened to the inchoate shape of a "night-black sea."

Howitt's poem draws in phrasing and prosody upon a greater

one: Coleridge's "The Rime of the Ancient Mariner." It has puzzled many readers that the Mariner shoots the albatross when it is universally perceived as a bird of good omen, one that uniquely has the power to speed the ship through the restraining ice of the southern pole. But from the perspective of our discussion we can appreciate that the Mariner slays the bird precisely because it enforces gratitude upon the lonely sailor by its angelic, indeed Christic, character. That which reminds man of his limitations by rescuing him from them is subject to vengeful violence, the ineradicable instinct for destruction that Freud located in the child's resentment of the omnipotent parents. Because the Mariner has no concrete motive the reader must actively discover his own motive in recognizing (as all readers do) the dramatic rightness of the Mariner's action. The reader sees through the preposterous rationale of the crew – (" 'Twas right, said they, such birds to slay, / That bring the fog and mist") which implicates them in the murder. But that recognition of spurious reasons for sympathy makes the reader's sympathy more discomfiting. The guilty identification forces the reader, like the Mariner, to feel the weight of the albatross's corpse until a spiritual conversion is effected in the poem.

It may be useful to look at one of the longest poems on the subject of birds in the nineteenth century to appreciate the kind of elegiac action appropriate to what might be called the Ancient Mariner motif in bird literature. James Grahame's *The Birds of Scotland*, published in 1806, is a poem of some 1500 lines in the georgic tradition that purports to "delineate the manners and characters of birds."[14] The volume is not so much a celebration of birds, however, as a catalogue of their destruction by "savage man" (p. 12). Beginning with a familiar topos in eighteenth-century literature, the sentimental regret for the death of an innocent animal, the poem, by constant repetition and variation, finally becomes a haunted and morbid-minded lament for the extermination of a whole part of the Creation. The severe indictment of humanity reminds one more of Swift than Thomson, and anticipates the twentieth-century poetry of this mode, culminating in works like Ted Hughes's *Crow* and *Cave-Birds*.

The rhetorical movement of mind in each verse paragraph is virtually the same. The poet identifies the bird, praises its winning features, and then dramatizes its cruel death at the hands or guns of mankind. The following example is introduced by a landscape of dancing flowers and greensward:

> Hither the long and soft-billed SNIPE resorts,
> By suction nourished; here her house she forms;
> Here warms her fourfold offspring into life.
> Alas, not long her helpless offspring feel
> Her fostering warmth; though suddenly she mounts,
> Her rapid rise, and vacillating flight,
> In vain defend her from the fowler's aim.   [p. 19]

Shortly before this passage we have read of the murder of the gorcock's covey by an especially sadistic hunter ("many a gory wing, exultingly he sees, / Drop, fluttering"), and shortly afterward Grahame remembers the inexplicable malignity of his young companions toward the yellowhammer ("Fair plumaged bird! cursed by the causeless hate / Of every schoolboy"). As in the passage above, frequent cries of "Alas" or "Poor bird" resonate throughout the poem.

In a world where "murder roam[s] at will" (p. 15), a psychological landscape very different from that of most bird poems emerges. From Grahame's perspective the birds are "falsely secure" (p. 12) because they are helpless against human intervention. Boys steal the young from the lark's nest – a scene reminiscent of the nest-robbing episode of Wordsworth's *Prelude* – and set snares for other birds; the farmer kills the partridge with his scythe; the landscape gardener cuts down trees which protect hundreds of birds; songbirds like the linnet are caged ("Oh, crime accursed!"); and hunters threaten every bird in the sky. The activity of man, in short, is to abrade the efforts of the Creation to fly. Man cannot tolerate the spectacle of a free spirit; he must and will encage or destroy it for various reasons, most of them, like the Mariner's, "causeless."

If the tendency of Grahame's contemporaries is to deny the physicality of the bird in favor of its idealized song, this poet contributes a corrective dose of realism. At times he pretends surprise at his own dark obsession. "Where, fancy, hast thou led me?" he exclaims at one point, and answers, "No, stern *truth*, / 'Tis thou hast led me" (p. 46). Fancy, the power he calls upon at the poem's opening to assist him, cannot help but avert its eyes at slaughter; Fancy cheats the mind, as Keats acknowledges in the Nightingale ode, by painting what should be rather than what is. Our fancy forms a conception of birdsong as, in Shelley's phrase, "an unbodied joy," but the truth is that joy is engendered by a physical apparatus. Grahame calls upon the hunter, "O, let not the leaden viewless shower, / Vollied from flashing tube, arrest [the thrush's] flight, / And fill his tuneful, gasping bill with blood!" (pp. 40–1). To a poet operating on the reality principle, exclamations more often are directed at man than bird, for the bird's survival depends on the man's capacity to reform his actions. The "viewless" object, for the same reason, is not the bird, as in the great Romantic odes, but the gunshot quicker than any flight which drowns the song in blood. Whatever rich resonance of association Shelley and Keats can give to song, there is a ceiling provided to their own flight by the audience which cannot tolerate the sight of free movement in the sky. In this sense the realistic mode shades into the symbolic, though Grahame does not exploit the correspondences he reveals. Blake certainly does in "Auguries of Innocence":

> A robin redbreast in a cage
> Puts all heaven in a rage.
> A skylark wounded in the wing
> A cherubim does cease to sing.

Every abridgment of the divine presence is a recapitulation of the Fall, a reinforcing of Satan's annihilating power to foil the Creator's scheme.

The enmity of man and bird is explored from a different angle in another book-length poem of this century, William John Courthope's *The Paradise of Birds* (1870), a verse drama much admired by Ruskin and W. H. Hudson. Mankind has annihilated all living birds, so a Romantic poet and a naturalist journey to the North Pole, where they believe a Platonic refuge of birds exists secure from human depredation. On the way they pass through a Purgatory of human souls who have helped to destroy avian life – a cook, a birdcatcher, a lady of fashion who coveted costume feathers – until they arrive at the bird community, where they successfully plead for two eggs of each species to repopulate the world. Courthope allows the birds their own voice in a "Song of Man" that expresses the bitter resentment of a race upon whom genocide has been practiced. The Nightingale delivers a characteristic speech:

> [Man's] heart, unforgiving,
> Grudged us the down on our coats,
> Envied the ease of our living,
> Hated the tune in our notes;
> And he snared us, too careless and merry,
> Or compassed our death with his gun,
> As we wheeled round the currant and cherry,
> Or bathed in the sun.[15]

Likewise, Elizabeth Barrett Browning gives the nightingale a voice in "Farewells from Paradise: Bird-Spirit" in which the immortal bird watches Adam and Eve leave the Garden:

> The creature-sounds, no longer audible,
> Expire at Eden's door,
> Each footstep of your treading
> Treads out some cadence which ye heard before.
> Farewell! the birds of Eden
> Ye shall hear nevermore.[16]

Nevermore. Like Poe's bird with its beak in the student's heart the nightingale torments man, who in turn torments all birds within his range as a condition of his unhappy exile from Paradise.

The nineteenth-century imagination insisted on seeing birds as a cultural group in danger of systematic destruction. James Fenimore Cooper's depiction of the slaughter of passenger pigeons in *The Pioneers* (1823) and Longfellow's cautionary poem, "The Birds of Killingworth" (1863), are the most famous texts of what can only be called a fabular literature of genocide. Birds tend to have a human face in such writings; poetic diction insists that birds are "the plumy people," "the feathered people of the boughs," "commoners of air," "tribes of the air," and so forth.[17] "Man and bird are brother," Mary Howitt affirms,[18] but the brotherhood of man and bird seems to be like that of Cain and Abel, a sibling rivalry between two irreconcilable states of being concluding in murder. Or put another way, Cain and Abel conspire against the bird-sister, as in W. H. Hudson's *Green*

Mansions (1904), where the narrator Abel intrudes into the Edenic sanctuary of the bird-girl Rima, and thus makes possible her murder by the Cain-like savages who fear her magical voice.

Another typical document on this subject is Percy Mackaye's masque of 1913, *Sanctuary*, performed for the dedication of the bird sanctuary of the Meriden Bird Club in New Hampshire. Mackaye himself played the part of Alwyn, the poet, who along with Shy, the naturalist, foils the attempt of Stark, the hunter, to slay Ornis, the bird-spirit. Stark is prevented from carrying out his deadly intentions by the establishment of the sanctuary, which preserves the birds and ushers in a new reign of love, what Shy calls "a greenwood partnership," between humans and birds.[19]

The bird's survival depends upon its *visibility*, its passage from a state of abstraction to that of recognizable, hence human character. Mackaye accomplishes this passage literally by means of the masque, in which the bird-spirit is personified and enacted by an actual woman. In a key bit of dialogue she approaches the hunter and reminds him that hers was the inspiring song he heard in the Edentime of his childhood. "Lo, I am Ornis, and I love you still!" her maiden speech concludes. Stark's reply is the most significant speech of the play:

> Yet – yet it seems I never heard your voice
> Till now; nor ever understood
> Till now; nor paused, as now in this still wood,
> To tremble and rejoice
> At greeting you, my sister. [p. 54]

This greeting of the spirit, to use Keats's phrase, occurs for the first time when the hunter comes face to face with his intended victim in the Sanctuary. The bird must be re-cognized as a moral creature subject to the laws and ethics that govern humanity, before the hunter can be persuaded to spare its life. Stark is not conscious of being a murderer because the plumage he seeks has a magical significance for him; he aspires to the beauty and charismatic power of the bird by taking its life. He must be rescued from the tyranny of idealization into the tradition of liberal humanism by the imposition of secular authority and institutional controls symbolized by the bird sanctuary.

In this chapter I have defined a pathology which underlies all writing about flying machines, including birds. The bird has attracted worshipful admiration because it seems to possess sheer life in such abundance it can be imagined as nearly divine. But the bird's status as a symbol could not survive the envy its quickness provoked. Vindictive hostility sought to spoil the enviable object, caging and killing it to such a degree that writers finally could not idealize the bird – set it apart from temporal action – without abrogating the responsibility to preserve it as a living creature. This is not to say that envy has disappeared, only that the ability to produce a mechanical imitation which could occupy the bird's place in the Paradise of the upper air permitted writers and readers to worship an object less frail, less of a memento mori to the imagination. That human technics, once injured by the bird's superior powers, could henceforth become the object itself of universal admiration, answered the desire of an increasingly industrialized civilization. What writers would now have to report is that when *Homo invidiosus* put on his knowledge of aeronautical being he did not leave behind the aggressive power which envy had nourished; rather, he took his enabling instinct for destruction into the sky.

4. Wells and *The War in the Air*

"The telephone bell rings with the petulant persistence that marks a trunk call, and I go in from some ineffectual gymnastics on the lawn to deal with the irruption. There is the usual trouble in connecting up, minute voices in Folkestone and Dover and London call to one another and are submerged by buzzings and throbbings. Then in elfin tones the real message comes through: 'Blériot has crossed the Channel.... An article ... about what it means.'"[1]

The date is 25 July 1909, and Louis Blériot has won the *Daily Mail* prize of five hundred pounds for being the first pilot to cross the English Channel in a motor-driven aeroplane. The recipient of the call is H. G. Wells, who has been contacted not only because he is a recognized pundit more than willing to comment on any significant current event, but because he has been writing fiction and reportage about aeronautics for some sixteen years. "Argonauts of the Air" (1895), for example, was a thinly disguised account of Otto Lilienthal's experiments with a glider; the fatal crash at story's end anticipated Lilienthal's death the following year. *When the Sleeper Wakes* (1899) and its closely related short story, "A Dream of Armageddon," had elaborated on the nightmare prospect of aerial warfare, not to mention *The War of the Worlds* (1898). More recently, Wells's polemical novel *The War in the Air* (1908) had electrified the English-speaking world by chronicling prospective dirigible raids against the United States and aerial combat by every kind of flying machine imaginable. Now in the stenographic syntax of the modern age – the ellipses in the quotation are Wells's – he is given the opportunity by journalistic fiat to construe an historical event of peculiar resonance for the British Isles.

One must pause to admire the way Wells introduces his finished article by calling attention to its origin. Telephone communications offer the estranging echolalia of station operators, and the high-pitched transmission he captures in the phrase "elfin tones." Yes, there is still something magical about these invisible voices, something belonging to the ethos of fairyland that the author of "The Door in the Wall" (1906) finds compelling. But the phrase "elfin tones" immediately precedes "the real message" which does come through; the sentence that begins in fantasy presents in its main clause a triumphant fact. Fantasy and fact coexist as framing contraries for the stark announcement on the other side of the colon: "Blériot has crossed the Channel." While one representative Englishman was performing his "ineffectual gymnastics on the lawn" a French mechanic – the French possessed the most advanced air technology of that time – had made an "irruption" that must give the insular kingdom considerable pause. Wells has anticipated the significance he will give to the flight in the article's title, "The Coming of Blériot." His readers would hear a clear echo of the nineteenth century's most famous heroic poem, Tennyson's *Idylls of the King*, whose first book is "The Coming of Arthur." Camelot and Fairyland are summoned for an identical rhetorical purpose: as recollections of the irremediably lost dream-worlds of the nineteenth century, which now must yield to the "real" wonders of scientific enterprise. By 1909 Wells is the undisputed prophet of that transformation in history of which the airplane threatens to become the chief technological symbol.

"What it means" is that England is in mortal danger. In the Darwinian struggle among nations for supremacy in strength and ingenuity, England has lost its lead. It has failed to cross the fin de siècle with the momentum of its earlier achievements. In his fiction and journalism Wells tends to confront what in *The War in the Air* he calls the "hallucination of security" (XX.337) – security based on the undeniable fact that things had gone well for the English – with new machinery of such devastating power that it could overwhelm the old civilization with one swift genocidal attack. In many nineteenth-century works a sentimental attachment to a dying culture is mortified, a hallucination of security shattered, in order for "modernity" to emerge in a recognizable form. The classic statement is King Arthur's in Tennyson's elegiac poem: "The old order changeth, yielding place to the new, / And God fulfills himself in many ways, / Lest one good custom should corrupt the world." Like Tennyson, Wells was capable of affirming that change was progressive, a boon to the aspiring modern spirit. The author of books like *The Outline of History* and *The Work, Wealth and Happiness of Mankind* expected great benefits from the supersession of cultural behaviors. And yet such changes enter Wells's fiction in a pessimistic form. Here we see them in the narrator's comment – from a future prospect of nearly a century – in *The War in the Air*:

> Up to the very eve of the War in the Air one sees a spacious spectacle of incessant advance, a world-wide security, enormous areas with highly organised industry and settled populations, gigantic cities spreading gigantically, the seas and oceans dotted with shipping, the land netted with rails and open ways. Then suddenly the German air-fleets sweep across the scene, and we are in the beginning of the end. [XX.341]

The coming of Blériot signals The Passing of Arthur, the presence of national exhaustion, depopulation, and death – "The stillness of the dead world's winter dawn" as Tennyson evokes the aftermath of the "Great Battle of the West." The distance from Tennyson's poem to Wells's novel is precisely measured by the flying machine itself.

If Wells needed a warning sign, the Hague Conference of 1899 and 1907 provided him with a sufficiently chilling one. In the first meeting the Conference prohibited balloons and airships from discharging projectiles and explosives; all European nations subscribed to the prohibition, which they agreed to renew at the next Conference. In 1907 amendments enforced by the chief powers prevented the prohibition from being made a permanent one; rather, a five-year renewal encouraged the nations to speed up the armaments race. It was obvious that expediency – to Wells's mind the law of natural selection – would determine the use of aerial bombardment in future wars. Blériot appeared, then, as the anti-Arthur, the harbinger of ruin, for he symbolized the capacity of foreign nations to cross the Channel and overwhelm England by means of a superior machinery. When Napoleon had threatened such an invasion a hundred years earlier he possessed no such machinery, though it is worth remarking that after the first balloon crossing of the Channel in 1785, by Jean-Pierre Blanchard, abundant engravings, cartoons, and popular literature appeared in England and France which entertained the notion of aerial invasion. Likewise, a century later, a French journal published a cartoon showing the ghost of Napoleon gazing upon Blériot's landing in England and saying, "Pourquoi pas cent ans plus tôt!"[2] The coincidence in the 1900s of a hostile European power (Germany) and an epoch-making advance in aerial technology revived and intensified apocalyptic fears.

Before Wells, fantasy writers had imagined the danger to England in the form of overseas invasion, with all the necessary stages of docking, shoreline battles, gradual advance through countryside toward the centers of population, skirmishes, siege and blockade, and so forth. The whole of European literature from the classical period to the present had established a narrative tradition upon which nineteenth-century writers – usually hacks providing sensational copy for cheap magazines – could draw consciously or unconsciously. Wells perceived clearly that the old paradigms of war literature were insufficient, and that once aircraft outgrew its infant forms war would become three-dimensional, obliterating the "front line" and with it the distinction between civilian and soldier. A nation's entire population could very quickly be brought into jeopardy by a blitzkrieg. *The War in the Air* is best seen as a statesman's manual, like *The Prince*, which makes its recommendations in the conditional grammar of threat. The extremity of violence in the novel is calibrated to offset the resistance to change. If most readers, including the country's leaders, suffer from the hallucination of security, then the strong medicine prescribed must be a hallucination of equal and opposite power. Nothing but the new form called scientific romance could conjure a spectacle sufficiently shocking to penetrate the torpor of the English public.

One must add that even the forward-looking Wells was surprised by the rapid development of the airplane, and this may account for the fervor of his proselytizing. As late as 1901, in *Anticipations*, he predicted only that "long before the year A.D. 2000, and very probably before 1950, a successful aeroplane will have soared and come home safe and sound" (IV.168). The flights of the Wright brothers, Blériot, and others indicated that advancement would be rapid. Wells was especially impressed with the achievements of Count Zeppelin in Germany, who had been developing his dirigibles since the 1890s. In 1907 he sailed his rigid airship LZ-3 for ten hours over Lake Constance at an average speed of twenty miles an hour. By contrast, England launched her very first airship, small and non-rigid, the same year; it landed at the Crystal Palace where, buffeted by strong winds, it had to be deflated, ripped up, and carted back to its factory in Aldershot: no mean symbol of England's incapacity. "Can England Be Raided?" – a chapter title in a book on airships published the same year as *The War in the Air* – must have been a common question of the period. Wells's antennae were always uncommonly responsive to new figures for the Zeitgeist, new images that enforced irrevocable changes in the historical moment. His new literary task was, in Karl Marx's phrase, not to interpret the world but to change it, by presenting the case for the airship's dangerous preeminence in the immediate future.

The plot of *The War in the Air* is best seen as a framework flexible enough to support Wells's frequent discursive asides, presented as the jeremiads of an indignant narrator gazing back upon the the stupidities of the early moderns. The novel's protagonist, Bert Smallways, is a young Cockney who works (like the Wright brothers) in a bicycle shop, and enjoys modern inventions, unlike his gardening, greengrocer father. The magus of the new century is Alfred Butteridge who invents and pilots an airplane from the Crystal Palace to Glasgow early in the novel. The first chapters give us a vivid picture of the ballooning and gliding vogue in the century's first years, for it seems that everywhere Bert goes The Aero Club is exhibiting its latest designs. Before transforming it into an emblem of apocalypse, Wells wants first to depict the flying machine as an instrument of pleasure – as he will do the next year in *Tono-Bungay* – a vehicle for enhanced enjoyment of life. The reader is at the turning point of some momentous paradigm shift. The flying machine is still the plaything of the old society; a chapter later it will become the invincible weapon of the new.

One day Butteridge lands a balloon on Dymchurch Beach where Bert is walking and when Bert complies with a request to hold onto it he is swept upward and conveyed, alone, across the Channel to Germany, where he views with surprise a fleet of dirigibles being readied for some sinister purpose. Captured by the Germans who think he is Butteridge, he is compelled to accompany the evil geniuses of the new German military machine, Prince Karl Albert and Lieutenant Kurt, on a transatlantic flight and aerial bombardment attack upon New York City. The City surrenders after City Hall, the Post Office, Brooklyn Bridge, and other sites are reduced to rubble. New York, the narrator tells us, is "the first of the great cities of the Scientific Age to suffer by the enormous powers and grotesque limitations of aerial warfare" (XX.200). "Limitations" refers to the fact that a city cannot be occupied by an aerial force; it can only be subdued by repeated bombings. When the population of New York begins a guerrilla movement against the raiders, the German air-sailors massacre civilians. In an ensuing period of indefinite length a worldwide war breaks out. Other countries had been secretly building flying machines in preparation for a first strike. The Eastern Confederation, Japan and China, sends many thousands of dirigibles and airplanes against the West. Famine and pestilence grip England. London is in ruins. The novel ends some thirty years later with the war still sputtering, while the survivors try to figure out how and why it all happened.

Unlike Wells's masterfully plotted scientific romances of the preceding decade, *The War in the Air* is more remarkable for spectacle than complex design. The reason is an important one for our purposes, however. The narrative exists principally to highlight the image of the airship. Wells has exercised the minimum amount of extrapolation in portraying this "monster" – to cite a favorite epithet. Indeed, he provides a genealogy rooted in events every reader of 1908 would recall from recent headlines: "the great airships with which Germany attacked New York ... were the lineal descendants of the Zeppelin airship that flew over Lake Constance in 1906, and of the Lebaudy navigables that made their memorable excursions over Paris in 1907 and 1908" (XX.91). Bert acts as the common reader's stand-in; his dramatic role is to observe the mysteries of the dirigible, and to testify by his wonder ("GAW" is his recurring ejaculation) to its unprecedented magnitude.

The dirigible belongs to the tradition of the technological sublime which became so popular during the nineteenth century. Wells makes use of every rhetorical device available that would enhance the *mysterium tremendum* of the new machine. Adjectives like *great*, *vast*, *gigantic*, *astonishing* and *overwhelming* recur frequently, often in combinations. The amount of space in the dirigible staggers Bert — for it is capable of carrying a troop of air-sailors in its compartments. The design in black of "the Imperial eagle ... an overwhelming bird in the dimness" (XX.110) decorates the outer skin of the machine, a sign of the magazine of explosives occupying the middle of the airship. The eagle carries forward the motif of the irresistible *uccello* to which visionary writers had given so much attention in the centuries preceding Wells — all the way back to the Rumor Bird which threatens great cities in Virgil's *Aeneid*. Unlike earlier writers, however, Wells has a scientific context, the Darwinian theory, appropriate to the emergent bird-machine.

The airship is often described by anatomical terminology. It has "a headlike fore part" and a "central backbone" and "big ribs like the neural and haemal canals" (XX.136), as if it were a living being, a new avian creature in evolutionary history superseding those other bird forms which by 1908 were disappearing as a result of human technology. Wells's language tends toward a vulgarized Darwinism when he describes the airship: "a most complete adaptation of the fish form to aerial conditions" (XX.92) or "The apparatus of warfare, the art and method of fighting, changed absolutely every dozen years in a stupendous progress toward perfection" (XX.101). Wells's "science" is not always solemn. He delights in the prolific variety of new species in the air, and catalogues them by name and similitude: the "bladders" (balloons) of The Aero Club, Butteridge's "gas-distended elephant," the "fly-like mechanism" of a smaller airplane, the "altogether fishlike" German airships, the "Colt-Coburn-Langley pattern" of the American airplane with its front propeller screw, and so on. There is even a moment during the aerial battle over Niagara Falls when the comic aspect of these immense hybrid forms overcomes the author (not the narrator, I think), and he remarks how they are "like clouds fighting, like puddings trying to assassinate each other" (XX.262). At such moments we hear behind Wells's profundities the playful mockery of Samuel Butler, whose application of evolutionary theory to machines in *Erewhon* (1872) expertly fused elements of the satiric and prophetic.

At least one function of the Bert Smallways episodes is to tone down associations with the prophetic tradition. By keeping Bert at the center, Wells maintains a connection with the kind of story boys' weeklies popularized at the turn of the century: the adventures of an energetic juvenile in the sophisticated intrigue of the adult world. As he often does, Wells draws upon his own childhood anxieties as a model for the protagonist. Albert Peter Smallways is a version of Herbert George Wells in his formative years. Known as "little Bertie," the young Wells drank in an abundance of millenarian symbolism from his mother's depressed conversation and favorite religious texts, the Bible and *Pilgrim's Progress*. "The fundamental impress was that of a fearful religion upon a fearful child," his biographers remark.[3] They add that "these fears were intensified by a feeling that he was physically weak and vulnerable." Wells compensated throughout his childhood by war fantasies in which he cast himself as a dictator, necromancer, or demigod. As a novelist Wells shared his former envy of virile action with readers uninitiated into the technological rites of passage, which he often renders in the grammar of sexual conflict. The central fantasy of *The War in the Air* is the Oedipal yearning for mastery over one's "Motherland" (XX.31). Scopophilia (instinctual gratification from looking) abounds. Bert always seems to be peeking surreptitiously at the forbidden – a favorite motif in Wells's fiction. "He was quite involuntarily playing that weird mysterious part [when he observes the dirigibles] – the part of an International Spy. He was seeing secret things" (XX.90). Bert's appreciation of the phallic dirigible is clearly meant to be a moment of erotic awakening into manhood.

Bert receives an education from Lieutenant Kurt and Prince Karl Albert. The Prince might be described as the paternal will of the flying machine. The likely source for this figure is Jules Verne's imperious pilot Robur the Conqueror, in the 1886 novel of that title and its sequel of 1904, *Master of the World*. Like Leonardo's necromancer, Robur achieves mastery by means of his flying machine. "With the invention of this airship," he exults, "I hold control of the entire world, and there lies no force within the reach of humanity which is able to resist me."[4] Likewise, the narrator of Wells's novel remarks of the Prince that "to many, he seemed Nietzsche's Overman revealed" (XX.104). Whereas both Butteridge and Bert continually plot to make some money out of their experiences – a nation of shopkeepers to the end – the Prince's vision is determined by the selfless national mythology that shapes his vision. He has commissioned a portrait of the Viking War God for the dirigible *Vaterland* in which Bert recognizes the Prince's own features. It is precisely his desire to imitate the divinities of Valhalla that causes the Prince to plot his course toward the New World.

Germany had become the great modern state because it found a means to take advantage of England's superannuated gentility. Germany is post-civilized, one might say, whereas England is merely civilized, cultivating its garden rather than sharpening its claws. By 1907 it was obvious to everyone that the Germans were developing the dirigible in order to bomb London as soon as hostilities broke out. As far back as 1887, Prince Kraft zu Hohelohe, who had commanded the Grand Artillery in the Franco-Prussian War, remarked about that war, "The manner in which the campaign was opened on the part of the Germans will ... remain a standard pattern so long as new inventions do not create new strategical means, *such as aeronautics might do.*"[5] When the opportunity arrived in 1914 to make use of such means, the Chief of Naval Staff in Germany wrote in a memorandum: "I hold the view that we should leave no means untried to crush England and that air raids on London, in view of the already existing nervousness of the people, would prove a valuable means to this end."[6]

It seems clear that the choice of target proceeds from the fact of the airship itself, and Wells's desire to publicize it as the essential expression of the modern world. The feasibility of a London bombardment could most easily be demonstrated by dramatizing the dirigible's capacity to achieve a much more difficult task. The airship must be apotheosized by increasing its destructive power to the limits of the imagination – and beyond. An air raid on New York was called for precisely because it seemed incredible.

There is another reason for the choice of New York City. In Chapter VI New York is called "the modern Babylon" and likened to "the apocalyptic cities of the ancient prophets." Wells does everything he can to establish, and insist upon by repetition, the topos of the Fall of Empires. If the positivist view emphasizes the slow accumulation of skills and arts that fosters a unique culture, Wells's prophetic eye looks back at modern history and sees only the apocalyptic downfall. And that downfall cannot help but have a providential character. In an earlier paragraph Wells renders the armada approaching New York in these terms:

"Clouds veiled the sea again, and the long straggling wedge of airships rising and falling as they flew seemed like a flock of strange new births in a Chaos that had neither earth nor water, but only mist and sky" (XX.170). In this parody of Genesis, the dirigibles will give form to the new century and the New World. The birds cannot escape association with the holy spirit: primal creator, sponsoring figure of Annunciation and presumably of the Second Coming as well. Wells entertained the possibility that the inevitable apocalypse Germany was preparing would produce from its ruins the phoenix of a disciplined worldwide social system made orderly by aircraft, the argument of his postwar book, *The Shape of Things to Come*.

The dirigible, then, becomes the harrow of the Almighty, his "strange" bird sent to punish the iniquity of London and New York. That Wells was not alone in his feelings can be demonstrated by quoting from one of the few poems relating to aerial warfare in *War Verse*, a widely-read patriotic anthology of English poetry published in 1918:

> *Song of the Zeppelin*
> Ship without sails am I,
> Bird without wings am I,
> Lord of the gales am I,
> Terror of Kings am I, –
> I am the Zeppelin!
> . . . .
> Mark well the flight of me,
> Ships! Have a care of me!
> Shrink at the sight of me!
> Cities! Beware of me!
> I am the Zeppelin![7]

What, we wonder, would cause Violet D. Chapman, whoever she is, to celebrate the speed, power, and efficiency of the enemy aircraft very probably bombing her own country at the time of composition? The poem's obvious source, W. E. Henley's "Song of the Sword," gives us one clue. "Clear singing, clean slicing; / Sweet spoken, soft finishing, / Making death beautiful. / I am the Will of God: / I am the Sword." Because the Will that destroys also creates, it is possible to welcome the divine instrument as a figure of personal and cultural redemption. By figural correspondences between sacred (scriptural) and secular events, writers sought to mitigate the terror of the flying machine. They accommodated its powers to a predetermined historical design that offered some cheerful promise in the midst of crisis and widespread destruction. Some such motive informs D. H. Lawrence's description of the Zeppelin as an apocalyptic symbol, in a letter of 1915:

> Last night when we were coming home the guns broke out, and there was a noise of bombs. Then we saw the Zeppelin above us, just ahead, amid a gleaming of clouds: high up, like a bright golden finger, quite small, among a fragile incandescence of clouds. And underneath it were splashes of fire as the shells fired from the earth burst. Then there were flashes near the ground – and the shaking noise. It was like Milton – then there was war in heaven. But it was not angels. It was that small golden Zeppelin, like a long oval world, high up. It seemed as if the cosmic order were gone, as if there had come a new order, a new heaven above us: and as if the world in anger were trying to revoke it. Then the small, long-ovate luminary, the new world in the heavens, disappeared again.[8]

"So it is the end – our world is gone," Lawrence concludes. As Blake and Shelley made the lark into a redemptive force a century earlier, so Lawrence and his contemporaries observed in the "bright golden finger" of the Zeppelin an index of Annunciation. A change in the *form* of events, not just in the fortune of national destinies, could be sighted in the heavens.

Despite the eschatological subtext, however, Wells sympathized principally with the victims of aerial technology, the smallways of his origins. His prewar writings argue that history would sustain a definition of the flying machine as an essentially demonic invention. His prophecies remained the most influential writings on the airplane throughout his lifetime, and well into the Atomic Age, which he foresaw in his novel *The World Set Free* (1914), a narrative comparable in many ways to *The War in the Air*. Whenever a later writer wished to express the anxiety attendant upon an exploded hallucination of security, Wellsian imagery came to his aid. Rudyard Kipling imitated Wells's conceptions in describing the Aerial Board of Control, which enforces its will upon Chicago in the futurist fantasy, "As

Easy as A.B.C." (1912). W. H. Auden in "Journal of an Airman" (from *The Orators*), has his diarist record, "The faint tang of irretrievable disaster; as if Lake Constance were outside the window and had destroyed all countries and human beings," an entry illuminated by a later one: "Read . . . the life of Count Zeppelin (obtainable in Air and Airways Library)." Olaf Stapledon opens his epic novel of 1930, *Last and First Men*, with an aerial version of Armageddon clearly borrowed from Wells. And V. Sackville-West concludes her novel *Grand Canyon* (1942) with a German blitz against New York City: "It seemed that the combat of civilization could go no further, could reach no higher peak of dread than in this whirling, screaming vortex of war planes over and between the skyscrapers of the towering city."[9]

As World War II approached, William Rose Benét looked back upon the history of aviation in his book-length verse chronicle of flight, *With Wings as Eagles* (1941), a sequence that accents the positive, and recalled Wells in his "Ballad of Louis Blériot":

> He flew – and England's prophet
> Wells, as he strained his eyes
> Out toward the windy Channel,
> Saw the hooded future rise,
>
> Saw England's fleet-walled island
> Dissolve into idle words –
> Her day of reckoning coming
> Far off, in a swarm of birds.

At the end of the poem the power of prophecy is appropriately shifted from Wells to Blériot's airplane, "Whose dragonfly floating wings / Prophesied a united world / Or else – the end of things?"[10] It is the one moment in Benét's book when he dares to peer into the abyss. Wells gave him and his generation the strength and imagination to do so by being the first to chart out all possibilities of the airplane's intervention into history, and especially the events mankind could expect if the flying machine were given privileges in keeping with its omnipotence as a weapon.

5. "Tumult in the Clouds": The Flying Machine and the Great Crusade

In *The Great War and Modern Memory* Paul Fussell argues that the hostilities of 1914–1918 necessarily caused a revaluation of writers in the preceding generation, and that the chief beneficiary was Thomas Hardy. The name of H. G. Wells can certainly be added to Hardy's. For those who apprehended a new social order in the making, specifically because of the airplane, Wells seemed in retrospect the one eye among the blind. Technological advances from the beginning of the century had persuaded many writers that anything was possible. As early as 1905, Henry Adams remarked that "bombs educate vigorously, and even wireless telegraphy or airships might require the reconstruction of society."[1] When bombs and airships united in a single form, Wells's prophecies made the unprecedented results at least semi-intelligible. If, as Fussell maintains, the myth-history of the Great War half-created the war literature that succeeded it, how much more recognizable are the apocalyptic fictions of Wells – which Fussell ignores – than the memoirs of Sassoon and Graves!

By 1918 the bombing of cities was a realized nightmare that would haunt the human imagination ever afterward. In Wellsian fashion convoys of Zeppelins (after 1916 Gotha airplanes) had raided England repeatedly, dropping nearly 9,000 bombs and leaving 1,414 dead and 3,408 wounded. There were 51 airship and 52 airplane attacks. London was bombed 12 times by airship and 19 times by airplane, at a cost of 670 killed and 1,962 wounded. And, as W. H. Berry pointed out in a widely read report, New York City was just as vulnerable to aerial attack as Wells said it was, albeit by different means. A typical submarine of 1918 could house six seaplanes which, an hour's flight from the eastern American seaboard, could unload heavier and more devastating bombs than any dropped on London. The planes could return to the submarines for more bombs, and inflict horrifying damage to New York in a single night. Berry borrows an idea from another Wells novel, *The First Men in the Moon*, for a prediction of his own: that in the future cities may have to be constructed underground in order to defend themselves against aerial bombardment.[2] Perhaps Berry knowingly overstated his case, but the extremity of destruction throughout the Great War gave a latitude to alarmist rhetoric. No doomsday scenario could be entirely dismissed in an era of stupendous technological progress.

In terms of actual effect, the air war was a sideshow, and widely acknowledged as such. English citizens resolutely stiffened their resistance after air raids. But to state the matter so simply is to conceal the enduring trauma engendered by the bombings. Anti-aircraft guns were sufficiently crude that airplanes were in little danger from them, but the bombers did have to stay above 10,000 feet for protection, and at that height, in the dark of the moon, precision bombing was impossible. Bombs might fall anywhere and kill anyone, so that the sound of engines in the sky harrowed even the most stoical. Arnold Bennett recalls a conversation of 1917 with Wells in which "he said that in air raids he was afraid of going to pieces altogether."[3] It is this personal fear that Wells, and Bennett, located as the unique fatality of the wartime period.

Bennet provides a description of the bombings in his novel of 1918, *The Pretty Lady*:

> He thought about death and maiming and blood. The relations between him and those everyday males aloft in the sky seemed to be appallingly close. After the explosion perfect silence – no screams, no noise of crumbling – perfect silence, and yet the explosion seemed still to dominate the air! Ears ached and sang. Something must be done. All theories of safety had been smashed to atoms in the explosion.
>
> . . . . .
>
> True, it was an explosion. But the previous event had been an explosion, and this one was a thousandfold more intimidating. The earth swayed up and down. The sound alone of the immeasurable cataclysm annihilated the universe.

The sound and the concussion transcended what had been conceivable.[4]

In one chapter the main character shines an electric torch on "a child's severed arm, with a fragment of brown frock on it and a tinsel ring on one of the fingers of the dirty little hand" (p. 232). The arm, like the "dissevered legs and arms ... being thrown into buckets" (p. 160) noted earlier, is an image that focuses the horror otherwise lost in the language of sublimity quoted above. The death by shrapnel in the brain of the protagonist's adored young female friend brings the terror of the raids home to him, for all his efforts to stand apart from the war or view it as a delectable spectacle. His friend's death represents to his mind the extinction of the society she and he embody: the genteel leisure class which the Zeppelin raids forcefully deliver from its boredom. Similarly, the German bombers at the conclusion of Shaw's *Heartbreak House* are welcomed by the dead souls in that play – they turn on the house lights to give the planes a target – as a means of shocking them from their absurd dream-life.

The Great Crusade, as David Lloyd George called it in his wartime book of that title, was "great" because of the breadth of its boundaries, the magnitude of its statistics, and its momentous implications for the future of the race. It took on the semblance of sublime history, horrible and bewitching to the imagination. "In a deep sense he was enjoying it," Bennett writes of his protagonist, "the immensity of it, the terror of it, the idiocy of it, the splendour of it, its unique grandeur as an illustration of human nature, thrilled the spectator in him" (p. 217). By breaking down psychic as well as geographical boundaries the sublime event liberates the instincts and effects a profound sense of community. Edmund Burke, a scholar of the sublime, noted that the guillotine became a folk hero during the French Revolution for enabling this frenzied binding. Aircraft, more than any other instrument of warfare, involved spectators in a display of force that awed and threatened them.

Vulnerability to danger is part of the sublime, as egoistic control dissolves during the onset of an overwhelming stimulus. When such rapture is the effect of a natural event, as most often in Romantic literature, the spectacle is cherished for its revelation of profound depths of feeling, including the sense of immortality. But when the external stimulus is an afflictive and manmade one, the sublime can lead downward through exciting terror into an abyss from which there is no cathartic escape. One of Rudyard Kipling's "Epitaphs of the War" makes the crucial point:

> *Bombed in London*
> On land and sea I strove with anxious care
> To escape conscription. It was in the air![5]

Every living thing is drafted into the condition of danger produced by a machine with infinite extension and devastating firepower. The writer's response, then, must always be to locate the human "text" in the context of the sublime; not merely to enjoy the spectacle but to pass judgment on its horror by insisting upon its toll in terms apprehensible by sympathy – as Bennett does in *The Pretty Lady*. Otherwise, there is nothing but the Futurist religion of force.

The civilian view of the air war is one thing, the airman's view is another. It is an odd fact of literary history, however, that this view has not been allowed entrance to the canonical literature of The Great War. Anthologies such as Eugene Löhrke's *Armageddon: The World War in Literature* (1930) and George A. Panichas's *Promise of Greatness: The War of 1914–1918* (1968) hardly notice the airman, and the principal critical studies of Great War literature – by John A. Johnston, Bernard Bergonzi, Paul Fussell, Jon Silkin, and John Lehmann – devote their entire attention to writings about the trenches. It is unquestionably true that almost the totality of first-rate poems and memoirs about the war were written by Owen, Rosenberg, Sassoon, Blunden, Read, and Graves. But I would argue that some of the aviation literature has a complexity of theme and imagery worthy of comparison with work by infantrymen. Aviators experienced a sensation of speed and power unprecedented in history, and the moral ambiguities of their situation challenged their capacity to articulate that firstness. What we miss in their work is the gritty concreteness and the range of feeling captured by men who endured the wretched trial of combat day after day. We have a popular image of the Great War created mainly by the poets named above, and writers who discovered a different kind of war may seem irrelevant to the one we acknowledge as our "modern memory." Mud and stench and boredom and the overwhelming presence of the dead – these are what we "remember" from the war. When Billy Bishop opens his memoir, the most famous of the air war, "It was the mud, I think, that made me take to flying," we cannot help but feel that his choice of service abrogated his right to speak of the authentic war we have canonized.[6]

But in compensation we get something of unique value from the aviators: an anatomy of the lordly privilege derived from elevation itself. The war provided an enlistee with alternatives that conformed to the radical opposition of heaven and earth I have charted in the imaginative writings of nineteenth-century authors. There is the familiar terrestrial world, made repulsive by war activities. Bishop renders it thus: "Everything was dank, and slimy, and boggy. I had succeeded in getting myself mired to the knees...." Bishop is preparing to describe a pure experience of envy, and he adjusts his environment to his morbid sense of inescapable bondage in the element of creatureliness. Then comes a vision:

> ... when suddenly, from somewhere out of the storm, appeared a trim little aeroplane.
> It landed hesitating in a near-by field as if scorning to brush its wings against so sordid a landscape; then away again up into the clean grey mists.
> How long I stood there gazing into the distance I do not know, but when I turned to slog my way back through the mud my mind was made up. I knew there was only one place to be on such a day – up above the clouds and in the summer sunshine.

The visitation of the plane is like that of the butterfly in Hawthorne's tale, "The Artist of the Beautiful." Because the healthy psyche, as Shelley remarked in his poem on the skylark, is a "scorner of the ground," Bishop's word "scorn" is the proper one for the dramatic context. From the "sordid" the mind naturally aspires to the "clean," and the flying machine provides the most effective means of making that purifying ascent.

And how exactly does one feel after earning wings? Bishop's account is simply a boastful scorecard of successful kills; a text of more intense moral questioning is required. I shall examine in some detail a long poem by Captain Paul Bewsher, D.S.C.,

R.A.F. – as he is described on the title page – called "The Bombing of Bruges."[7] It was published in a volume of that title in England in 1918, with a number of short poems mainly on aerial bombardment. Though Bewsher also authored another book of poems on the same theme – *The Dawn Patrol* (1917) – and a highly readable memoir, '*Green Balls*' (1919), he is unmentioned in every literary history of the war.

"The Bombing of Bruges" is a poem of 296 lines, in heroic couplets, describing a single bombing raid against the German-held city of Bruges, in Belgium. In narrative action the poem derives from Bewsher's earlier account, "The Night Raid," in *The Dawn Patrol*, but the astonishing advance in skill within a single year shows us that Bewsher no less than other war poets matured very fast during those harrowing months. The earlier poem is slightly more than half the length, and devotes only ten lines to the actual bombing of the target, while indulging in longer descriptions of leaving and returning to home base. The later poem begins as the bomber approaches Bruges, and describes the bombardment moment by moment. When compared with the account of this raid in his memoir, it is clear that Bewsher has telescoped in the poem experiences and feelings from different raids during his career in the Royal Air Force, especially his first bombing runs into Germany and the Lowland countries. Though a competent pilot in his own right, Bewsher acted as navigator and bombardier on this run. The distinction is important because the separation of functions placed an increased responsibility upon Bewsher, who had to make all the split-second decisions which determined how lethal the bombings would be, and whether the plane's crew would escape death from anti-aircraft fire. The success of a bombing raid, for example, depended upon cutting the motor at just the right time so that anti-aircraft crews would not hear the plane overhead. If the motor was cut too soon the plane would lose too much altitude before reaching its target, not only making it vulnerable to guns at the target's perimeter but wasting its chance at a successful strike. The tension and anxiety of the flight, and the joyful release once the bombs were dropped and the plane escaped the searchlights, make up an arc of emotion more capable of sustained narrative development than trench experiences could encompass. A long poem of infantry life – setting aside special cases like David Jones's *In Parenthesis* – is likely to be antidramatic, a depiction of exhaustion, entropy, and futility. But aerial bombardment presents Bewsher with a pattern of rising and falling action within which both ruminative and expository elements can be effectively set.

The couplet form is well-chosen for the lengthy narrative. This excerpt will suggest the whole:

Now I can see the target for my load
Which hangs behind me ready to explode: –
Fourteen great bombs which are the friends of Death,
Of battered bodies and of bubbling breath –
The weapons which are foreordained to slay
Men I have never seen – yet I will pray
That their poor souls may rest in lasting peace
Since I this load of evil must release.
Now I am almost o'er the crowded docks –
Far from the ground, inside a wooden box,
Alone and unprotected in the sky;
Aware that I perhaps may have to die
In a few moments . . . but the men below
Will die before me, for with movement slow
I push the wooden lever by my side,
And hear a click as four bombs slide
Into the darkness . . . hang . . . and turn around,
And rush in screaming progress to the ground.
Again, again I pull the lever back
And push . . . and hear the clatter of the rack
Behind me as the yellow bombs drop clear
And shriek towards the ground, and bring swift fear
To many a man that knows not where to hide,
But crouches – motionless and terrified.
Then I look far below with eager eyes
To where the unsuspecting country lies . . .
Sleep on no more! The bombs are screaming down,
And sleep is murdered in the little town!

[pp. 11–12]

The chief virtue of the couplet is that the rhyme-unit gives a sense of completion to each two lines, so that the poet can maneuver swiftly from action to action ("Now . . . Now . . . Again, again . . . Then I look . . .") or from action to comment and back to action with a quickness that mimics not only the flight but the excited reverie which gives each moment meaning. Also, the couplet has been at least since Dryden's and Pope's time a means of expressing the tension between a highly ordered or civilized rhetorical form and a disordered skein of events which mocks or threatens its stable container. Couplets, too, are designed to brand themselves with epigrammatic force upon the memory:

> *Sleep on no more!* The bombs are screaming down,
> And sleep is murdered in the little town!

There is superb concentration of effect here. The first half-line is an exclamation directed both at the "unsuspecting" target, and, by means of the allusion to *Macbeth*, at himself; the next half-line is a declarative sentence rising in pitch because of the emotive (and very precise) verb, and then the second line makes the sentence a compound one by adding effect to cause, fulfilling the action in a way that both satisfies the reader's expectation and disturbs him for seeking a violent completion.

By this I mean that the reader wishes the "screaming" to stop, yet when it does, both bombardier and reader know that other screaming will begin. It is screaming that cannot be heard by either party, and that silence is more harrowing than explosions, as we shall see. The "screaming" of this line appropriately repeats a usage nine lines back – "And rush in screaming progress to the ground" – for the experience of bombing is one of mechanical and repetitive action: pulling the lever again and again as the various targets are approached. One notices also the pun on "progress," perhaps the most ubiquitous cant word of the prewar period. The effect is that of poetic kenning: bombs = screaming progress. The repetition of word and phrase, echoing as it does the sequence of murders, makes Macbeth's progress in crime a controlling metaphor. In Bewsher's couplet the allusion to the murder of Duncan, the horrible act which unravels not only sleep but the whole community, provides a perspective on bombardment that one will not find in official histories of the war in the air.

The allusions to *Macbeth* are the only sustained ones in the poem and for that reason worth pursuing as a model of Bewsher's use of a familiar narrative to give increased complexity to his own story. The speeches of Duncan and Banquo upon arrival at

Macbeth's castle have become the classic expression of the hallucination of security. Duncan speaks the language of trust when he says, "This castle hath a pleasant seat, the air / Nimbly and sweetly recommends itself," and Banquo sees a good omen of hospitality in the nesting of the martlets in the castle walls. Macbeth is tormented by the depth of this trust; to violate it by his "black and deep desires" will bring upon himself the "deep damnation" reserved for acts of Satanic iniquity. The tragedy of Macbeth is that his nature compels him to yield to "vaulting ambition" and to seek the highest eminence, the most elevated station, by acts of violence.

In Bewsher's poem the governing image of the first section is that of the "unsuspecting country" around Bruges, and the complacent city itself:

> Sleep on, pale Bruges, beneath the waning moon,
> For I must desecrate your silence soon,
> And with my bombs' fierce roar, and fiercer fire,
> Grim terror in your tired heart inspire:
> For I must wake your children in their beds
> And send the sparrows fluttering on the leads!
>
> [p. 7]

Like the martlets in *Macbeth* the sparrows are the celestial visitants who signify the peace of the community. The airplane which seems to be of their kind is in fact their unnatural enemy. Again, the situation can be interpreted as an allegory of "progress" in which the birdlike machine alters the natural balance toward increased predation. Macbeth knows he does evil, but Bewsher is not entirely sure, for the rhetoric of patriotism assures him that he does good to resist the encroachment of evil by the enemy. He knows only that he and his machine are Death ("And Death is creeping toward them through the sky"); the rest of the poem must resolve his identity further, in case the searchlights discover his secret design, "And I perhaps must die to-night as well, / To meet *your* souls in Heaven or in Hell" (p. 8).

The searchlights receive more metaphorical elaboration than any other image in the poem. A night bomber must act in darkness in order to survive; when threatened by the German lights at Bruges Bewsher prays, "O that Night could fold / Its velvet wings around us," a metaphor summoning the Holy Spirit to make him invisible. (The obvious allusion is Psalm 91: "He shall cover thee with his feathers, and under his wings shalt thou trust. . . . Thou shalt not be afraid for the terror by night.") Light is described as murderous – the searchlights are "keen bright swords" or the arms of an octopus, or a monster or genie, or (in his memoir) "long weeds in an evil pool." That is his perspective, but he is also able to look upward with enemy eyes:

> They see a little bird-like shape which seems
> Fixed on the apex of a dozen beams
> Of slender light – a little bird at bay
> Which tries and tries in vain to get away . . .
>
> [p. 15]

In traditional iconography the dove of peace is pictured at the apex of a painting, rays of light emanating from it to interpenetrate everything below. Here the bird is pierced by the light which belongs to the enemy. Bewsher, as a bird with a human face, is a signifier of all birds humans have destroyed, and also the will to destroy them, as in Billy Bishop's gloating claim in his memoirs that aerial attack "was not like killing a man so much as just bringing down a bird in sport" (p. 198).

The dual perspective reveals again the dual character of the flying machine, which gives man greater powers of destruction than ever before, but also imprisons him in a state of precarious physical dependence and moral uncertainty in that superior world. Searchlights can illuminate the deformity of desire, even in a patriot, as that desire is realized in the act of flight. Bewsher describes the experience this way in his memoir: "It is as though you stood in the corner of a dark room and an evil being with long arms came nearer and nearer, sweeping those arms across the velvety darkness and you knew that there would come a time when they would touch you."[8] Bewsher uses childhood fears directed at the father, and the sexual timidity basic to the Oedipus complex, as a means of expressing the embarrassment of his ethical position:

> . . . And I feel stripped and naked in the sky:
> I feel ashamed, as though caught on the sly
> Upon some evil work . . .
>
> [p. 14]

If the citizens of Bruges resemble Leonardo in his memory of violation by a bird, their violator, too, feels a form of sexual distress when the lights reveal his presence. All epithets are reflexive because both sides in the conflict mirror each other's destructive intentions; he too is an "evil being" that seeks to touch the terrified city with his long arms of fire.

A further complication is the light of the bombs as they explode:

> One after one these flaming flowers bloom
> And scatter scarlet pollen thick with doom.

[p. 12]

These flowers of evil are the result of "screaming progress" in the new century, which has transformed the grammar of Romantic imagery. Taking Keats's Nightingale ode as a model, we see how the tender night of that poem has changed to an inky cloak enabling widespread devastation; how instead of the mystical trance in which "I cannot see what flowers are at my feet" we have the visible flowers of night scattering their murderous seeds; and for the nightingale itself the "throbbing monster" (as he calls it in another poem) which brings eternity to earth-dwellers in a most unromantic form. Max Ernst's famous painting, *Two Children are Threatened by a Nightingale* (1924), which summons the modern memory of aerial bombardment for its wry critique of Romanticism, expresses the metaphorical connection precisely.

"And all this horror I shall never know" (p. 8). This is the crucial line of the poem, and the sentiment most relevant to Bewsher's understanding of his unique aerial situation. Expressions of this guilty detachment are common in the literature of World War II and afterward, but Bewsher is one of the first to link the anesthetizing quality of aerial bombardment to the religious experience. Flying gives an *"almost divine* point of view," he remarks in his memoir (p. 39), and later, "I live through one of those rare *moments of divinity* which come to men when they see before them for the first time some sublime spectacle which perhaps has never been seen before" (p. 247). As he undertakes mission after mission the experience becomes more intense:

It seems incredible that my soft right hand has actually this night caused damage and brought death to the far, far remote place, which even now is in a state of confusion. Vividly I realise the amazing wonder of flying; vividly I feel the strange fascination of night-bombing, with its long journeys and sense of domination – *its sense of being almost divine.*

[pp. 258–9]

I have italicized phrases which reflect the common view of aviators that their actions transcend the normal boundaries of moral judgment – not only because they are warriors in a Great Crusade, but because their supreme power over earthly creatures gives them the historical authority of gods. Only a decade before the war, Henry Adams had remarked in "A Dynamic Theory of History" that "To the highest attractive energy, man gave the name of divine, and for its control he invented the science called Religion."[9] It was the Great War that made the flying machine a symbol of that highest imaginable force, and compelled pilot-authors like Bewsher to forge a scriptural mode of identity for the airman.

"The Bombing of Bruges" does not simply collapse humanity and divinity into one, however. By allusions to *Macbeth* and sincere statements of remorse, Bewsher acknowledges his guilty kinship with his victims. Nevertheless, the last lines resolve the question of his identity by expressing an exculpatory judgment:

> I thank my God that He has brought me back
> And feel Him by me ... then my thought grows black.
> Sleep kisses me upon each shuttered eye
> And God smiles on me from His quiet sky.

[p. 18]

The conclusion substitutes the language of reconciliation for that of self-accusation, but one does not feel this as a moral evasion so much as a deepening of the moral perplexity. The sleep that "kisses" him is the same sleep he has "murdered" in the town. (The word "shuttered" makes the connection explicit.) God's sky is now quiet because the noise of engines has disappeared; God reigns where the bird-like shape which is apparently the instrument of His will formerly wrought destruction. The smile of God, then, is like the smile of Blake's creator in "The Tyger." War is God's will; his light a sword or flaming flower; his means of annunciation a winged structure of linen, steel, and wood. Bewsher has successfully articulated these disturbing metaphorical crossings, but finally surrenders them to the reader as "thought grows black" (i.e., God finally enfolds him in velvet wings) and the sleep denied to Bruges is given to the bombardier as a sign of favor.

Studies of Great War literature have revealed how thoroughly the notion of the war as a Great Crusade was repudiated by its foot-soldiers in the trenches. But the new machinery that effaced the infantry made aviators spectacularly visible to a public familiar with the literature of chivalry. The image of knighthood, so powerfully impressed on the English imagination in works from Malory and Spenser to Tennyson, had suffered somewhat from Mark Twain's *A Connecticut Yankee at King Arthur's Court* (1889), but Twain's point was arguably that the insufficiency of the Arthurian myth lay in the machinery of knighthood, especially the outdated armor and horse which was so easily annihilated by Hank Morgan's dynamo-fed weapons. Knighthood itself, then, might arise in a new form with updated machinery.

Certainly David Lloyd George subscribed to this view; the air war formed a crucial part of his vision of the machine-age Crusade:

The heavens are their battlefield; they are the Cavalry of the clouds. High above the squalor and the mud, so high in the firmament that they are not visible from the earth, they fight out the eternal issues of right and wrong. Their daily, yea their nightly struggles, are like the Miltonic conflict between the winged hosts of light and of darkness. They fight the foe high up and they fight him low down; they skim like armed swallows, hanging over trenches full of armed men, wrecking convoys, scattering infantry, attacking batallions on the march. Every flight is a romance; every report is an epic. They are the knighthood of the war, without fear and without reproach. They recall the old legends of chivalry, not merely the daring of their exploits, but by the nobility of their spirit, and, amongst the multitudes of heroes, let us think of the chivalry of the air.[10]

It hardly needs demonstrating that this myth became a powerful element of our modern memory of the war. A glance at the bookshelf reveals that biographies, autobiographies, and journalistic accounts of the air war take their titles, as they do their informing vocabularies, from the chivalric tradition: *Knight of Germany* (about Oswald Boelcke), *The Red Knight of Germany* (about Manfred von Richtofen), *Guynemer: Knight of the Air* (by Henry Bordeaux), *Germany's Last Knight of the Air* (Carl Degelow's memoirs), *Knights of the Air* (by A. Bennett Molter), *The Knighted Skies* (by Edward Jablonski), and so on, not to mention *Heroes of the Sunlit Sky* (by Arch Whitehouse), *The Great Adventure* (by Laurence La Touriette Driggs), *King of the Air Fighters* (about "Mick" Mannock), and kindred glamorizing titles. The mythology is self-referential, like the *imitatio Christi* of former centuries. Often the contents of these books reveal not saintliness or chivalry but a predatory cold-bloodedness hardly compatible with our image of a Lancelot or Galahad. And yet the air war did have a personal face. The invention of the synchronized machine gun which could shoot between propeller strokes made possible the engagement of single combatants in aerial duels of infinite tactical variety. Many pilots emblazoned personal insignias on their planes so that opponents would recognize them, and in consequence the record of kills which made each champion an "ace" could be verified and respected on both sides. The pilots underwent an exhaustive period of initiation into the unique technical features of aerial flight: cross-country flying, forced landings, handling of controls during specialized maneuvers, recovery from a spin, reconaissance and aerial photography, bombing, and air fighting, to name a few. At each stage the recruit had to pass tests before he could advance, but once he completed training he was treated with the privileges owed to a nobleman. He lived in comparative luxury behind the lines, in billets, served by an abundant ground crew and idolized from afar for his courage and mastery of the rules of flight and war alike. If ground warfare marked the absurdist conclusion of a military ethos stretching back to the Homeric period, the air war could be presented, and not just by Lloyd George, as the legitimate "epic" of the modern world. W. H. Auden was not the only poet to claim that the closest modern equivalent to the Homeric hero was the ace fighter pilot;[11] the pilots too idealized themselves according to heroic models made available to them by the literary tradition.

In addition, the popular media seized upon the exploits of airmen for morale purposes, and to aggrandize their own powers of making celebrity fictions. Newspapers gave the air war coverage disproportionate to its strategic importance. And the movies took up the myth as well, capitalizing on the superb cinematic possibilities of aerial warfare. (*Wings* won the first Academy Award in 1928 as Best Picture of the Year.) Pulp and other magazines ran fiction and non-fiction about the air war from its very beginnings. After the war the memoirs of air aces became the closest approximation one can find to the knightly tales in Malory, an association the authors underlined explicitly. Here is Cecil Lewis, for example:

.It was like the lists of the Middle Ages, the only sphere in modern warfare where a man saw his adversary and faced him in mortal combat, the only sphere where there was still chivalry and honour. If you won, it was your own bravery and skill; if you lost, it was because you had met a better man.[12]

One cannot read in these memoirs very far without noticing structural features similar to Malory's accounts: the catalogues of warriors, the repeated trials by combat, the attention to gestures and the set pieces of dialogue, the relishing of all mechanical description, and the avowal of moral purpose throughout. As so often in heroic literature, the sense of fraternity shared by pilots on all sides transcended national loyalties. The duellings between British and German aces resemble the battles of champions like Aeneas and Turnus.

Not all writers embraced this new myth, of course, and especially not those who had drunk deep of the myth in its older form, by means of Tennyson, Morris, and the Pre-Raphaelite artists. I am thinking here of W. B. Yeats, whose poem "An Irish Airman foresees his Death" deserves extended commentary, not only for its high literary quality, but because it is the only poem about flight during World War I to achieve a status in anthologies and among critics equivalent to the best work of the trench poets.

The poem's occasion was the death in January 1918 of the only son of Yeats's friend and patron, Lady Gregory. First reports were that Robert Gregory, a fighter pilot, had fainted while in flight, but later it was learned that he had been shot down mistakenly by Italian allies. Yeats wrote three memorial poems, and the differences between them show us a poet hostile to machinery adapting his rhetoric until it becomes an authentic report of an airman's fate. Yeats's first poem on the event is "Shepherd and Goatherd," an eclogue that reaches back to Theocritus for a model of mournful commemoration. Two country figures meet in a timeless rural landscape and speak about the brilliant young man who "died in the great war beyond the sea."[13] No mention is made of how he died; rather, the poem emphasizes his mother's sorrow and the pathos of early promise cut short. The poem is artful, but Yeats was clearly dissatisfied with its evasions, and with the whole genre. He wrote two other elegiac poems – the dating is uncertain – which chose a more contemporary language for the recent event.

"In Memory of Major Robert Gregory," which I suspect came first (it is dated May 1918), speaks more directly, eschewing the conventions of pastoral elegy. Here we get an elaborated portrait of Gregory as a Renaissance figure, "Our Sidney and our perfect man." And yet the attitude is a mixture of the critical and the complimentary. In "Shepherd and Goatherd" the shepherd had remarked that the deceased "knew himself as it were, a cuckoo, / No settled man." "In Memory" also emphasizes Gregory's flighty and reckless nature:

> When with the Galway foxhounds he would ride
> From Castle Taylor to the Roxborough side
> Or Esserkelly plain, few kept his pace;
> At Mooneen he had leaped a place
> So perilous that half the astonished meet
> Had shut their eyes; and where was it
> He rode a race without a bit?
> And yet his mind outran the horses' feet.

[p. 134]

Gregory's desire exceeded his possession; in life he ceaselessly violated rules and limits. Gregory was one who "may consume / The entire combustible world in one small room." Certainly his volunteering for the air force was in keeping with his attraction to the dangerous life. Yeats is obviously sympathetic to

Gregory's aristocratic temperament. More than one veteran reported that the ritualistic fox hunt served volunteers as a paradigm of the air war, because it combined disinterestedness in pursuit with the thrill of successfully completing the kill. "Our lives were touched by the exciting spirit of the chase," recalled Gordon Taylor after his years as a pilot, "each one of us keyed to his own private discovery of war. We felt no real hate against the Hun. He hardly existed as a human individual. He was simply the Hun, the opponent, the impersonal enemy. For myself – and I believe I was typical – I was not incapable of killing Huns, but I was certainly incapable of hating them."[14] The fox-hunting ethic precisely! The sport featured a code of manners germane only to skilled professionals, whose reward was the pleasure of self-mastery and the ecstatic outrunning of the horses' feet. Yeats's phrase "A lonely impulse of delight" looks toward the Dionysian ceremonies of foxhunting and flying alike.

And so Yeats came to write the third elegy, which confronts directly the facts of Gregory's death as a pilot.

An Irish Airman foresees his Death
I know that I shall meet my fate
Somewhere among the clouds above;
Those that I fight I do not hate,
Those that I guard I do not love;
My country is Kiltartan Cross,
My countrymen Kiltartan's poor,
No likely end could bring them loss
Or leave them happier than before.
Nor law, nor duty bade me fight,
Nor public men, nor cheering crowds,
A lonely impulse of delight
Drove to this tumult in the clouds;
I balanced all, brought all to mind,
The years to come seemed waste of breath,
A waste of breath the years behind
In balance with this life, this death.

[p. 135]

Yeats's dilemma is obvious. The whole force of an elegy is the cherishing of an individual whose life and work make him a model for the close-knit community that survives him. The pastoral form of the elegy sees this community as a shepherd's flock, and his death as a diminishment of the very Nature to which shepherd and flock belong. The personified figure of Nature usually appears in such poems to bewail the loss of her devoted priest. But Gregory desired to ascend above the earthly realm, to rid himself of the constraints represented by mother, land, and country. The airplane made possible, as the horse did not and could not, an unnatural speed suited to a violent nature. Yeats, who artfully lost his speech in "In Memory" when the need for consolation arose in the last stanza, removes himself from the awkward role of memorialist altogether in this poem. The Irish airman narrates his own story, which begins at a low altitude ("the clouds above") and then climbs lyrically toward the highest sphere with the rapidity and vitality of a lark. The "tumult in the clouds" is very likely the noise and perturbation of engines and gunfire as well as the thrill of ascent. Like Shelley's lark the airman is a scorner of the ground, but unlike the Romantic bird he cannot outdistance the historical conditions which answer his violent desire. When he refers in the last line to "this life, this death," the final two words apparently announce the moment of death itself. No external enemy kills the airman within the drama of the poem; rather, he slays himself by indulging his aristocratic disdain and tragic gaiety, as if he knew all along that the machine he rode into the clouds was Death. Thus Yeats avoids the mercenary implications of the patriotic myth, and turns the notion of a chivalric Crusade to his unique, neoromantic purposes.

It is significant, however, that Gregory's abdication of his pastoral duties continued to gnaw at Yeats, so that when Ireland underwent civil war Yeats looked backward bitterly, and addressed to Gregory the poem "Reprisals," which he never collected in book form.[15] He begins by noting Gregory's record of nineteen German planes downed before his accident. "We called it a good death," he remarks, but on the same line begins his reconsideration: "Today / Can Ghost or man be satisfied?" Gregory and Yeats had both been satisfied, or satisfied *enough* for "An Irish Airman" to preserve the balance of sympathy and criticism. But now Yeats, in his own voice, denies the Airman's claim that "No likely end could bring them loss." Soldiers are murdering Gregory's tenants, men who respected Gregory's father are being shot at, women suckling their babies are driven indoors by armed men. Gregory would not care now, Yeats implies, as he did not care about these people when the country was at peace. "Then close your ears with dust and lie / Among the other cheated dead." How cheated? Most likely self-cheated, by indulgence in a lonely (read selfish) impulse, like one of Bewsher's "moments of divinity" that lures humans from the limits – and benefits – of community.

We have seen that the airplane effectively divides the imaginative history of World War I into two histories: a sordid one of armies blindly battling on a darkling plain, and a sacred history governed by the metaphor of the Crusade and the heroic example. But even within this latter category two kinds of crusade can be discerned. One is defined by *engagement* with an enemy. Lloyd George's reference to "the Miltonic conflict between the winged hosts of light and of darkness" is the locus classicus of this patriotic myth. But a second form of the crusade exists, the way of *transcendence*. As the airman ascends he yearns to escape the burden of history altogether and linger in what Bewsher calls "the cloudy chapels of the sky." In this mystical phase of sacred history, a specific technological achievement – the progressive development of the airplane – makes possible an unprecedented discovery of the upper reaches of the human spirit. Thus, in the midst of an aviator's memoirs we are sometimes struck by mystical passages which point directly toward an unmediated apprehension of divinity made possible by the solitary ascent of the flying machine. Just as earthly landscape becomes increasingly abstract in such descriptive passages, indeed cubist and surrealist in appearance, so the human image is estranged from its familiar shape and spiritualized. These are significant moments, and form a subgenre of statement within the sacred literature of technology.

Perhaps the most striking example occurs in Cecil Lewis's *Sagittarius Rising*. It is a long passage but because it illustrates the complete cycle of beatific possession and dispossession, worth quoting nearly in full:

I sailed on for a time, alone in the wonderful skies, as happy as I have ever been or ever shall be, I suppose, in this life, looking lazily for some rift in the white floor; but there was none. It was complete, unbroken, absolute. I was about to turn west again when I saw, in the distance, a cloud floating above the floor, small, no bigger than a man's hand; but even as I looked, it seemed to grow. It swelled, budded, massed, and I realized I was watching the very birth of a cloud – the cumulus cloud that chiefly makes the glory of the sky, the castles, battlements, cathedrals of the heavens. What laws had governed its birth at that moment, at that place, amid the long savannahs of the blue? Heaven, that bore it, knew. Still it was there, creating a growing loveliness out of nothing! A marriage of light and water, fostered by the sun, nourished by the sky!

.   .   .   .   .

Wisdom said: Keep distance and admire. Curiosity asked: How much closer without losing the illusion? I edged nearer. I was utterly alone in the sky, yet suddenly against the wall of the cloud, I saw another machine. It was so close that instinctively, as an instantaneous reaction to the threat of collision, I yanked the stick and reeled away, my heart in my mouth. A second later, I looked around and laughed. There was nothing there! It was my own shadow I had seen, the silhouette of the machine on the white cheeks of the cloud. I came back to observe the strange and rare phenomenon. There on the cloud was my shadow, dark, clean-cut; but more than the shadow, for around it was a bright halo of light, and outside that a perfect circular rainbow, and outside that again another rainbow, fainter, reversed.

From the ground the rainbow is an arch spanning the visible heaven. From the next hill-top, so it seems, one would be high enough to solve the riddle of where it ends. But here it was small, bright, compact, a perfect circle, and at the centre the shadow of the Parasol, like the stamped image on a golden coin.

I shut off, turned east, and came down. The white floor, several thousand feet below, rose up, towards me, turned at last from a pavement of pearl to just a plain bank of fog. I plunged into it. I might be going back from paradise to purgatory, so grey and cold and comfortless it was. And as I sank through it, listening to the singing of the wires, I was thinking how some day men might no longer hug the earth, but dwell in heaven, draw power and sustenance from the skies, whirl at their will among the stars, and only seek the ground as men go down to the dark mysteries of the sea-floor, glad to return, sun-worshippers, up to the stainless heaven. [pp. 150–2]

The vision is comprised of a highly conventional iconography. The ascent into a landscape of clouds belongs to the Romantic fascination with distance and the *beyond* that Ruskin inflated into an aesthetics of the sublime. Here within the veil of God Lewis is granted a vision of his machinery spiritualized, the airplane ringed with a "bright halo of light," and that circle enclosed by a "perfect circular rainbow" – the symbolic figure of God's covenant with mankind. The radiant sunlight upon the cloud must be contrasted with the searchlights that threaten Lewis, as they do Bewsher, from below. Significantly, halo and rainbow belong to that *place* alone; they are symbols ringing the insubstantial shadow of Lewis's own machine. The shadow belongs to the cloud, so that the pilot cannot possess it except by visual epiphany. The machine that made possible the vision drags him down from the show of ideal creation. In his forlorn Icarian descent he undergoes the realization that fancy cannot cheat so well as it is famed to do; he cannot avoid the "grey and cold, and comfortless" world of the exile from paradise, though his sensitivity to the bleakness of the lower world accounts also for his aesthetic moment in the higher. The machine does provide constant access to the "glory of the sky," however, and so remains a friend to man whenever his craving for views of eternity becomes irresistible. In fact, no literary or graphic image of the airplane was more popular in the postwar period than that of a solo flight among clouds.

Lewis's vignette is a spot of time we can set beside his more jejune evocation of aerial life as a medieval tournament. If his comparisons to knightly jousting look backward for an appropriate model of warfare, his mystical fascination with the perfect images of paradise allows him to look forward to a peaceful millennium amidst "the stainless heaven." He summons aerial perspective constantly in this memoir of 1936 to discover some means of confidence in social recuperation. From a height of 10,000 feet one does not see the disfiguring images of man, he reminds the reader, but the eternal woods and fields of the original Creation. Those who are earthbound in the 1930s may be obsessed with the ugliness of industrial technology, and overcome with despair because daily battered by reports of oncoming war and present Depression. But the veteran who has experienced the joy possible to man by his escape from the bounded horizon can provide consolation, as a mentor and prophet. Lewis urges a one-world political philosophy in keeping with the new vision of earth endowed by the flying machine, and recommends that world order be enforced, violently if necessary, by aerial patrols. The tremendous popularity of Lewis's memoir suggests that his vision was shared by a war-weary public. But there is another point to be made, that Lewis's effort to distinguish patriotic crusade from spiritual quest, to locate the sacred history of flight in a non-combatant situation, and to foreground the pilot as a figure "sailing godlike above [the] clamour" (p. 161) and linking the earthbound community with the imperial "castles, battlements, cathedrals of the heavens," depended upon the prestige of a singular event which altered the mythology of flight decisively: the transatlantic flight of Charles A. Lindbergh in 1927.

6. Lindbergh in 1927: The Response of Poets to the Poem of Fact

A miraculous mood transformed the whole civilized world when the wheels of the *Spirit of St. Louis* left the earth.

For the first time within the memory of mankind an adventure bringing high rewards was undertaken and no human being envied the adventurer. The minds of humanity in an instant surged and flowed into one great, common ocean in which anxiety and pride were intermingled.

—*The Boy's Story of Lindbergh*[1]

More than half a century has passed since Charles A. Lindbergh's transatlantic flight to Paris, and even at this distance the event seems to belong as much to the triumph of that inflated rhetoric we have come to recognize and distrust as media hype as it does to the history of aviation. "Now is the most marvelous day this old earth has ever known," proclaimed the soon-to-be Chief Justice of the United States, Charles Evans Hughes, at a banquet for the young pilot, adding, "This is the happiest day of all days for America."[2] The official account of the flight prepared for the Boy Scouts of America called it "all things considered, the greatest feat undertaken by a single man."[3] A historian must back away from such eulogies, but not so far that he loses sight of their contribution to the essential character of the event.

Lindbergh himself recognized that the authors of such words did not praise him so much as their own Platonic conception of greatness, which they thrust upon him. Those who worked themselves into a frenzy of celebration were not, he felt, responding to his achievement, about which he had no false modesty, but to the hangover of journalistic practice in nineteenth-century America. It was as if nothing had changed

97

in either aerial technology or public attitudes since 1844, when Edgar Allan Poe astounded readers of the *New York Sun* by reporting a transatlantic balloon flight. The reporter who describes the event in Poe's sketch, afterward known as "The Balloon Hoax," calls the flight "unquestionably the most stupendous, the most interesting, and the most important undertaking ever accomplished or even attempted by man."[4] The idealizing tendency of popular discourse created a cultural need for actual figures of stature, who, when they emerged, were fated to be perceived and consumed as nothing more than eidolons of the journalistic imagination. Lindbergh's enduring war with the press has this historical situation as its basis.

In this chapter I wish to consider two related questions: whether the poetry, and to a lesser extent the prose, that remarked on Lindbergh's flight perpetuated the false conception of greatness he resisted, and the degree to which the effusive flattery aimed at Lindbergh's machine brought the *Spirit* into conformity with exalted models we have already studied. Never in history did an event so brief provoke so many poems in so short a time. Principally because of a widely publicized national contest, the number of poems written in 1927 about Lindbergh – thousands were printed in local newspapers before the summer had ended – probably exceeds ten thousand. Examination of an anthology of these works may tell us something about how poets, amateur and professional alike, assessed a turning point in the history of aviation, what standards of judgment they applied, what attitudes they bequeathed to later writers on aerial technology. Such an analysis should reveal something about the viability of poetic language itself in a journalistic and scientific age. A year before Lindbergh's flight I. A. Richards, in *Science and Poetry*, had disturbed the literary world by entertaining what he called "the representative modern view"[5] that poetry had no future at all because it could not compete with the precision of creative design that *The Spirit of St. Louis* later came to symbolize. The outpouring of verse that greeted Lindbergh's action, then, can be viewed in retrospect as a denial of the oblivion that many poets saw as threatening their art. Lindbergh's flight became a test case of the poet's traditional role – at least since Homer – as a praiser of heroes, the true historian of a culture's epic achievements.

Lindbergh's own attitudes are best revealed by a close reading

of one passage from his autobiography of 1928, "*WE*". He cites
a newspaper account of a crash landing he made in 1923 while
flying an old Curtiss Jenny in Minnesota. The news item
concludes, "Lindbergh says he will be flying again in three
days." The statement implies an extreme foolhardiness, and
Lindbergh's immediate comment allows a certain justice to that
implication:

> After reading this and similar accounts of equally minor
> accidents of flight, it is little wonder that the average man
> would far rather watch some one else fly and read of the
> narrow escapes from death when some pilot has had a forced
> landing or a blowout, than to ride himself. Even in the post-
> war days of now obsolete equipment, nearly all of the serious
> accidents were caused by inexperienced pilots who were then
> allowed to fly or attempt to fly – without license or restriction
> about anything they could coax into the air – and to carry
> any one who might be beguiled into riding with them. [pp.
> 75–6]

Lindbergh apportions equal blame to machine and man, just as
he will give himself and *The Spirit of St. Louis* equal credit. In
this instance the judgment is accurate: three cylinders of his
Jenny stopped firing, and he had recklessly flown through several
storms to meet an appointment with his father. To an outsider,
like the news reporter, Lindbergh by his persistence seems to be
courting doom for himself and for a plane that had already
shown some infirmity in the air. The passage seems to flatter
the "average man" for his prudent refusal to endanger life and
limb for a momentary thrill.

But Lindbergh's praise is qualified, in fact transformed into
irony, by the context of this passage. He describes on the previous
page how the inhabitants of Savage, a nearby town, hear that a
barnstormer has crash-landed and that two boys, in the local
speech, "had gone up and felt of his neck and that it was stiff
and he was stone dead." The townspeople rush excitedly to the
swamp, but find Lindbergh alive and well. He comments drily,
"They were undoubtedly much disappointed at having come so
far on a false alarm." This sentence is crucial to an understanding
of Lindbergh's lifelong hostility to the common man. In it he
reveals what every daredevil knows, that people do not come to

see a performer defy the law of gravity, but to fail to do so. When the trapeze act, the high-wire walk, or the loop-the-loop ends successfully the public disguises its morbid hopes by manic applause. The townspeople of Savage really wanted him dead, as punishment for escaping natural law "without license or restriction." Here Lindbergh touches on a subject we have examined in Leonardo da Vinci's career, and in the premodern literature of flight: the desperate envy of the earthbound for those things which rise to a superior element.

In his study of Leonardo, Freud remarks suggestively of the flying dream that "the wish to be able to fly is to be understood as nothing else than a longing to be capable of sexual performance."[6] Flying releases instincts that social upbringing has repressed and returns man to the "heaven" from which social constraints have exiled him. In Lindbergh's formulation, the "average man" prefers to let others enjoy the ecstasy of deeper penetration into open space, knowing he cannot lose this vicarious game: he shares in the thrill if the aviator successfully conquers the air, and has the satisfaction of self-congratulation if the aviator crash-lands. Whatever the outcome, the spectator, the voyeur who uses his eyes only (witnessing and reading) while the aviator makes use of his whole sensorium, is by nature an adversary of the "bird-man," as the pilot was called in those days. The onlooker hangs nets of restriction, tradition, moral conformity, which the aviator seeks to escape.

Immediately after the passage on the average man, Lindbergh describes his reunion with his father:

> My father had been opposed to my flying from the first and had never flown himself. However, he had agreed to go up with me at the first opportunity, and one afternoon he climbed into the cockpit and we flew over Redwood Falls together. From that day on I never heard a word against my flying and he never missed a chance to ride in the plane. [p. 76]

Lindbergh's movement of mind in this entire passage now becomes clear. Aviation is a means of individuation, an achievement of desires that society, personified as his father and the townspeople of Savage, considers self-destructive. Lindbergh acknowledges their conventional wisdom by appealing, as they do, to historical record – many pilots did crash-land, and, yes, a death wish did exist in some cases. (One thinks of Faulkner's Bayard Sartoris.) But Lindbergh challenges that wisdom by focusing on his father, who "had been opposed to my flying from the first" but was converted by physical experience to a new truth. It is a peculiarity of the machine age that son must initiate father into the mysteries, a rite in which the achievement of ecstasy overcomes the mortmain of repressive tradition. The title of Lindbergh's autobiography, the so-called aeronautical pronoun "WE," warns the public that traditional structures of kinship, such as father and son, must yield in the twentieth century to the more perfect union of man and machine. The machine is the birdlike *Spirit*, which carries an individual into heaven, into the achieved pleasures formerly denied by parental and social authority.

It is necessary to emphasize this point because the father-son relation of the Lindberghs represents a cultural transformation in the new century. (Wells had dramatized the change by opposing the aviation-minded Bert Smallways to his greengrocer father in *The War in the Air*.) The pilot's father was a farm owner, and as a Congressman in Washington he drafted legislation with the same purpose as his didactic verse, to defend Nature's Nation from the titanic forces of the coming machine age. His son, however, recognized that new values needed expression. In college Lindbergh turned his imagination against the culture of literacy he identified with his father and the whole nineteenth century: "Why should one spend the hours of life on formulae, semi-colons, and our crazy English spelling? I don't believe God made man to fiddle with pencil marks on paper. He gave him earth and air to feel. And now even wings with which to fly. I'd like to stop taking English, and concentrate on engineering."[7] Engineering was faithful to the new consciousness created by new modes of transportation. As for the "average man" who no doubt taunted the young pilot with slurs about the flying machine, Lindbergh's revenge would be the ecstasy of actual flight when he came into his true birthright as a child of the century:

I began to feel that I lived on a higher plane than the skeptics of the ground; one that was richer because of its very association with the element of danger they dreaded, because it was freer of the earth to which they were bound. In flying, I tasted a wine of the gods of which they could know nothing. Who valued life more highly, the aviators who spent it on the art they loved, or those misers who doled it out like pennies through their antlike days?[8]

This later, lyrical recreation of his state of mind, however, contrasts to his earlier writings on the subject of flight, which dwell on technical matters almost exclusively. In the 1920s Lindbergh measured his distance from the earthbound precisely by the matter-of-fact language of his craft. At public occasions orators might speak of the "wine of the gods," but Lindbergh typically responded by statistics on motor design, oil consumption, and the necessity of new airports.

Of the more than four thousand poems about Lindbergh's flight submitted to a national contest, it is doubtful if any made reference to oil consumption by *The Spirit of St. Louis*, which gave its name to the anthology resulting from the contest. The editor commented that in Lindbergh's act "the rather slipshod prose of daily life has been transmuted into poetry."[9] His rhetorical opposition of daily life and poetry is faithful to the antagonism of birdman and public already described. The poets in this anthology have drunk from the same ethereal fountains of Romantic speech as the journalists and orators. Nineteenth-century poets constantly exemplified the exaltation of aerial ascension in their bird poems, and these dazzling flights satisfied the envious public until reality usurped fantasy, until the poem of fact displaced the poem of words. Lindbergh's flight was heralded as one such change, "the rune of youth sung in a new language and in the dawn of a new age."[10] And the deference paid to it by poets represents a yielding of their prestige and example to the pilot's art, to engineering.

Since the heyday of the Romantic period poets had watched the development of amazing machines, and chose in the main to withdraw support from their rivals in making. At least one eminent scientist urged poets to enter this brave new world and adapt it to their ongoing spiritual concerns. Charles Steinmetz, in an introduction to Charles M. Ripley's *Romance of a Great Factory*, asked, "Is there no poetry in this world of ours? Do we really lack romance in this scientific and engineering twentieth century? Or is it not rather that the ignorance of the average literary man disables him to see the romance of our age!"

Steinmetz's "average literary man" is comparable to Lindbergh's "average man" – both alienated from modern sources of power. Harriet Monroe, editor of *Poetry* magazine, cited Steinmetz's critique and wistfully agreed: "It is evident that the man of science is the romanticist of our age – the poet is a hard and cold seeker of truth in comparison with the modern fire-bringer."[11] Monroe, faithful to her admission, contributed a poem to *The Spirit of St. Louis* that shows Lindbergh singing an old Romantic sentiment as he flies:

> For me!
> The sun, the moon,
> The night and the day and the sea
> For me!

[p. 180]

The notion of Lindbergh uttering these lines is ludicrous, but Monroe's placement of them in his mouth represents her conviction that the man of science had inherited the Romantic artist's vision with his wings.

Since none of the poems in the 1927 anthology outlived its occasion, it may be that the event that prompted a greater immediate outpouring of verse than any in American history will finally go uncommemorated by a significant poem. This reminds us how very few poems on historical events come down through the generations. When something happens that touches every life and challenges prevailing ideas of order, it causes adjustments of consciousness that many people feel compelled to express in verse. In songs, hymns, ballads, elegies, all the traditional forms of popular art, the writers state as best they can what the event means in terms of their previous understanding of the dynamics of history. This very insistence on assimilating the event into the familiar, the shared experience of the culture, limits the ramification of poetic feeling. Seeing the event in terms of some earlier sublime text prevents the glory-starved author – and public – from responding to its unique features. In this sense the anthology is typical of its era, for no period in history shows such a pandemic of strained allusions to exalted texts and figures as the postwar decade in America.

In *The Spirit of St. Louis* Lindbergh is compared to a multitude of gods and heroes in the Western tradition. He is Jehovah and Christ, Apollo, Prometheus, Hermes, Bellerophon, David, Moses, Roland, Lancelot, Adam, Columbus, Ulysses, Beowulf, Marco Polo, Galahad and Lohengrin, to name a few. The first poem proclaims, "far removed from earth he reigned / A king of air" (p. 11). He is a "Master of the empyrean" (p. 42), a "Lord of the air" (p. 118). Though the most frequent comparison is to Christ, it is not the Incarnation but the Resurrection that we find everywhere. A few passages equate Lindbergh's landing in Paris with Christ's descent – "He stepped out stiffly on that ancient sod / And was a god" (p. 128) – but on the whole he is kept as securely immaterialized as possible. Lindbergh entered, as one poet puts it, "the new world of the upper air" (p. 158). By finding a passage through the skies he achieves the primal dream of the race, to be as gods:

> I cannot die
> Who have flown as eagles fly
> Into the blue unknown.
> I have throttled oblivion.
> I have fathomed the myths
> Of space and time. . . .
>   I am one with immensity
>   I cannot die.
>
> [p. 163]

This helps to explain the frequent comparisons to King Arthur's knights who sought the Holy Grail, and especially to Galahad whom God took directly into Heaven. (Here, as in the Christ comparison, Lindbergh's virginity came to the poet's assistance.) Purified of the violent associations of the former knights of the air – the aces of The Great Crusade – Lindbergh retains the glamor they helped to create for the act of flight. Writers could believe, as in the epigraph to this chapter, that envy itself would dissolve in the light of such a divinized presence. To the extent that Lindbergh is a "pilgrim to the future" (p. 215), opening new passages for the human spirit, he releases his admirers from the prison of envy and mortality alike.

If Lindbergh's destination is a New World of the spirit, his point of origin must be a place of intolerable horror. And so it is in these poems, which speak to a cultural paralysis with as much fervor, though considerably less art, as any single volume of the 1920s, including *The Waste Land.* "The world was grown a sorry place," writes R. P. Tristram Coffin (p. 49). Nathalia Crane opens her First Prize poem, "The gods released a vision on a world forespent and dull" (p. 65). Royall Snow laments, "We are devoured by petty things and trivial ways / That feed in hurried hunger, ant-like, on our days." Gertrude Scott Jewell's poem reaches the furthest point of self-laceration: "We stupid ant-like things / Plodding along in our accustomed paths" (p. 138). As the insect imagery makes clear, the poets see themselves as the pilot sees them from his aerial perspective. To their uplifted eyes he is not an avatar of the new science, not a mechanic, but an angry god. The paradox of the envious eye seems inescapable. The desire of the earthbound to escape envy leads to an identification with the superior figure, but the act of identification intensifies the invidious response to the envier's own ground.

And yet Lindbergh had to return; that was the explicit purpose of his flight. He had to make his Icarian descent and confront the frenzied crowds that welcomed, and threatened, him in European and American cities, crowds that one reporter compared to a "gigantic human tank which swept ruthlessly on its way" and which Lindbergh feared would tear him and his plane to pieces. Reporters testified that when Lindbergh saw such mobs approaching him he would scream to the police, "For God's sake, save my machine!"[12] One could find no better example in aviation history of the envious spoiling of the object that succeeds upon the process of idealization. Behind the reception of the pilot in the cities was a suppressed contempt for his inability to stay aloft, for his humanity.

This fact adds poignance to the poets' frequent comparison of *The Spirit of St. Louis* to Pegasus, for poets can be assumed to know the whole story of the legendary flying horse: that it was engendered from the blood of the dying gorgon Medusa; that it created the fountains of Hippocrene on the Muses' mountain by a kick of its hoof; that it was tamed by the noble rider Bellerophon who was thrown to his death when he, like Icarus, guided his new wings higher than mortals are allowed; and finally that it became the carrier of thunderbolts for Jupiter. The "gallant Pegasus, cleaving shades for the goal of a deathless dawn" (p. 110) carried its modern Bellerophon – to what? The pilots of the Great War had introduced into the public imagination horrific apparitions associated with the airplane that no poet in 1927 could honestly overlook as a tradition pressing upon the subject of aerial technology. Pegasus had become a frightening creature, its deadly thunderbolts an essential subtext of *The Spirit of St. Louis*, whether Lindbergh's admirers liked it or not. Poets like Paul Bewsher who bombed European cities a decade earlier had warned their generation that the blood of Medusa clung to the mechanical realization of the poet's dream, but no poet in the anthology pursued the disturbing questions raised by their mythological references. Though the volume seems to engage the subject of modern machine technology, as Harriet Monroe and others advocated, the poets simply turned backward to the most positive Romantic bird poems as models. By insisting that the flying machine carries Lindbergh *beyond* the confines of nature and history they abdicated their prophetic responsibility to alert readers to the dangers of idolatry. Their failure to probe the full implications of Pegasus's increasing mastery reflects their failure as artists to comprehend the historical period in which they lived and wrote.

We see the failure most clearly in the comparison of Lindbergh to Icarus. The legendary Icarus, lacking the good sense of his father, fell into the watery chaos he sought to overleap. Remembering Lindbergh's initiation of his father into the mysteries of flight, we might perceive his career as a modern inversion of the classical story. Certainly most of the poets take pains to contrast the two gilded youths, seeing the pilot as an avenger or redeemer of the doomed flier. But the poets ignore a darker aspect of the resemblance, one that the *New York Times* spelled out explicitly. In an editorial titled "Lindbergh Symbolizes the Genius of America," it remarked that Lindbergh "is, indeed, the Icarus of the twentieth century; not himself an inventor of his own wings, but a son of that omnipotent Daedalus whose ingenuity has created the modern world."[13] The pilot, in other words, benefited from an inheritance that he does not entirely control. Engineers constructed the *Spirit* that exalted Lindbergh. The Master of the Empyrean, then, could be said to have a master of his own, like Victor Frankenstein. *The Spirit of St. Louis*, in poet Babette Deutsch's phrase, is his "dear monster" (p. 83), liable to carry him down if he neglects or mistakes the least of its needs. The machine has transported the pilot from the labyrinth of modern life, but only because of Lindbergh's unfailing solicitude for its welfare. The condition of keeping a high station above the mobs who sooner or later overwhelm and vandalize all human handiwork is that the newly created creature be gradually perfected by engineering knowhow. Power and control must be reserved for the elite custodians of a new technological civilization. Lindbergh's commitment to a new form of life, a symbiotic union of man and machine, made him a test case for the validity of science's claims upon the future.

For this reason, the American public watched Lindbergh's gravitation toward Nazi Germany with a kind of spellbound horror. His visits to German airfields and airplane factories in 1937 convinced him that Germany would soon possess the most powerful military force in the West. In 1938 he accepted the Order of the German Eagle from the leader of the Luftwaffe, Hermann Goering. He sent back favorable reports about his meetings with Germany's new leaders. He admired the "virility" and "efficiency" of the Germans, and contrasted their national virtues to the "softness" and the "stupidity" of the British. Americans knew that Lindbergh included them in this latter category (hadn't his flight exposed their "stupid, ant-like" lives?). Lindbergh did not favor the domination of European countries, and certainly not of America, by the German supermen, but he did think that Germany deserved to lead the West in a *Kulturkampf* of global proportions. In a *Reader's Digest* article of November 1939, "Aviation, Geography, and Race," Lindbergh wrote, "It is time to turn from our quarrels and to build our White ramparts again. ... It is our turn to guard our heritage from Mongol and Persian and Moor." Our civilization, he wrote, depends "on a united strength among ourselves; on a strength too great for foreign armies to challenge; on a Western Wall of race and arms which can hold back either a Genghis Khan or the infiltration of inferior blood." Lindbergh assures his readers that scientific knowhow can stop the annihilating menace of the East. Aviation "is a tool specially adapted for western hands ... another barrier between the teeming millions of Asia and the Grecian inheritance of Europe."[14] What must Lindbergh's former admirers have thought of this turn, this strophe, in his personal saga? The flight of 1927 had been generally interpreted according to the Whitmanian gospel – that advances in transportation would have the effect, as one poet put it, of "Quickening beyond reason's slow control / The nations' brotherhood, the racial soul"

(p. 171). Lindbergh and his wife had suggested such global solidarity by their flight in 1931 to the Far East, described in Anne Morrow Lindbergh's chronicle *North to the Orient* (1935). Aerial technology at that time was not "another barrier" but a means by which "Bright viewless bridges of linked light are flung" (p. 251).

On the other hand, the war took on a clan or narrowly racial definition, as some poets had described Lindbergh's former triumph. They had praised his flight as "the stupendous effort of the race" (p. 117), an expression of "The Spirit of the Valor of the West" (p. 119). Hegel had saluted Napoleon as the world-spirit on horseback; to Lindbergh's admirers the world-spirit in aircraft stirred an abased yearning that looked from the perspective of 1939 fascist in character. Lindbergh himself began to understand, as the war progressed, that his self-image as an avatar of the new science and the (seemingly opposed) view of him by poets and public as a messianic leader were essentially one.

My purpose in raising the connection between Lindbergh and fascism is not to demean Lindbergh, who certainly combatted the Axis powers during World War II with admirable zeal. Rather, I wish to highlight the habits of mind shared by ideologists of all nationalities who embraced aerial technology because it validated their self-conception as autonomous, purified, indeed godlike beings. Lindbergh may have scorned Hitler and Mussolini for their political goals, but what strikes us in reading his prewar speeches and *Wartime Journals* is the eerie compatibility of his neoromantic sentiments with their artfully crafted public images. Notice the movement of mind in this journal entry of 1941, for example:

> To me solitude means beauty and distance and uninhabited places. I feel a city around me, even though no one knows where I am within it. There seems to be an atmosphere of people and unhappiness and the uninspired drabness of everyday life. I feel it as I feel the smoke in my lungs and the concrete under my feet. I sometimes think I can feel the tension and turmoil of a city as I fly over it 5,000 feet in the air.

In the first sentence Lindbergh assumes a stock Romantic pose that seems to invite identification, but as soon as he links together in one prepositional phrase people, unhappiness, drabness, and everyday life he levies a distinction that exalts him dramatically. Literally he begins to soar above the "atmosphere" of ordinary life until he reaches an altitude of 5,000 feet. He remains in somatic contact with the inchoate masses around and beneath him – the phrase "I feel" is repeated four times – but it is assumed in the passage, as in all of his writings, that Lindbergh the pilot and inventor belongs to the elite group of farsighted planners who will create the new order in which others are to live. What is "uninspired" needs reshaping by one whose expertise in making constitutes a warrant for political control. In her controversial book of 1940, *The Wave of the Future*, Anne Morrow Lindbergh had underlined the necessity of adaptation to "a highly scientific, mechanized, and material era of civilization," an era not favorable to democratic values.[15] Her diaries of the period recur to her husband's solo flight as a figure of the commanding leadership required by the nation. One thinks inevitably of the opening scenes of Leni Riefenstahl's film *Triumph of the Will* (1935) in which Hitler looks downward from his airplane upon the assembled multitudes in Nuremberg awaiting his descent and his authorization for a crusade against the reactionary enemies of the thousand year Reich.

In his brief trajectory across the public scene, Lindbergh posed the same questions to the writers of the 1930s as the Futurists did in the previous generation. If the religion of technology required a god who symbolized the energies and destinies of machines, what counterforce would prevent that god from treating his worshippers as drones or robots? If dreams of aerial glory breed monsters of the state, what down-to-earth discourse would lend the makers of aviation history a human face?

7. Origins: Some Versions of Kitty Hawk

To say that Lindbergh's flight marks the turning point in the history of the flying machine is an understatement; in effect, it *created* that history by giving it a pattern and meaning intelligible to a worldwide audience. To a public that had understood the airplane variously as a toy, a sporting device, or the scourge of cities, Lindbergh's flight established its "true" nature as a figure for the triumphant modern spirit. This signification usurped all others because it enabled its believers to imagine that history had a *telos* consonant with their most profound hopes for a harmonious world community. As the enabling event for such a belief, his flight represented a resurrection of the heroic ideal itself, and in that sense was a landmark not just in aviation history but in modern history. Indeed, to the extent that the twentieth century has taken its form from the pressures exerted by technological innovation, the two cannot be separated. During the decade following Lindbergh's flight writers continually sought to establish the authentic tradition of the flying machine as the locus for a new and energized social order.

One of the first writers to recognize the mythic character of Lindbergh's crossing was Harry Crosby, who witnessed the landing at Le Bourget Airport in 1927. His diary entry is a paradigm of a modern gospel:

Then sharp swift in the gold glare of the searchlights a small white hawk of a plane swoops hawk-like down and across the field – C'est lui Lindberg, LINDBERG! [sic] and there is pandemonium wild animals let loose and stampede towards the plane and C and I hanging on to each other running and the crowd behind stampeding like buffalo and a pushing and

110

a shoving and where is he where is Lindberg where is he and the extraordinary impression I had of hands thousands of hands weaving like maggots over the silver wings of the Spirit of Saint-Louis and it seems as if all hands in the world are touching or trying to touch the new Christ and that the new Cross is the Plane and knives slash at the fuselage hands multiply hands everywhere scratching tearing it and it is almost midnight when we begin the slow journey back to Paris (traffic like traffic in the war) and it takes us three hours to cover eight miles and it is freezing cold but what an event! Ce n'est pas un homme, c'est un Oiseau![1]

The passage is remarkable for its concentration of themes surveyed in the last chapter. Crosby captures not only the hunger for some kind of sky-god, but the destructive frenzy of that hunger. In trying to exalt itself through tangible contact with the hero and his machine, the mob actually becomes subhuman, like "maggots," a mass with no light of its own save what the Leader or "new Christ" expresses by his radiant presence. The stream-of-consciousness style collapses these elements into the unity they clearly are, for the slashing at the fuselage results directly from a perception of the plane as the "new Cross"; the mob, that is, revenges itself upon the "Oiseau" or bird figure for illuminating its limitations in the act of transcending them. One is reminded of the Ancient Mariner and the albatross.

Crosby's infatuation with Lindbergh and subsequently with flying must have seemed excessive to his friend Hart Crane, who was writing the second half of *The Bridge* while living with the Crosbys in France. In his earlier poem "For the Marriage of Faustus and Helen" (1922), Crane had rendered the meaning of the airplane by associating it with the Great War. The pilot or "religious gunman" perpetuates by aerial bombardment the warfare between male (machine) and female (earth), as opposed to the unity represented by the marriage of Faustus and Helen. The poem satisfied Crane, except that it falsely cast him as a technophobe. Attracted as he was to images of modern industrial society, Crane began to feel his way in the 1920s toward a more sophisticated interpretation of modern technics. Like some of his contemporaries – Carl Sandburg and Vachel Lindsay especially – he sought a resonant historical image that would embody the humane tradition of technics, earth-centered and organic, rather than one afflictive to humanity. In poems like "Smoke and Steel" Sandburg had located the romance of modern life in factory production, and Vachel Lindsay, in poetry and prose, had idealized the motion picture as a means of salvation for the masses.[2] Crosby's proposition that Lindbergh was the new Christ seemed no less viable a myth. Yet Crane could see in Crosby's own experience how the airplane's appeal derived from its potential for violent domination. It would not have reassured him to hear Crosby tell how he was seized by desires to bomb farming villages when he overflew them.[3]

The sacred history inaugurated by Lindbergh could not be dismissed; it had to be engaged in whatever competing myth Crane might enunciate. As he acknowledged in a letter to his father just after the 1927 flight:

> For over a month we haven't heard, read, eaten or been permitted to dream anything but airplanes and Lyndbergh [sic]. After reading a good deal about it I've decided that the world is quite mad. I'm sure it will take months for people to get their eyes out of the sky and their necks uncrooked and back to their stomachs. Time and space is the myth of the modern world, however, and it's interesting to see how any victory in that field is heralded by the mass of humanity. In a way my Bridge is a manifestation of the same general subject. Maybe I'm just a little jealous of Lindy.[4]

"Jealous" rather than "envious" is the precise word in this context. Lindbergh has stolen away the poet's audience by his superior craft. Crane's response will be to create a work in which figures of mechanical flight and bardic power confront each other and struggle to achieve preeminence as masters of time and space. Lindbergh never lost an opportunity to defer to the Wright brothers as his spiritual parents – he visited Orville shortly after the flight to make the point – just as Crane deferred to Whitman as his precursor. The poem that would provide a forum for the struggle of these powerful figures is "Cape Hatteras" in *The Bridge* – a poem Crane composed in the months immediately following Lindbergh's flight.

This rivalry is further complicated, however, by the presence of a common ancestor, Leonardo da Vinci. Orville Wright had stated in a biographical deposition of 1920 during a patent suit,

1. Darius Green and his Flying Machine. Illustration of 1910 for John Townsend Trowbridge's poem.
Wallace Goldsmith.

2. *The Annunciation*, c 1478 by Leonardo da Vinci.
Uffizi, Florence.

3. *Leda*, c 1504, Ceśare da Sesto, after Leonardo da Vinci, Wilton House.
By kind permission of The Earl of Pembroke, Wilton House, Wiltshire, England.

4. *The Lark*, illustration (after 1818) for John Milton's *L'Allegro* by William Blake.

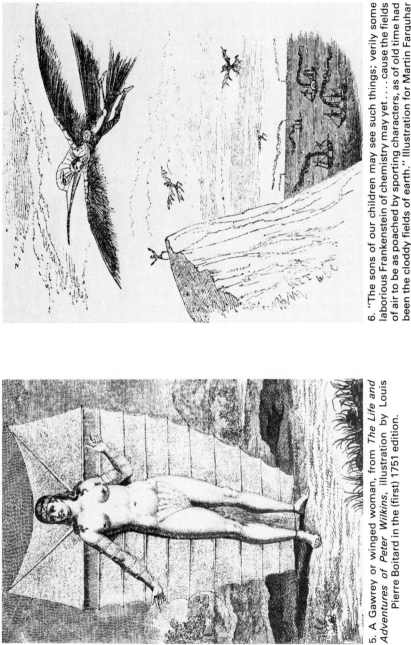

5. A Gawrey or winged woman, from *The Life and Adventures of Peter Wilkins*, illustration by Louis Pierre Boitard in the (first) 1751 edition.

6. "The sons of our children may see such things: verily some laborious Frankenstein of chemistry may yet . . . . cause the fields of air to be as poached by sporting characters, as of old time had been the cloddy fields of earth." Illustration for Martin Farquhar Tupper's "A Flight Upon Flying" (1842) by George Cruikshank.

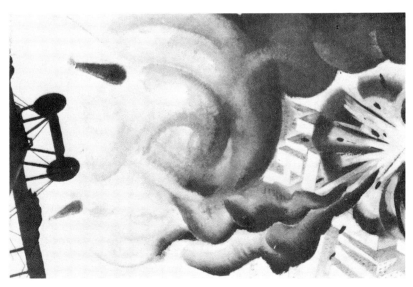

7. (above) *Homage to Blériot*, 1914 by Robert Delaunay. *Kuntsmuseum, Basel.*

8. (right) Bombing a City in the Great War: A Pilot's-Eye View by Cosmo Clark. Reproduced from *Sky Larking, The Romantic Adventures of Flying* by Bruce Gould

Courtesy Liveright Publishing Company.

9. *Two Children are Threatened by a Nightingale,* 1924, by
Max Ernst.
The Museum of Modern Art, New York.

10. *War in the Air,* 1918 by C. R. W. Nevinson.
The Canadian War Museum, Ottawa.

11. *"Master of the Empyrean," "WE"* by Einar Kverne.

12. "A Human Wave Deluged the Field." *The Spirit of St. Louis* threatened by the crowd.
Brown Brothers.

The
FUTURE
"A New Heaven and a New Earth"

Drawing By
H. RAYMOND
BISHOP

13. "A New Heaven and a New Earth": The Airplane as an Apocalyptic Symbol, from Francis Trevelyan Miller, *The World in the Air,* II, 328.

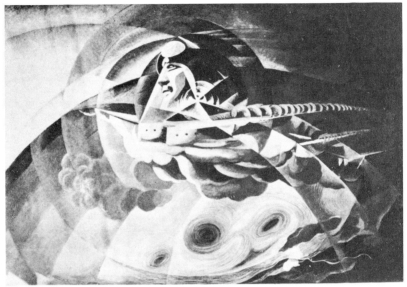

14. *The Aviator,* 1933 by Gerardo Dottori, from *Dottori: Aeropittore Futurista* by Guido Ballo.
Courtesy Editalia: Edizioni d'Italia, Roma.

15. Benitoi Mussolini from Guido Mattioli, *Mussolini Aviator.*

16. "She stood for a holy thing, the world of human happiness." A pilot's wife hears that her husband is lost in a storm. Illustration to Antoine de Saint-Exupéry, *Night Flight* (1931) by Chapelain-Midy.

17. "Pure destruction, achieved and supreme." Recruitment poster of the 1930s.

18. The Fantasy of Firebombing, *Marvel* cover of 1939. Illustration by Wesso.

19. *Guernica,* 1938 by Pablo Picasso.
Museo del Prado.

20. *Spectre of Kitty Hawk*, 1946–47, by Theodore J. Roszak. Welded and hammered steel brazed with bronze and brass, 40¼" high, at base 18"×15". *The Museum of Modern Art, New York.*

21. "That high perfection of all sweetness." Illustration to Jules Verne, *All Around the Moon* (1870).

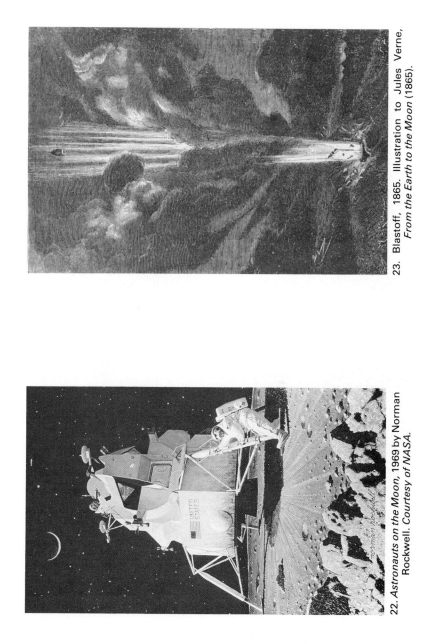

23. Blastoff, 1865. Illustration to Jules Verne, *From the Earth to the Moon* (1865).

22. *Astronauts on the Moon,* 1969 by Norman Rockwell. *Courtesy of NASA.*

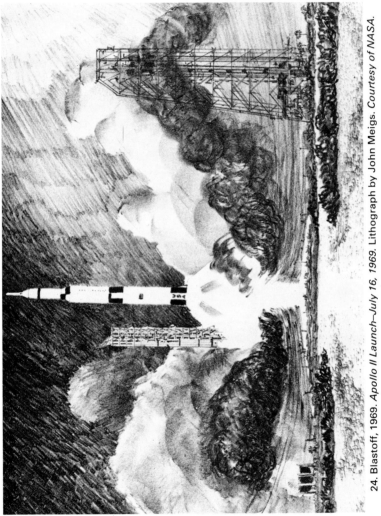

24. Blastoff, 1969. Apollo II Launch—July 16, 1969. Lithograph by John Meigs. Courtesy of NASA.

that he and his brother were impressed by "some of the greatest minds the world has produced," including "Leonardo da Vinci, one of the greatest artists and engineers of all time."[5] Indeed, in their prolonged study of birdflight on Cape Hatteras in order to learn the best way of constructing a flying machine, the Wrights self-consciously imitated the practice of Leonardo. For Crane's part, he had received a letter from Yvor Winters just before Lindbergh's flight comparing him [Crane] to Leonardo. Winters's letter is lost, but Crane's response makes it clear that Winters charges him with spotty work habits and a clouding of moral vision in his myth of the Bridge, both sins reminiscent of the Paterian version of the Renaissance artist. Crane defends Leonardo in a letter of 1 May 1927, in terms that clearly foreshadow his apotheosis of Whitman in "Cape Hatteras." Crane sees that Winters objects to the exaltation in *The Bridge* (Crane had been sending him drafts of the sections) of what might be called a "homosexual" vision, as Freud defined it in his book on Leonardo. That is, an egocentric narrative which idealizes a mother-figure (Pocahontas) in psychosexual terms. Whitman, whom Winters detested, is really the issue between them, for Winters could see that Whitman, supreme egotist and moral anarch, was the source and hero of Crane's sacred history of the progressive American spirit. Was Whitman virile enough to fulfill such a role? That may well be the burden of Winters's insinuations and Crane's bristling defense of Leonardo:

> ... I don't think your reasons for doubting his intelligence and scope very potent. – I've never closely studied the man's attainments or biography, but your argument is certainly weakly enough sustained on the sole prop of his sex – or lack of such. One doesn't have to turn to homosexuals to find instances of missing sensibilities. Of course I'm sick of all this talk about balls and cunts in criticism. It's obvious that balls are needed, and that Leonardo had 'em – at least the records of the Florentine prisons, I'm told, say so. You don't seem to realize that the whole topic is something of a myth anyway, and is consequently modified in the characteristics of the image by each age in each civilization.[6]

Lindbergh's flight the next month, then, challenged Crane on the delicate point Winters had raised. Is Lindbergh the fulfilling type of Whitman's prophetic question in "Passage to India": "Are thy wings plumed for such far flights?" The question was not an abstract but a personal one for the anxiety-ridden Crane. Lindbergh is the consummate man of action, whereas the poet is commonly stereotyped as the dreamer whose work makes nothing happen. Could a person his masculine-minded culture doubly condemned, as a fairy and poet, compete for wings with someone like Lindbergh? Crane answers this question by constructing an alternative, counterculture myth. "Cape Hatteras" in effect transfers to Whitman (and hence to himself) the credit given by the public first to the Wright brothers and then to Lindbergh.

The Bridge is an odyssey through American history that concludes, as it begins, with a rapturous hymn in celebration of the Brooklyn Bridge. Though technology has played no happy part in the nineteenth century – in fact it has created an "iron-dealt cleavage" between land and land, land and person – Crane chooses to believe that the Bridge rejoins what the railroad put asunder; the Bridge is one of those symbols of connection that Whitman championed in poems like "Passage to India," and therefore an emblem of spiritual resurrection for an America grown deaf to the prophetic speech of its most original bard. Where does the airplane fit into all this? "Cape Hatteras" marks the transition in the myth-history of the poem from the age of great ships (Columbus through the late nineteenth-century) to the Air Age. In a letter Crane identifies the space between this poem and the preceding one, "Cutty Sark," as the "'center' of the poem, both physically and symbolically."[7] "Cape Hatteras" likewise falls into two parts: the first an evocation of Kitty Hawk, the Wright brothers' flight and its sequel, the carnage of the Great War; and the second an evocation of Whitman, whose idealistic vision of America remains potent and nourishing to Crane and his generation despite the perversion of machinery Whitman lauded. Whitman, in fact, becomes a symbol of flight ("Who has held the heights more sure than thou, / O Walt! Ascensions of thee hover in me now") which is usable in the modern century precisely because it *is* a vision of connections. At the end of "Cape Hatteras" Crane reaches out his hand to Whitman, his guide, and they move into the second half of *The Bridge*, where Whitman will be transformed again into the risen figure of the Brooklyn Bridge itself. The structure of *The Bridge*, then, decanonizes the so-called miracle of Kitty Hawk.

The genuine surprise of "Cape Hatteras" is the scant treatment accorded the inventors who made the landscape of the poem so world-renowned. Crane notices the "warping" which constituted the fliers' breakthrough in aircraft design, but the few lines given to the events at Kitty Hawk are really only one sentence, which ends in a question-exclamation as to the meaning of this epochal act:

> There, from Kill Devils Hill at Kitty Hawk
> Two brothers in their twinship left the dune;
> Warping the gale, the Wright windwrestlers veered
> Capeward, then blading the wind's flank, banked and spun
> What ciphers risen from prophetic script,
> What marathons new-set between the stars!

The answer is a pessimistic reading of the nativity:

> The soul, by naphtha fledged into new reaches
> Already knows the closer clasp of Mars, –
> New latitudes, unknotting, soon give place
> To what fierce schedules, rife of doom apace!

The Popean couplet suits the Neoclassical practice of testing every event by its moral implications, rather than suspending judgment in the interests of applauding an abstract rationale. (Thus Edmund Burke measures the rhetoric of the French Revolution by its actual crimes, its pretext with its text.) Crane's collapsing of the events at Kitty Hawk with the Great War is justified in part by the slight lapse of time dividing those two events, but also by the fact that from the moment the heavier-than-air machine was conceived in the new century it was linked to military usage, not least by the Wright brothers. If Crane knew of their negotiations with the War Department – which he almost certainly did, for he studied their lives before writing "Cape Hatteras" – he would have regarded this deformation of the creative spirit as similar in kind to the spiritual corruption by materialistic values he exposes in "The River," "Quaker Hill," and elsewhere in the poem.

Crane's next step is to demythologize the conception of pilots as Arthurian knights. Rather than seeing the air ace as St. George going out to do battle with the dragon, the formation itself is imaged as a "dragon's covey"; and to the extent that spectators idealize it – "While Iliads glimmer through eyes raised in pride" – they worship the Satanic spirit or Antichrist summoned in the next line as "Hell's belt" usurping "heaven's plumed side." Similarly the "Cetus-like" dirigible, Crane claims, has "splintered space!" This blimp has both comic and serious links to the Leviathan of the Bible – as Melville exhaustively documented in his chapter of cetology in *Moby-Dick*. Its ascent into the heavens, like the dragon's, reveals an inverted moral universe that needs a greater champion than the debased knight of the air.

But here Crane confronts the paradox of the Whitmanian gospel essential to his myth-history. Just as Whitman could affirm during the Civil War that the smash-up of his dream of brotherhood would give way to even greater democratic vistas, so Crane needed to affirm that the air war recently past would lead to some kind of spiritual renewal. As Lawrence Dembo has pointed out, Crane's friend Eugene Jolas very likely influenced "Cape Hatteras" at this rhetorical crux by means of his neoromantic doctrine of "Verticalism," which glorified aviation as a new opportunity for the aspiring spirit.[8] Crane does momentarily attribute to the predatory pilot the powers Blake and Shelley gave to the lark:

> Remember, Falcon-Ace
> Thou hast there in thy wrist a Sanskrit charge
> To conjugate infinity's dim marge –
> Anew ... !

He then brings down the ace by means of a modern equivalent of the Mariner's crossbow: "The benediction of the shell's deep, sure reprieve!" Though Crane is obviously thinking of the Great War, his pilot falls "into mashed and shapeless debris ... / By Hatteras bunched the beached heap of high bravery!" The bad magic of the Wright brothers' science returns back upon their own favoured landscape, where it must remain until Whitman, summoned in the lines immediately following, appears to lift the airplane by his wizardry in "Easters of speeding light." Thus

Crane drowns the book of machines he finds within *Leaves of Grass* in favor of the Christic artificer of the Word.

Crane responds in advance, then, to the later career of Lindbergh, whose attraction to fascism, like that of the Futurists who influenced Jolas and Crane himself, revealed the dark side of the "Falcon-Ace." Crane's poem redeems the pilot by bringing him down to earth in a fiery crash; after the fall the pilot can be resurrected by pastoral means, by Whitman the "Panis Angelicus" (the loaf of God). As Whitman and Crane advance onward, the future of America is seemingly secured by the covenant of "the rainbow's arch" above the Cape. It is the Bridge-form and not the airplane's which finally glorifies Kill Devil Hill. The flying machine, with its inventors, simply disappears from the poem, left behind like the dinosaur to which Cape Hatteras is compared at the poem's beginning. Crane's revenge upon Lindbergh is complete: he has humiliated the flying machine and its succession of virile pilots in favor of the unmarried Logos to whom he plights his troth, and whose gospel he perpetuates in his own.

MURIEL RUKEYSER'S "THEORY OF FLIGHT"

Crane's attention to the Wright brothers' flight provoked other poets in the 1930s, younger and older than himself, to offer their competing versions of the same, virtually contemporary event. Muriel Rukeyser's long poem, "Theory of Flight," the title work in her Yale Series of Younger Poets volume of 1935, both imitated and corrected Crane's hymn to the Brooklyn Bridge. The imitation is undisguised, apparent in the structure, allusions, and bardic tone of voice. In her study of Rukeyser, Louise Kertesz provides a commentary and chart comparing sections of the two poems, from their opening invocatory passage to their closing hymn. Kertesz's misreading of "Cape Hatteras," however, which she interprets as unadulterated praise of the airplane, prevents her from distinguishing Rukeyser's attitude from Crane's.[9] Rukeyser, in fact, seeks to resurrect the smashed symbol on the shores of Cape Hatteras and reconstruct it as a religious figure comparable to Crane's Bridge. It is a classic case of a younger poet – Rukeyser was 21 when her book was published – challenging an older poet on his own turf, a duel of metaphors she believes she can win because hers is the more dynamic, the more assimilable to the rich tradition of Romantic utterance she shares with Crane.

Rukeyser's strategy is to embrace the masculine, machine-minded Whitman whom Crane had rejected in favor of the feminine, pastoral Whitman. She waves away "frail mouthings," "weakness' loveliness," "Peter Ronsard finger-deep in roses" and urges instead the hard-edged and demonstrative language of contemporaries aware of their role in an industrial civilization.[10] Her culture has been obsessed with images of ruin and defeat, of entrapment in history, of the Wheel of Fortune. The Preamble of *Theory of Flight* cautions against the habit of mind whereby "we replica / ourselves in hieroglyphs and broken things." Rather, she recommends the nourishing model of perfectly functioning new inventions as subject and metaphor for her turbulent decade. "Distinguish the metaphor most chromium clear," she advises. Like its subject, a poem must be considered a practical act of navigation into the future. For this movement it needs a "gyroscope" – the title of section 2 – to keep it from being turned end over end. A distinct industrial metaphor like the airplane serves this function: it gives the poem historical stability and direction; it can absorb the buffetings of wind that threaten to blow it off course.

The muscular posture has a superficial resemblance to the manifestos of Futurism, but the differences are most significant. Like Crane, Rukeyser is fascinated with energy but suspicious of power; she seeks creative forms not destructive ones, and therefore is attracted to historical modes where the Futurists seek to smash them up. Rukeyser draws the line of force, in her dynamic theory of history, between the fifteenth and twentieth century:

Leonardo's tomb
not in Italian earth
but in a fuselage
designed
in the historic mind
time's instrument
blue-print of birth.

[p. 22]

To see the airplane in this humane light is no longer to feel threatened, as Crane did, by the new invention's overwhelming presence. Rather, one can take charge of the *novum*'s destiny, as, to cite Rukeyser's constant comparison, one does of a child. If we return to the model of the Annunciation scene discussed in the second chapter, it might appear that Rukeyser identifies with the Virgin. Leda-like, she invites in the poem's second line ("how violate we experiment again"), a forceful change in her condition by a holy spirit. Here that spirit is a scientific one, a "blue-print of birth" engineered by experimenters like Leonardo. M. L. Rosenthal comments, "The plane's image brings release to the personality 'praying' the poem; the plane's phallic power must bear her away, reveal new vistas, teach her and the reader to 'fly' on their own."[11] Clearly this is true, but to say as much is to identify the speaker's voice as the angel's as well as the Virgin's. Like Leonardo, but unlike the airplane-hating Crane, Rukeyser performs both masculine and feminine roles as a representative figure of her century's re-naissance.

But Rukeyser cannot advance very far in her "dynamics of desire" (p. 24) before she encounters an etiological vexation. "Leonardo's tomb" contains the seeds of the airplane but by analogy to Jesus' tomb it also reminds her of the defeat of desire as well. The "blue-print of birth" calls for a new energy to be crucified in history before attaining transfiguration. By 1935 the airplane already had a history longer than Jesus', or about the same length if one took the Wright brothers' flight in 1903 as the true nativity. And that history had a trajectory as familiar and inflexible as the ballistic curve of a rocket. Hardly have we entered the poem when "Icarus' phoenix-flight" (p. 24) becomes the commanding figure, with its associations of defeat for the aspiring spirit. The confident section titled "The Gyroscope" gives way to "The Lynchings of Jesus." History is collapsed according to the law of entropy that Rukeyser seemed to deny in her hopeful figure of Leonardo:

Kitty Hawk is a Caesar among monuments;
  the stiff bland soldiers predestined to their death
  the bombs piled neatly like children's marbles piled
  sperm to breed corpses eugenically by youth
  out of seductive death [p. 37]
. . . .

Failure encompassed in success, the warplanes
dropping flares, as a historic sum of knowledge,
tallying Icarus loving the sun, and plunging,
Leonardo engraved on the Florentine pale evening
scheming toward wings, as toward an alchemy
transferring life to golden circumstance.
Following him, the warplanes travelling home,
flying over the cities, over the minds
of cities rising against imminent doom.
Icarus' passion, Da Vinci's skill, corrupt,
all rotted into war   [p. 44]

Leonardo himself, as we have seen, was satisfied with acts of human depravity as "a historic sum of knowledge," for he delighted to see all actions governed by necessity, holding true to a constant rhythm perceptible in repeated experiment. The adaptation of art to weaponry did not seem a perversion to him but a natural and predictable tropism. Rukeyser has no such tolerance, and her rejection of a view of life based on blind *physis* is present in every section of her poem.

It is, in fact, the entrance of a social conscience into the poem that vitiates its coherence, for ideology has the effect of tarnishing the chromium-clear distinction of the metaphor; once the airplane yields its central place the poem becomes destabilized by conflicting moral intentions. The clear image of the flying machine is first derived from Leonardo, thence to Icarus (not Daedalus), thence by analogy to the doomed Jesus, and from Jesus to figures who have been victimized in Rukeyser's own time by oppressors. Thus the lengthy sections devoted to the Scottsboro Boys, the miners suffering from poverty and silicosis, and various other cases, darken the central metaphor into a final obscurity. And her conclusions become foregone and pessimistic, for if the test of the flying machine's viability as an artifact is the Scottsboro Boys, then little of positive value can be derived from the analysis. The airplane loses its identity as a "new special product of mortality" (p. 21) and becomes equivalent to any active expression of desire. Despite Rukeyser's considerable research for the poem, including ground school instruction, she has not provided a historical scheme capacious enough to isolate the airplane in character and function – as Crane did the Brooklyn Bridge. Crane's poem can be accused of naivete of historiographical judgment, but its compensatory value is clarity of iconography. Whitman and the Bridge provide concrete and credible alternatives to the kind of technological messianism represented by Lindbergh. Given Rukeyser's enthusiasm for the airplane, however, she needs a figure like Lindbergh as a fulfilling type of Leonardo's "blue-print of birth" or the Wright brothers' primal invention.

When Rukeyser begins the section on the Wright brothers with the passage already quoted, in which "Kitty Hawk is a Caesar among monuments," she denies to the airplane the great destiny she had conceived for it in the opening sections of the poem. Her approach to them is wary and deferential. She keeps the description of their achievement factual for many lines in the notebook style the Wright brothers shared with their admired Leonardo:

> "To work intelligently" (Orville and Wilbur Wright)
> "one needs to know the effects of variations
> incorporated in the surfaces ... The pressures on squares
> are different from those on rectangles, circles, triangles, or
>   ellipses ...
> The shape of the edge also makes a difference."
>
> [p. 37]

This is the enabling terminology of flight. As Lindbergh tirelessly reminded his audiences, all of which preferred the language of sublimity and heroism, aviators care more about data than anything else. In the section of "Theory of Flight" preceding this one on the Wright brothers, Rukeyser dramatizes the misunderstanding between a departing pilot and his pregnant wife. She tells her husband that he is "a hero in mysteries which all the world has wanted." But he resists the word "hero" because of its associations with the god-privileged who are masters of their fate. The aviator knows better; he is vulnerable to many destabilizing forces, including the kind of strong winds that are recorded at the end of each stanza. These winds, we surmise, are responsible for the pilot's death reported at the conclusion. His Icarian falls comes back to haunt the passage on the Wright brothers, for after some frenzied lines of celebration of the brothers' achievement – "We burn space, we sever galaxies" – comes this allusive passage:

gentlemen, remember these incandescent points,
remember to check, remember to drain the oil,
remember Plato O remember me

Like Ishmael aboard the Pequod, or any other "sunken-eyed
young Platonist" (Melville), we may be tempted to idealize until
we lose our connection with the "real" world of physical matter,
but the plane will not permit such indulgence; it will, in Ishmael's
words, "drop through that transparent air into the summer sea,
no more to rise for ever." The tag from Hamlet's father's ghost
("remember me") recalls the narcissist to his duty to others, a
duty so simple as changing the oil. No "blue-print of birth" can
succeed, as the Wright brothers demonstrated by their repeated
experiments, without devotion to technique.

If the pregnant wife and the efforts of the Wright brothers
figure forth the drive to bring new life into a world yearning to
be transformed by Eros, then the final dramatic scene of
the poem, "Night Flight: New York," expresses the force of
Thanatos. In this description of a mock air raid on New York
City we confront the Futurist airplane, no longer lover but rapist:
"hard frames of aircraft ... incisive angles ripping evening ...
bare / fatal battalions ... shark-bodies." The airplanes have no
human face, only a "clean strength" evoked as "a metaphor of
death." Here the angel of annunciation is also the exterminating
angel. Just as Hart Crane had measured the Wright brothers'
achievement as "ciphers risen from prophetic script," so Rukeyser
renders this after-effect of the events at Kitty Hawk as "Pregnant
zero breeding annihilation." Zero is a complex word in aviation.
It is the setting of a firearm that allows it to shoot accurately;
by this angle of vision every person is a target. All victims are
zeros (made nothing by annihilation), dispatched at zero hour
as the fulfillment of a mission. In the Airman's Alphabet of
W. H. Auden's "Journal of an Airman," there is this definition:

Zero – Love before leaving
and touch of terror
and time of attack[12]

A theory of history that equates the Wright brothers with Caesar
seems to demand that eroticism be rendered by the dissemination
of bomb-seeds. Rukeyser and Auden, like H. G. Wells before

them, expose this yearning for the madness it clearly is, the madness of the fantasist who insists upon heroic proportion as a measure of his potency. For such a person the "calculated dance of war" enacted by the planes over New York City is "climax to superbest flight," that is, a debased sexual consummation that satisfies the dynamics of desire in the masses.

"Flight is intolerable contradiction" (p. 45), Rukeyser confesses in the poem's final section. What makes it intolerable is that history had swiftly branded an irresistible, negative meaning on the Wright brothers' wonderful invention – and very much with their assistance. Whichever way she turns in her ambitious poem, she confronts the victims of other people's desire, including the victims of the Wright brothers themselves. But despite the powerful case she has made against the flying machine, Rukeyser returns in the last section to the spirit of Kitty Hawk for inspiration. "We cry beginnings" she proclaims. History is made by repeated, imperfect experiment, which takes its toll, martyr by martyr. But Eros cannot be extinguished. Rukeyser's question, "Shall we then straddle Jesus in a plane?" (p. 30) sounds impious, but is a sincere attempt to fuse into a complex figure the redemptive impulse in Christian and modern societies. The last, often-quoted verse paragraph of the poem attempts to resolve the contradiction of flight, which is the historical opposition of air and earth, the imagined male and female entities:

Master in the plane shouts "Contact" :
master on the ground : "Contact!"
he looks up : "Now?" whispering : "Now."
"Yes," she says. "Do."
Say yes, people.
Say yes.
YES

[p. 46]

The Joycean Yes hopefully foresees a new social solidarity on the order of earth-to-air intercourse. The childless Wright brothers, whatever else they had bequeathed to the twentieth century, had given it a compelling offspring of satisfied desire.

LANGUAGE AND ORIGINS

In the ostentatious matter-of-factness of Rukeyser's descriptions of the flight at Kitty Hawk we see the same problem that Lindbergh's admirers confronted and could not overcome: the fabrication of a language of praise both appropriate and dramatic. The Wrights were remarkable for methodical observation and testing on thousands of occasions of each detail pertinent to their machines. Their journals and letters contain almost nothing but research data, and even their accounts of the first flight eschew sublimity of phrasing for rigorous documentation. Imaginative writers found such material intransigent, for the Wrights had not just been silent – which would have permitted their followers to speak for them – but had insisted upon the privileges of scientific speech. Others must defer to its authenticity, as Rukeyser did, or speak in a different tongue and thereby violate the spirit of the achievement.

No sooner were writers ready to propound a sacred history of aerial flight, then, than they were stymied by the essential problem of answerable style. To the extent that aviation history will differ from traditional religious history by being uniquely modern and mechanical, the return to a conventional idiom must seem a failure of the literary imagination. And yet the adoption of a scientific style would appear to be a surrendering of the poet's prerogative to the engineer. No wonder modern writers envied Whitman, who had the best of both worlds by being one of the first poets to name the previously forbidden "Appearances" of the industrial era. Objects of human technics are some of the "dumb, beautiful ministers" summoned in "Crossing Brooklyn Ferry." He could make them beautiful because they *were* dumb, because they required his purposeful noticing to reveal their high function in the new society. By the 1930s, however, a mechanistic language had been forged and popularized; the imposition of a "poetic" idiom upon a literature of fact sufficient to its purposes would be a ludicrous breach of decorum, similar to that of the eighteenth century when well-meaning poets were ridiculed for lines like "INOCULATION, heavenly muse! descend!"

In effect, the language of prose rather than the high diction of verse seemed more appropriate to describe a machine increasingly domesticated to commercial purposes. In the 1920s Gorham Munson, Hart Crane's friend, wrote a textbook in which he distinguished "Scripture" from "prose." "Scripture is 'superhuman' or 'godlike'," he wrote, but "Prose deals . . . with human and interhuman affairs, the relations of man to man."[13] Scripture, prose or verse, would be the desirable mode for a text that directly challenged Lindbergh's apocalyptic act, like *The Bridge*. But a "reasoning prose," as Munson calls it, one that persuades logically by marshalling data, would be the preferred form in a period when Lindbergh's achievement was socialized and translated (by the accelerated evolution of mechanical forms) into passenger routes and mail services; in which airplanes like the Boeing 247, a ten-passenger plane of unimaginable comfort and style, replaced *The Spirit of St. Louis* as the popular icon of contemporary aeronautical design. For such a machine the language of scripture might enter into advertising copy but made an ill fit for the mode of documentary or chronicle so popular in the 1930s.

"Reasoned prose" of the kind Munson recommends tried to make a peace with dynamic historical forces, so that writers would have an enduring niche in whatever systems evolved as a result of new technology. But American writers were aware that if dreams of flight and real flight were to go together, accommodation must be on the dreamers' part, for the American temperament cannot be altered by a style, or stance, that eschews the visible world as the eyes and ears of an accurate transcriber report it. Experimental writers for the most part, had to emigrate to Paris if they wanted to take part in the new artistic movements that privileged non-mimetic forms. The American public would listen to Sinclair Lewis and Carl Sandburg, and honor them for representing familiar reality in recognizable ways, but it had little tolerance for the makers of works like *The Waste Land* and *The Cantos*. The rhetoric of much 1930s literature is propitiatory, a deferring to things as they are in the plainest of plain styles. Abundant manifestos declared that writers must respect the authority of fact, and surrender the temptations of authorial sovereignty to the preeminent shaping power of history itself, for history is as much the donnée for a narrative of events as physical materials are the donnée for inventions in the primary realm of the world.

John Dos Passos's use of the Wright brothers in *The Big Money* (1936) is a case in point. The entire trilogy *U.S.A.* is a superb example of that surrendering to the authority of historical fact that realism demanded. Barbara Foley has remarked that "while *The Big Money* clearly consists primarily of fictional narrative ... it could be argued that it is essentially, in its generic nature, a historical document rather than a fictional one, since its structure is molded by the shape of historical events and its goal is to illuminate the truth of the reader's world."[14] By means of the camera eye and biography sections, Dos Passos keeps history in the foreground of the novel. The Wright brothers are part of the pantheon of inventive figures who bequeath a world of immense force influencing the fate of some characters for the better and most for the worse. If John William Ward is correct in his suspicion that the character Charley Anderson in *The Big Money* is a conscious inversion of Charles Lindbergh, "the names, of course; both fliers, both Minnesota boys," then Dos Passos is offering an ironic reading of aviation history.[15] Anderson's decline into grasping materialism is meant to represent America's corruption in the new century. Like Rukeyser, Dos Passos traces an Icarian pattern of tragic descent following upon the first exhilarating ascent at Kitty Hawk. But Kitty Hawk itself is treated with extraordinary piety. In "The Campers at Kitty Hawk," Dos Passos relates the story of the Wrights in their own notational style, as if to make the point that their minds and acts are so close to the workings of nature they seem to be part of the *physis* of nature:

> There with a glider made of two planes and a tail in which
>   they lay
> flat on their bellies and controlled the warp of the planes by
>   shimmying
> their hips, taking off again and again all day from a big dune
>   named
> Kill Devil Hill,
>   they learned to fly.
>
> Once they'd managed to hover for a few seconds
> and soar ever so slightly on a rising aircurrent,
> they decided the time had come
> to put a motor in their biplane.

Language cannot get more factual, more unadorned. "The Campers at Kitty Hawk" allows Leonardo da Vinci to make an appropriate appearance as another champion of the empirical method shared by author and subjects.

The Wright brothers are featured in another book of 1936, *Prelude to 'Icaros'*, widely distributed but now sunk without trace. Its author, John Williams Andrews, designed it as the introduction to an epic poem on Lindbergh's flight, though the epic was never published. This is another book of origins, a chronicle of fact and legend that traces the enduring and polymorphous desire for ascent. The poem begins with a Whitmanian catalogue of birds, proceeds to Icarus, then to Chinese, Babylonian, and Christian stories related in some way to flight legends (the latter an imaging of Christ as a birdman), then a long section on the balloonist Pilatre de Rozier, whose sublime ascent just before the French Revolution is offered as a figure for the rise of the masses against social constraints in Andrews's own era. The book concludes with the Wright brothers and the triumph of aircraft in the generation following their achievement. The poem represents, like the prose histories of flight which proliferated in the 1930s, a sacramental chronicle of its subject, in which foretypes are canonized in a sequence of model biographies.

The dramatic construction of Andrews's poem is sound, or at least feasible, but the poem is vitiated by his failure to find a language, a sustained register, in which the patternings of his vision can be artfully expressed. On the one hand he is constantly trying to inflate the narrative to a scriptural pitch by biblical echoes. In the Icarus section: "the hand of Icaros / is a stubborn hand!" (p. 29), and in the Kitty Hawk section: "the gales came down and smote [the *Flyer*]." This is awkward enough, but the lines following the smiting are these:

> And when they seemed ready at last,
> The welded heads of the screw-shafts turned in the hubs,
> And were patched with cement, and held; but then the shafts
> broke;
> And new shafts were sent from Dayton, which also twisted;
> And Orville packed up his bag and went back to Dayton,
> Five-hundred long weary miles to the metal-lathe,
> And new shafts were turned, of solid blue steel this time;
> And Orville came back to the Banks and the shafts were
> installed.[16]

The Bible can be matter-of-fact as well, but it *is* the Bible, a repository of divine speech acts authorized in an archaic era close to the beginnings. Andrews's hectic alternation of the dithyrambic and the prosaic is altogether too crude. If flight were finally accepted as the true Church, *Prelude to 'Icaros'* might find its way into the assemblage of sacred writings, but it is not a work to solemnize the tradition.

A step down even from Andrews is William Rose Benét's *With Wings as Eagles* (1940), another book-length poem ranging from man's ancient dream of flight to the most immediate events of the late 1930s. Two things impair this historical chronicle. One is Benét's deliberate proscription of any unfavorable portraits from his gallery of aviation history. In an audacious lapse, for example, he simply leaves out World War I as he traces the development of the airplane and its various uses; similarly the horrific bombings of cities in Spain and China, the subject of forceful poems by W. H. Auden, Archibald MacLeish, and others at the time Benét was composing this sequence, go unmentioned. The second problem derives from the first, that Benét – who could and did write better than this – adjusts his poetic function to suit a mass audience. No scriptural intentions here, he constantly refers to his "rhymes," "this swaggering verse," his "banjo tune," and so forth. And the low point is the section on the Wright brothers, written in doggerel couplets meant for speedy consumption. His book must stand here for a multitude of uninspired newspaper and magazine verse in honor of the Wright brothers – not excluding Robert Frost's feeble epigram, "The Wrights' Biplane" in *A Further Range* (1936). The desire to honor the nativity continued, but the great poem of Kitty Hawk would not be written till the 1950s – by Frost himself.

The last typological treatment of the Wrights in this decade is Selden Rodman's book-length poem, *The Airmen* (1941), which offers lengthy accounts of Daedalus and Icarus, and Leonardo da Vinci, before taking up the Wright brothers. A fourth section is devoted to Lauro de Bossis, a young Italian poet who, inspired by Gabriele D'Annunzio's act of dropping pacifist leaflets on Vienna from an airplane during The Great War, dropped anti-Fascist pamphlets on Rome in 1931. De Bossis sacrificed his life in the act of redeeming the flying machine from its Futurist-Fascist associations. He thus performs the same Christic function in Rodman's myth-history that Lindbergh would have performed in Andrews's poem had the epic of Lindbergh's flight followed his *Prelude* as intended.

"The Brothers" is the longest narrative of the poem (forty pages) and the longest verse passage ever written on the subject. Several sections are devoted to a chronicle of experiments by the Montgolfiers, Cayley, Pilcher, Maxim, Lilienthal, and Langley. As in so much writing about the airplane, this obsessive recapitulation of the honored tradition, the naming of ancestors and the ritual recording of their achievements, serves a biblical function, like the counting of generations in Chronicles. Whereas Daedalus and Leonardo are shown as serving the Pharaonic will of tyrants like Minos and Cesare Borgia, however, these inventors are depicted as disinterested, motivated by curiosity in the highest, Arnoldian sense. The *sporting* character of their experiments is emphasized throughout, the element of play as a value in itself. Once again, however, the industrial muse fails to provide satisfactory wings to the poet. Rodman clearly feels constrained by the diaries and letters of the Wright brothers, as well as the testimony he gathered while researching the book. The poem sinks into the documentary style the author conceives to be the truest wedding of form to content:

> Encasing all surfaces and crossbars in a covering of muslin,
> All wires tightened simply by shortening two,
> They shift the frame's main cross-piece to the cutting edge;
> Run after it in the wind, warping the wings by rope; find the
>   response true.
>
> If the glider balks on the beach, at Kill Devil Hill
> Two volunteers from the Life Saving Station will get under
>   the tips.
> It floats on the up-currents. It slides in the eddy of the slopes,
> Wilbur maneuvering the wingtips from the cradle with his
>   hips.[17]

Rhyme heightens the awkwardness of the passage, calling attention to the prosaic language by a noticeable poetic device. By deferring so entirely to the authority of fact, Rodman yields up his own prerogative as an inventor. Like other writers discussed in this chapter, he permits his respect for the machine to make him susceptible to its inventors' literary style. He imagines himself to be joining hands in common brotherhood with his fellow technicians, but they have usurped his power of making by his consent.

These writers are the victims of a self-conscious modernism. Jacques Ellul notes that "nothing belongs any longer to the realm of the gods or the supernatural. The individual who lives in the technical milieu knows very well that there is nothing spiritual anywhere. But man cannot live without the sacred. He therefore transfers his sense of the sacred to the very thing which has destroyed its former object: to technique itself."[18] The posture of reverence toward figures who embody the supreme creative powers of the modern world prevented these authors, as it did Lindbergh's admirers, from locating an individual voice and unique poetic structure sustainable beyond brief successful passages. Although poets desired to spiritualize machinery in order to sustain and modernize the civil religion in America, Mystery had become matter-of-fact to a public increasingly accustomed to technological breakthroughs and a rhetoric of instruction. And how matter-of-fact can poets become before disappearing into the workaday information systems characteristic of a consumer society? Crane's reactionary decision to cling to the bardic sublime seems in retrospect the wisest one, given his mythologizing intentions. But credit must be given to his successors as well, whose dogged persistence in hammering out a language of technique helped to make the sacred history initiated at Kitty Hawk visible to multitudes.

8. "The Nearest Paradise": Forms of Flight in the 1930s

REDEEMING THE TIME

There is something comic in the encounter between the poet and the airplane in the aftermath of Lindbergh's flight, a masquerade of language that reflects a crisis of vocation. Writers who honored the airplane as an apocalyptic symbol, a break in human time, were compelled to seek in the obsolescent past the sacramental tradition without which events at Kitty Hawk and Le Bourget could not be understood in their "true" significance. To the degree that writers mimicked that tradition they could be accused of trying to enhance their own importance by acts of afflatus upon the flying machine; Scripture requires divinely inspired scribes. On the other hand, if they deferred to an empirical mode of speech hostile to the miraculous, if they transcribed the *novum* in its own reasoned prose, they flattened the object and themselves in the effort at authentic homage.

The kind of historicist surveyed in the previous chapter, then, resembles the figure of Crispin in Wallace Stevens's "The Comedian as the Letter C." Vatic claims that the poet is a "Great Navigator" and the pilot a seer who can "conjugate infinity's dim marge – / Anew" (Crane), or that both together can "cut with ... certain wings; engrave space now / to your ambition" (Rukeyser) are like Crispin's pretense of being "preceptor to the sea" (of reality) which finally overwhelms him. If scriptural language made such a poor fit to mechanics, some skeptics argued, then perhaps the airplane ought to be taken less seriously. Nineteenth-century writers had legitimate reasons for celebrating new machines, the argument ran, but weren't modern poets making themselves ridiculous by repeating the clichés of

131

mechanisme? Shouldn't the airplane be treated as just another mode of transportation, a convenience rather than an exalted type of the modern?

In general, the answer was NO. Whatever the rhetorical problems, writers were loath to abandon their hopeful claims for the flying machine's extraordinary possibilities as a fact and metaphor. Though many of F. T. Marinetti's proclamations in the first decade of the century appeared naive and dangerous by the 1930s, his later assertion that "the changing perspectives of flight constitute an absolutely new reality, one that has nothing in common with the traditional reality of terrestrial perspective," offered a working hypothesis useful to modern artists.[1] Aerial perspective enjoyed a vogue in the literature, as in the painting and photography, of the 1920s and 1930s. In turn, the expansive forms of aerial perspective were introjected into the literature of terrestrial perspective, so that grounded observers increasingly looked upward to the airplane as a symbol of the liberated consciousness they *might* enjoy if and when aloft. The community of desperate souls that gazes rapturously at the skywriting plane in Virginia Woolf's *Mrs Dalloway* (1925), for example, experiences momentarily the redeeming sense of otherwordliness that comes with new vistas.

That aerial perspective tended to justify a neoromantic language in modern poetry can be seen in a poem like Frank Ernest Hill's "Upper Air," from *Stone Dust* (1928), the first significant book of verse by an American to give substantial attention to flight:

High, pale, imperial places of slow cloud
And windless wells of sunlit silence . . . Sense
Of some aware, half-scornful Permanence
Past which we flow like water that is loud
A moment on the granites. Nothing here
Beats with the pulse that beat in us below;
That was a flame; this is the soul of snow
Immortalized in moveless atmosphere.

Yet we shall brood upon his haunt of wings
When love, like perfume washed away in rain,
Dies on the years. Still we shall come again,
Seeking the clouds as we have sought the sea,

Asking the peace of these immortal things
That will not mix with our mortality.[2]

The first lines echo the two great Romantic odes of timelessness,
Wordsworth's "Ode: Intimations of Immortality" and Keats's
"Ode on a Grecian Urn" (which calls the urn a "foster-child of
silence and slow time"). Having evoked this "Permanence" as
only a pilot can see it, in the octave, the poet is pulled into the
orbit of its wonderful attraction in the sestet. That "we shall
brood upon this haunt of wings" (rhyming with "immortal
things") allows the poet to associate himself with the holy spirit,
until subject and object are momentarily one: a mirror reflection
between flying machine and Permanence of cloud that recalls
Cecil Lewis's scene already described in *Sagittarius Rising*. The
image of "return" which dominates so much writing about the
airplane, and usually refers to an inescapable natural cycle, here
is skillfully reversed so that it is the immortal object constantly
revisited by the lucky birdmen. The flying machine is a friend
to man because it grants him intimate participation with the
"peace" and wonder of heaven.

Hill's most ambitious statement on this subject is "Earth and
Air," a manifesto poem that exploits the same radical opposition
of terrestrial and celestial modes of being. Here the author gives
the opposition a historical character. Earth is not depreciated in
the poem; it is eulogized as all-creative and utterly beautiful,
and yet "Earth is our yesterday." Earth had a secret purpose
during all its prehistoric and historic periods, to foster the "Men
with the vision of air" who because "they envied the wind
and the eagle" continued to improve their technological skills,
spanning space in various forms until the twentieth century
crowned their efforts: "Air is today." In the modern century
man has become a god, Hill says explicitly in the poem, and has
thereby achieved the Paradise from which pastoral myths like
those of Judaism and Christianity exiled him.

Hill, who later collaborated with Allan Nevins on the standard
biography of Henry Ford, was widely read and anthologized in
the post-Lindbergh era. One sees the community of views in a
typical book of 1929, *Sky Larking*, by Bruce Gould, in which
Hill's work is cited as a model of excellence. Gould's tone is
reverential as well:

Whatever be the reasons, the facts are that flying satisfies deeply rooted desires. For as long as time these desires have hungered vainly for fulfillment. The horse, and latterly the motorcar have merely teased them. The upward sweep of the airplane signifies release. It is as though one cut the umbilical cord which has bound humanity to Mother Earth and in that instant is born into another, and to those who know its boundaries and color, more glamorous and romantic world than the accustomed earth.[3]

Gould was a journalist who covered the Lindbergh flight, and in this passage he summarizes the meaning of that flight as the public imagination finally determined it. The pilot, as Gould says, can skim "the indefinite borderline of eternity" and derive from his ascent a deep and permanent thrill different in kind from any ever experienced. "The air is the nearest Paradise we shall know in this life," (p. 30) he asserts. In his view, literary history has amounted to nothing more than the blind thrashings of Mankind frustrated by its earthly entrapment. Gould praises Leonardo as the ancestor of the modern Prometheans, as well as Shelley for understanding the impulse to break free:

Shelley, lying on his back, envied the skylark with all his poet's imagination, never dreaming that future poets could be the skylark instead of merely voicing their lyrical envy of it. [p. 22]

As one might expect, *The Spirit of St. Louis* emerges, in this orthodoxy, as the redemptive type of the modern, integrating the devotion to technique represented by Leonardo with the Romantic dream of wings.

Gould complains that modern writers have not elaborated the deep meanings of this new invention. He praises H. G. Wells's *The War in the Air*, and acknowledges in another chapter that "Given an hour or two, a sizable air fleet moving swiftly and unexpectedly on New York could reduce the proud and beautiful city to an uninhabitable shambles, hardly worth re-erecting" (p. 203), a scenario so familiar through Wells's example that by 1929 it could be summoned in one sentence as an unconscious *hommage*. And there is the obligatory allusion to the air aces of the Great War as "a race of heroes whose names shine out like those in the knightly age" (p. 62). But Gould argues that the imagery of warfare more properly belongs to the primitive phase of the airplane's evolution, and criticizes the kind of air-war narratives popularized by James Warner Bellah as derivative and formulaic. His book is directed specifically at youth, and it is clearly to the next generation that he looks for masterpieces on the subject of aviation.

Indeed a vast number of boys' books were published in the aftermath of Lindbergh's flight which carried forward the major themes of aviation literature to the generation that would fly in the European and Asian theatres of World War II. A representative title from the early 1930s that belongs to this programmatic excitement about the historical moment is *The Red Eagle: A Tale for Young Aviators*, by Alexander Key, a color-illustrated and expensively produced book aimed at fourth- to sixth-grade pupils. The story opens with two boys, Ned and Richard, awaiting the arrival by plane of their dashing Uncle Jim who visits them occasionally in his monoplane *The Red Eagle*. A former "ace in the Argonne" with a scar on his face, he flies a plane raised to exalted status by its associations with the already legendary figures of flight: "The ship was powered with a Wright Whirlwind Motor, one of the same type that took Charles Lindbergh across the Atlantic."[4] Similarly, the motif of the ecstatic first flight is rendered here as in so much aviation literature: "[Richard] felt exhilarated and completely master of himself. He was a great bird soaring across the field, no longer a mere being like others who could only look enviously at a swallow overhead and regret they themselves were earthbound" (p. 45). The devaluation of earthly existence is tempered by a plot that emphasizes the social utility of flight. On one glider flight the boys spot two murderers who have escaped from prison and report their location to a posse beating about vainly in the bush. In the longer story-line, they accompany Uncle Jim on a race at the flying club. He unexpectedly passes out during a thunderstorm due to a recurrence of shell-shock suffered during the war, and the boys pilot *The Red Eagle* to first place while he lies paralyzed in the cabin. Clearly an allegory of sorts is at work. The aviator's secret wound, of which his scar is an outward sign, represents the mixed effect of the war on the air tradition. If the conflict enabled the pilot to master his wings it also made an inward wound that sets limits upon his performance. He is redeemed by the children of promise who inherit his powers; he and their father present them with a plane of their own, *The Red Eagle II*, as a reward and sign of confidence in their future as pilots.

An English work of 1935 composed for similarly didactic purposes is C. Day Lewis's "A Time to Dance." Its first part is a long narrative of the flight of two lieutenants, Parer and M'Intosh, in 1920, from England to Australia. The poem is designed not only as a postwar exemplum, "a theme with a happy end," but as an allegory of the situation of the West in the mid-Thirties. The airplane is a rickety D.H.9 that after long military service ought to be junked; it deserves the end that so many prophets had called down upon the big machine of Western civilization. The condemned plane has been "patched up though to write an heroic / Line across the world."[5] The aviators have the power of preservation and resurrection, which in mechanical terms is the same thing. In fact, the resurrection myth informs the whole poem, for unlike some pilots who had no knowledge whatever of how to service the insides of their plane, Parer and M'Intosh have the skills needed to keep the plane going despite all failures and accidents: "they had power to repair / This good for naught but the grave: they livened her engine and gave / Fuselage faith to rise rejuvenated from ruin" (p. 148). Time and again the Christic fliers raise their birdlike structure, until their journey is completed.

In section 26 of a long sequence of 1933, "The Magnetic Mountain," Lewis had borrowed Gerard Manley Hopkins's rapturous language in "The Windhover" to praise the poet/aviator as a "saviour" whose courage will inspire the ill spirits of the modern world. In this later poem Lewis imitates the Old English and Icelandic narratives. Lewis admired in the sagas the unquestioning, unthinking hardihood of characters accustomed to overcoming challenges every day of their lives. One could say that the Anglo-Saxon ethos and narrative strategy of "A Time to Dance" represented a response to the ingenious modernism of a work like W. H. Auden's "Journal of an Airman," which had presented the airman as a severely paranoid character. There is a further connection here. Some critics have suggested that the model for Auden's airman is T. E. Lawrence in his Royal Air Force incarnation. Lawrence tells us, however, that he joined the R.A.F. precisely because he yearned to escape self-consciousness and rest within the disciplined ranks of an organization which depended upon technics rather than imagination. Parer and M'Intosh are certainly the kind of figures Lawrence looked to as models and which – a further irony – he himself had represented in his "Lawrence of Arabia" role. Whatever the ramifications back and forth, it is clear that Lewis's instincts were good ones. He generates respect for his vagabond-heroes by the skaldic form, summoning by imitation the phase of history he wishes to import into the present:

> Yet nerve failed never, heart clung
> To height, and the brain kept its course and the hand its skill.
> . . . . .
> Wrecked was their undercarriage
> Radiator cracked, in pieces, compasses crooked;
> Fallen all into confusion.
> Their winged hope was a heap of scrap, but unsplintered their
> courage.
>
> [pp. 147–8]

The poem is punctuated throughout with such praise, which functions as something more than a tonic. It reminds us constantly of the "courage, steadfast, luminous" (p. 146) a pilot requires to effect his task. That these veterans of war, urging their exhausted machine toward a distant, happy land, can achieve their aim gives the poet new hope for his personal and public situation.

Though Lewis's poem edges toward the mock-heroic, it still belongs to the class of neoromantic texts that emphasized the extra-ordinary aspects of flight. Perhaps the apex of Romantic sentiment is the philosophy of Verticalism (later Vertigralism) espoused by Eugene Jolas, who stated that his "romantic, cosmological and mystic theory of ascent was first conceived in Paris, in 1928."[6] Though he does not mention Lindbergh's flight the date and place tell their own story. In that year he published from Harry Crosby's Black Sun Press a fantasia of flight, "Secession is Astropolis," followed in the next decade by a manifesto, *Poetry is Vertical* (1932), more manifestos, an aesthetic theory of ascent in *Vertigralist Pamphlet* (1937), and finally an anthology, *Vertical: A Yearbook for Romantic-Mystic Ascensions* in 1941, containing work putatively (though not actually) on the theme by a variety of American and European writers. As the editor of *transition*, an influential literary magazine of the Twenties and Thirties, Jolas's manifestos are significant for their attempt to foreground the derivations of experimental movements like Surrealism from Romantic origins. For example, he collects specimens of flying dreams by Jean Paul, Victor Hugo, and others, in *Vertical*, and relates them to modern examples.

For Jolas the description of oneiromantic landscapes by pilots became the new scripture for a religion of ascent, and for an aesthetics vitally informed by aeronautical terminology:

> The poet, in an age of anguish, has as his principal task the rediscovery of the sacred character of expression ... Language must become vertical.... It may be possible that the much insulted vocabulary of technology may furnish us new symbols. Aeronautics, which is one element of ascension, should be able to renew the vertical speech. [pp. 94–5]

Like Hill, Gould, and Cecil Lewis (not to be confused with C. Day Lewis), Jolas sees history as little more than an evolution of the means and myths of continuous ascent, which when articulated in texts and universalized in act will perform the effective liberation of the soul. Unfortunately, Jolas is so wholly committed to one kind of experimental literary tradition that he will not acknowledge works that offer him precisely the material he needs as evidence. The writings of Antoine de Saint-Exupéry, to name the most obvious example, go unmentioned and unquoted in Jolas's anthology. Jolas never developed his notions coherently. He uses the term "ascent" honorifically, as nineteenth-century writers do, and ignores the actual literature of flight, despite his prescription quoted above, in favor of high-minded eloquence. For all his talk of modern technology Jolas's notion of ascent derives more from Petrarch's ascent of Mont Ventoux and the prospect poetry it inspired than from the new perspectives of aviation.

And for good reason. Jolas wants to praise the airplane as a transcendent symbol, lifting man above historical necessity, and yet his genuine concern about the rise of European fascism makes him conscious that his neoromantic philosophy may be a gesture of bad faith. The truth is that most of the literary movements of the 1930s which proclaimed their enmity to the machine and machinelike in culture – Surrealism, Herbert Read's Anarchism, "The Apocalypse" founded by Henry Treece, J. F. Hendry and G. S. Fraser – derived their tenets from Futurism, which had no more appropriate fulfillment than fascism and machine-worship. No writer in this period drew upon deeper unconscious wishes than Hitler and Mussolini, for whom the airplane came providentially to hand as a symbol for the triumph of the will. Mussolini especially had emphasized in his life and speeches the intimate connection between flight and imperial destiny. A propaganda biography published in Italy, *Mussolini Aviator*, made the connection explicit:

> . . . no machine requires so much human concentration of soul and will power as a flying machine to make it work properly. The pilot understands the fullest meaning of the word "control." Thus it seems that there is an intimate spiritual link between Fascism and Flying. Every airman is a born Fascist.[7]

The most effective resistance to the debased romanticism of such a claim was a commitment to its inevitable victims, which in historical terms meant the bourgeoisie. When Jolas proscribed from his canon writers like Saint-Exupéry who labored to domesticate the airplane in the interests of social solidarity he removed the voices that might have given it some measure of validity.

SAINT-EXUPÉRY

The work of Antoine de Saint-Exupéry is certainly the most sophisticated literature of aviation that appeared between the time of Lindbergh's flight in 1927 and the outbreak of World War II, events which have immediate bearing upon the shape of his imagination and the popular reception of his books. By this I mean that Saint-Exupéry sought to lead his readers from craven idolatry of the solo pilot – a species of hero worship he increasingly recognized as fascistic – toward a sharpened understanding of the fundamental conditions of life which bind together pilot and earthbound for their mutual benefit. The tendency in Saint-Exupéry's progress from his early novels *Southern Mail* (1928) and *Night Flight* (1931) to the memoir called in English *Wind, Sand and Stars* (1939) is toward a chastening of merely personal gratification in favor of love for his fellow creatures and a commitment to their happiness. He thus extends the ecclesiastical possibilities of the airplane announced by its disciples immediately after Kitty Hawk.

In Saint-Exupéry's earliest fiction human relationships are casual, lacking the profundity of feeling that the aviator-hero imbibes from the experience of flight. In *Southern Mail* nothing on the ground seems to give the protagonist, Jacques Bernis, any satisfaction. Compared to his rich childhood memories, the city is a "nameless confusion"; people dart around "like goldfish in an aquarium," and winter landscapes reveal mainly a heap of dead things. His mistress Geneviève cannot make authentic contact with him; both remain throughout the novel "images" not persons, like the insubstantial shades in Dante's Inferno. Their sexual coupling mimics the rhythm of aerial experience dramatized in the novel as a whole: brief soaring transports followed by that "little death" which marks the descent into postcoital sadness, the return to leaden life.

A change of emphasis is discernible in *Night Flight*, and in the preface for a book on flight published in 1933:

> The job has its grandeurs, yes. There is the exultation of arriving safely after a storm [as the pilot in *Night Flight* fails to do], the joy of gliding down out of the darkness of night or tempest toward a sun-drenched Alicante or Santiago; there is the swelling sense of returning to repossess one's place in life, in the miraculous garden of earth, where there are trees and women and, down by the harbor, friendly little bars. When he has throttled his engine and is banking into the airport, leaving the somber cloud masses behind, what pilot does not break into song?[8]

The imagery of cloud, air, and earth is the same as in Cecil Lewis's visionary scene in *Sagittarius Rising*, or Frank Ernest Hill's poem "Upper Air" – or, for that matter, the effusions of poets after Lindbergh's flight – but Saint-Exupéry inverts the value given to each image. The difference in attitude derives from seven years and thousands of flights for the Latécoère Airline Company, or "the Line," which Saint-Exupéry joined in 1926. He became part of a brotherhood which subscribed to an ideology of community service and international solidarity that made "the return," the reentry into "one's place in life," an occasion for joy as intense as the liftoff into the heavens.

"The Line" was initiated after the war by Pierre Latécoère, an airplane manufacturer who conceived the plan of a giant network of air routes joining Europe with Africa and South America. It was "a dream worthy of Jules Verne," according to one skeptical government official.[9] Mail between these continents was voluminous; two thousand tons of letters passed between Europe and South America each year, but at such a slow rate of progress (an exchange of letters between Paris and Buenos Aires required fifty days by boat) that cultural and commercial relations suffered considerably. Air mail, then, increased peaceful traffic among nations, and promoted closer relations between people whose happiness could be imagined as dependent upon the speedy delivery of correspondence. As Saint-Exupéry put it in *Southern Mail*, "The airline kept drilling it into you: the precious mail, more precious than life itself. Enough to keep thirty thousand lovers going."[10] By necessity, then, Saint-Exupéry emphasizes the civilizing stage of social evolution. He imagines his work with the mail service by metaphors of exploration and pioneering. His exaltation of the Line's international network evokes a latter-day Church, like H. G. Wells's syndicate, The Transport Control, in *The Shape of Things to Come* (1932). Pilots do not escape the social realm in his writing; they serve it like the shepherds to whom Saint-Exupéry sometimes compares them. And the pilots have their own shepherds, technocrats like Rivière, the chief of operations in *Night Flight*, who enforce responsibility to the humane values of an enlightened culture.

Rivière's most difficult task is to inform the doomed pilot Fabien's wife, by telephone, that her husband has lost radio contact after flying into a cyclone. When she appears at the airport to await further news, Saint-Exupéry is careful to balance the values of earth and air:

> The realization irked her that in this room she was the envoy of a hostile creed and almost she regretted having come; she would have liked to hide somewhere and, fearful of being remarked, dared neither cough nor weep. She felt her presence here misplaced, indecent, as though she were standing naked before them. But so potent was *her* truth, the truth within her,

that furtively their eyes strayed ever and again in her direction, trying to read it on her face. Beauty was hers and she stood for a holy thing, the world of human happiness. She vouched for the sanctity of that material something with which man tampers when he acts.[11]

Seldom does the earthbound receive such a favorable report in works by aviation enthusiasts. If the impulse of other writers is to recreate the pilot as a Romantic figure yearning to enter the nearest Paradise by repeated ascents, Saint-Exupéry, never denying the satisfaction of flight, offers in the figure of the pilot's wife a counterforce made "holy" by its claim upon human sympathy. The scene in the airport has the effect of a fairy tale in which those made spellbound by envious aspiration to the aerial element are redeemed by the power of a pure heart.

Saint-Exupéry's masterpiece, *Wind, Sand and Stars*, maintains the same delicate balance between opposed states of being, and does so by the most scrupulous intermingling of the prosaic and scriptural languages. It was not written consecutively at one time, but comprises for the most part a group of memoirs published in different periodicals after the success of *Night Flight* in 1931. Throughout the decade Saint-Exupéry tried to discipline his writing, which tended to rhapsodic overstatement, toward the goal of a genuinely Homeric style, less impressionistic and more transparent in its relation of thoughts and actions -- but without losing the grandeur of epic speech, the wonder at a life "fertilized by mysterious circumstances."[12] His literary model is not the familiar pilot's memoir but the kind of religious autobiography that renders ordinary events as occult stages of a spiritual education. Saint-Exupéry marshals religious imagery with an acute sense of its likely effect, especially on an audience (in France) that is principally Catholic. Traditional religion receives little attention in his work; Christian symbolism is almost entirely displaced into the "sacred rites of the craft" (p. 22). And nowhere is this more true than when Saint-Exupéry describes the conversion experience that forms the thematic center of *Wind, Sand and Stars*.

Saint-Exupéry and his mechanic André Prévot, have undertaken a flight from Paris to Saigon. While flying by dead reckoning they lose direction on the way to Cairo, and when Saint-Exupéry dives beneath the clouds to locate his position, they crash-land in the Libyan desert. A harrowing narrative follows in which the two men suffer the tortures of thirst as they explore, wait, signal, and hope vainly day after day for rescue. They undergo mirages, hallucinations, and physical ravages as dehydration empties them of defenses against the extremity of heat and cold. Finally, just as they are within hours of death, desert nomads, usually depicted in Saint-Exupéry's work as murderers of downed pilots in the unceasing war against colonialism, providentially appear and give them the water of life.

What is so fascinating about the scene, in the context of the literature of aviation, is the emphasis on water rather than air or earth. In his earliest fiction Saint-Exupéry uses water negatively as the presiding metaphor of earthbound existence. Alternating with this image is an equivalent one, the earth as desert. In this later work, Saint-Exupéry presents desert and water not as congruent elements opposed to air, but as contraries. Air is a means of transporting the pilot to a place where he can discover this fact. (Likewise in *The Little Prince* the aviator discovers vital truths from the title character after crash-landing in the desert.) The Moor who brings them water is called "this humble nomad with the hands of an archangel on our shoulders." He administers the act of communion to the aviators kneeling before him to take the water, and at that epiphanic moment he becomes to them a "god" who can "create life" (p. 234).

The turning point of the book, then, is Saint-Exupéry's realization while dying of thirst that "the essence of things" which he claimed earlier in the memoir (p. 184) was located in the upper air, in fact lies below the ground as a reservoir for pilgrims like himself. The adventure ends in a moral chastening of the desire for freedom; not liberation from the common human condition but bondage within its dense net of affections and needs becomes the ideal stance toward reality. "I have struggled to rejoin my kind, whose very existence on earth I had forgotten" (p. 228), he writes. It has been charged that Saint-Exupéry's code of hardship, duty, discipline, and sacrifice made him susceptible to the ideal of Airman-as-Fascist -- as embodied, for example, by Jean Mermoz, his good friend and fellow pilot on the Line, who as Vice President of the right-wing organization, the Croix de Feu, preached a militaristic code of social reconstruction that mirrored Italian and German fascist ideologies in significant ways. But *Wind, Sand and Stars* shows Saint-Exupéry mortifying his will to power by means of a fortunate fall into dependence upon the mercy of non-Aryan primitives. The book's final section takes Saint-Exupéry to Spain during the Civil War, where he commits himself to the saving of life, as his own life was saved in the desert.

In 1939, then, at a time when Lindbergh, imprisoned by the myth of the aviator-hero, was describing aviation as a "barrier" between peoples that would keep them in wholesome separation, and when the fascists had proclaimed to the world by their lightning bombardments that the essential meaning of the airplane lay in its use as an irresistible weapon, Saint-Exupéry was able to popularize a conception of the flying machine as essentially Christian, pacifist, humane. By doing so he made it an emblem of the anti-fascist spirit. Whereas Lindbergh had to fall silent during the war, Saint-Exupéry could speak out eloquently, in *Flight to Arras*, for the compassionate lessons enforced by aerial service. He learns (once again) from his entirely futile reconaissance flights that flying can never give the genuine sense of sovereignty that individuals crave. He finds that sense of power in his memories of childhood and in the sympathetic feelings of intimacy with the endangered villagers and refugees he overflies. In the most explicit Christic comparison in his books he speaks of his urgent belief in self-sacrifice as a model during this time of plague. He welcomes the Icarian death he foresees – he was in fact shot down in 1944 – as an authentic contribution to a world community in need of moral alternatives to the fascist fantasy of achieving lordship in the air. His life and work remained as pious *exempla* during a time when the patriotic myth of The Great Crusade once again tempted writers and pilots to relish their power to inflict death from above.

THE MODERN BIRD POEM

The history of aviation, as with any industry, is usually told in numbers, and during the 1930s these all point to a rapidity of development virtually unprecedented even in the modern world. How does one assess the implications of the statistic that domestic airlines in the United States alone, which had carried about 6,000 persons in 1926, were transporting almost three million people annually by 1941? If one adds to that the number of foreign airlines and private planes, one gets a sense of the hundreds of thousands of airplanes aloft during the decade following Lindbergh's flight of 1927. The changes wrought by the new invention are beyond the limits of this study, but it is appropriate to note that the effect on birdlife could only be negative. The annihilation of space and time which Saint-Exupéry praised as part of the colonizing spirit, whether engineered by plane, railway, or automobile, introduces into the environment substances and social habits inimical to the appreciably less dynamic cycles of birdlife. Lindbergh himself pointed this out in an interview shortly before his death in 1974:

> Lying under an acacia tree with the sounds of the dawn around me, I realized more clearly facts that man should never overlook: that the construction of an airplane, for instance, is simple when compared to the evolutionary achievement of a bird; that airplanes depend on an advanced civilization, and that where civilization is most advanced, few birds exist.
>
> I realized that if I had to choose, I would rather have birds than airplanes.[13]

Writers found it increasingly difficult to choose birds *rather than* airplanes as their subject matter. Instead one notes the increase in poems which accommodate the existence of the airplane as a not-so-secret sharer of the skies with birds. Such poems complete the tendency described in Chapter 3 of historicizing the bird by making it subject to human activities. Now instead of two actors in a poem – earthly observer, bird in flight – there tends to be three, for the airplane is always somewhere in the poet's psychic ken as a figure for that "advanced civilization" to which Lindbergh refers.

A simple example is Marianne Moore's "The Frigate Pelican."[14] The poem begins by praising the bird as resembling a primeval scheme for a flying machine:

> Rapidly cruising or lying on the air there is a bird
>   that realizes Rasselas's friend's project
>   of wings uniting levity with strength.

The allusion is a cunning one in a poem celebrating birdlife because the "project" described in Samuel Johnson's novel had such an unfortunate conclusion. The inventor climbed to a promontory with his glider-like contraption, leaped into the air and dropped immediately into a lake. No such fate awaits Moore's pelican, which is

> the fleetest foremost fairy
> among birds, outflies the
> aeroplane which cannot flap its wings nor alter any quill-tip.

(Moore excised these lines in a revision.) The poem is not a polemical one, and yet her point is made. The bird is adapted to its element, in a way that the airplane simply isn't. Moore dismisses the airplane as an ungainly mimicry of what is graceful in a natural creature.

A more complex example is Robinson Jeffers's poem "Pelicans," because it attempts to imitate the canonical nineteenth-century bird poem.[15] It begins with a grounded observer looking up to see four pelicans flying over his house. There follows a reverie in the manner of Keats in which the poet imagines that the birds' wings remember the oldest redwoods, the movement of continents, "the dinosaur's days" and the first European voyages into the unknown. Finally we have this passage:

> The omnisecular spirit keeps the old with the new also.
> Nothing at all has suffered erasure.
> There is a life not of our time. He calls ungainly bodies
> As beautiful as the grace of horses.
> He is weary of nothing; he watches air-planes;
>   he watches pelicans.

If this were a latter-day example of the Greater Romantic Lyric, the poem would return to the speaker's perspective; the pelicans would have flown out of view and the poet, affected by the sense of immortality of the sublime breaking of temporal and spatial boundaries achieved by the pelicans' symbolic flight, would ruminate on *his* moment in time. But the historicism of Jeffers's poem demands a different strategy. Like dinosaurs, these ungainly pelicans do not seem very likely candidates for survival. The balanced phrases in the last line claim an equivalent place for bird and airplanes. The secular spirit will not annihilate the old; it will conserve the organic and the mechanical in close proximity. (The form of the poem, a 14-line free verse structure, exhibits how the old and new can cohabit.) "Pelicans" is best seen as an argument for the expansion of historical perception beyond the blinders of a vain modernism. A public enthusiastic about the novelty of airplanes is asked to keep its eyes upon aerial figures of the world's experience in time.

Jeffers is better known for his poems about birds of prey, and indeed the principal modern innovation in the tradition of the bird poem is an increasing fascination with raptors – no doubt because of the recent history of aerial warfare. "Now the eagle dominates our days," Hart Crane had warned in "Cape Hatteras." In another sonnet, "Shiva" (1932), Jeffers unites the predatory bird and the Wright brothers' legacy into a single figure:

> There is a hawk that is picking the birds out of our sky.
> She killed the pigeons of peace and security,
> She has taken honesty and confidence from nations and men,
> She is hunting the lonely heron of liberty.
> She loads the arts with nonsense, she is very cunning,
> Science with dreams and the state with powers to catch them
>   at last.
> Nothing will escape her at last, flying nor running.
> This is the hawk that picks out the star's eyes.
> This is the only hunter that will ever catch the wild swan;
> The prey she will take last is the wild white swan of the beauty
>   of things.
> Then she will be alone, pure destruction, achieved and
>   supreme,
> Empty darkness under the death-tent wings.
> She will build a nest of the swan's bones and hatch a new
>   brood,
> Hang new heavens with new birds, all be renewed.[16]

The poem is a dark meditation on the evolution of avian life toward the sovereign raptor, the bird-machine. Given the context of Jeffers's other work, the figure of "pure destruction, achieved and supreme" can also be taken as a critique of American fascination with the airplane. Even in the 1920s, Jeffers had been appalled by an America "heavily thickening to empire," as he puts it in "Shine, Perishing Republic." How much more heavy, it must have seemed to him, after Lindbergh and his admirers charted continental and trans-continental routes for more and more powerful flying machines. "Nothing will escape her at last," he remarks with remorseful certainty.

That poets use the bird as a conceit for their most profound doubts about the enterprise of modern civilization can best be illustrated by two poems of Allen Tate's, separated by a decade.[17] "The Eagle" (1929) is Tate's version of Shelley's "To a Skylark," which located in the cultic image of the ascending bird the spiritual impulse to rise clear of historical detritus and break free to an immediate experience of infinity. Shelley's and Tate's birds are messengers to the divine source, "Shot out of the mind, / The windy apple.... The apple wormed, blown up / By shells of light." Tate's metaphors are mixed but comprehensible in a historical context. The modern mind is made sick by the corruption it undergoes because it is fastened both to a dying animal and to "the world's rot." The apple evokes the original sin of wordliness from which humanity seeks redemption. The "light" which explodes the diseased garden corresponds to the light of revelation the eagle perceives by the act of ascent. "The Eagle" expresses Tate's impatience with the conditions of human existence in time, like the poetry written to celebrate The Lone Eagle's flight two years earlier.

In a poem like "The Eagle," and its likely source, the caged eagle's dream-flight in Robinson Jeffers's *Cawdor* (1928), the neoromantic hunger to assert a pure spiritual force against the meaningless flux of historical change achieves its most compelling lyric expression. But the tradition of discourse on public themes did not go undefended. In his controversial pamphlet at decade's end, *The Irresponsibles*, Archibald MacLeish condemned a whole generation for seeking escape from its responsibility as social creatures. He imagines intellectuals of the future asking why writers and scholars of the 1930s did not oppose efforts by American philistines and by European fascists to destroy the life of the mind:

The answer we have prepared, the answer we have written out for history to find, is the answer Leonardo is said to have given Michelangelo when Michelangelo blamed him for his indifference to the misfortunes of the Florentines. It is the answer of our kind at many other times and places. "Indeed," said Leonardo, "indeed the study of beauty has occupied my whole heart." The study of beauty, the study of history, the study of science, has occupied our whole hearts, and the misfortunes of our generation are none of our concern. They are the practical and political concern of practical and political men, but the concern of the scholar, the concern of the artist, is with other, purer, more enduring things.[18]

Leonardo's beauty is the same that Tate celebrated in his "Sonnet to Beauty" (1929), the essence, of things toward which his and Jeffers's eagles plot their course. MacLeish's faultfinding stung Tate the scholar, but more so Tate the poet. MacLeish condemns the writer by saying, "He sees the world as a god sees it – without morality, without care, without judgment." The eagle had been Tate's emblem for godlike detachment. Very well, he would enter the fray by making obvious judgments upon the "historical" bird, the airplane. His "Ode to Our Young Proconsuls of the Air" (1943) responds directly to MacLeish's essay by caging the eagle within the historical process and observing the havoc of its beating wings.

The ode's principal complaint is that when the eagle-minded artist becomes a polemicist he has no choice but to endorse the predations of the airplane, which unlike that other bird of empire (the eagle) kills human beings and their cultures alike. The bombing of Pearl Harbor left American artists no choice; naturally they supported American forces against all others – but is that a sufficient morality? To Tate it seemed a Darwinian joke that

> Spirits grown Eliotic
> Now patriotic
> Are: we follow
> *The Irresponsibles!*

Tate adapts the strange stanza structure of Michael Drayton's "Ode to the Virginian Voyage" which compels a risible effect when used for satirical purpose. It insists upon demeaning its speaker and subject by its disordered rhyme scheme and the need for wild rhetorical leaps within its miniature stanzas. The compression conveys Tate's unease with a specious patriotism, and permits him to turn history into vaudeville blackouts stanza by stanza.

Tate jocularly confesses that self-absorbed artists *were* irresponsible. He is the more willing to do so because the alternative seems so loathsome. And so his call to arms is sarcastic. What can a crusade against fascists actually signify but an endorsement of a military solution to a moral and/or metaphysical problem (such as original sin)? Tate articulates the dilemma by use of two bird images. He advises "partisans / of liberty" to "Take pterodactyl flight" if they feel conscience-stricken by their former inaction. "Pterodactyl" is appropriate because of the size of modern bombers but it also summons a pre-human or more aptly non-human universe of pure predation, a Darwinian nightmare of the End. Tate could as easily have said "Take eagle flight" except that he once chose the eagle as a private symbol of transcendence, an irony he preferred not to highlight in the poem. (That is, his own scorn for the world is mimicked by the pilot's extermination of it.) In the poem's conclusion the "gentle youth" is told

> Dive, and exterminate
> The Lama, late
> Survival of old pain.
> Go kill the dying swan.

Tate remarked in a letter that "the Lama in my poem is the Liberal Artist,"[19] presumably figures like MacLeish who willingly granted the air arm moral power to annihilate all alien and diverse forms of life and impose a Pax Americana on the world. (Of course, MacLeish did no such thing.) "The dying swan" is probably borrowed from Jeffers's "wild swan of the beauty of things" in "Shiva" and refers specifically to artists of the beautiful like Tate himself, as well as Romantic and neoromantic poets – Wordsworth, Baudelaire, Mallarmé, Yeats – who used the swan as a favored symbol.

The dying swan may also be said to represent birdlife, which the airplane threatened to supplant in reality as in verse. A swanlike beauty, like the song of the lark, was increasingly eclipsed by images of heroes who approached closer to the sun than the eagle. As the mechanical bird gyred upward, invisible to the grounded observer's eye, the poet could not help but feel diminished, measured down by the access to divinity history had granted to the new pro-consuls of an imperial nation. Tate's self-mockery expressed despair at such a recognition. But if despair is the testimony of the failed Romantic, another interpretation of airflight emerged from the war, that of the pro-consul himself, endowed with powers hardly any writer except Leonardo and H. G. Wells had dared to imagine.

9. The Poetry of Firebombing

> Birds are now gods.
> It's they must have sacrifices.
> —Aristophanes, *The Birds*

THE CASE OF JAMES DICKEY

In James Dickey's controversial poem "The Firebombing," first printed in *Poetry* magazine of May 1964, a middle-aged American of 1964 interweaves sardonic remarks about his trivial, almost posthumous life as a suburban homeowner with an extended present-tense reverie in which his 1944 self, "some technical-minded stranger with my hands," flies over Japan and drops incendiary bombs on several villages. The speaker recalls the ecstasy of aerial conquest, and the great natural presences of the flight – moonlight, ocean, wind, rivers – but he cannot give a human face to the villagers who burned to death nor can he feel any guilt for killing them. He was then and still is a willing victim of "detachment / The honored aesthetic evil."[1] At the end of the poem he tries to imagine the Japanese dead at his threshold but confesses he cannot bring to mind anyone not like himself or his good American neighbors.

The poem had a tremendous impact upon publication, for unlike most recreations of the war experience during the 1960s, which emphasized its absurd and demonic qualities, Dickey's work seemed to claim that in the secret nostalgic core of ex-warriors the heroic mode prevails. Dickey wanted the poem to express the emotional plight of veterans, those who, as the Latinate word suggests, had grown old without repeating the elation of youthful adventures. Commenting on the poem, Dickey recalls that "there were a lot of people in the service ... who

cried when they were discharged because they knew they would
have to go back to driving taxis and working in insurance offices.
For them there wouldn't be any more of that *kind* of excitement,
and above all, there wouldn't be any more consequence. They
wouldn't be heroes or even potential heroes then; they would
only be ordinary human beings."[2] The Icarian descent of Dickey's
protagonist represents in miniature the downfall of a whole
American generation into the waters of complacent materialism.
Overweight and prosperous, given to a sardonic wit that borders
on self-contempt, the speaker cannot break through to genuine
compassion for the suffering of others.

And yet suffering is an essential part of his recollections, from
the opening lines of the poem:

Homeowners unite.

All families lie together, through some are burned alive.
The other try to feel
For them. Some can, it is often said.

Starve and take off

Twenty years in the suburbs, and the palm trees willingly leap
Into the flashlights,
And there is beneath them also
A booted crackling of snailshells and coral sticks.
There are cowl flaps and the tilt cross of propellers,
The shovel-marked clouds' far sides against the moon,
The enemy filling up the hills
With ceremonial graves.

The phrase "Homeowners unite," set off as a verse paragraph,
parodies the Marxist slogan adapted from the last sentences of
the *Communist Manifesto*, "Workers of the world unite. You have
nothing to lose but your chains." The speaker inhabits the
achieved bourgeois world from which a whole class of demobilized
humanity now, ironically, seeks liberation. He immediately
recalls other homeowners, those who burned to death in
bombardments which he, five lines into the poem, begins to
reenact in his imagination. In contrast to the fake pastoral of
the suburbs, the landscape of memory is exotic, filled with
natural objects of appealing strangeness. Palm trees "willingly

leap" into his flashlight, magically possessed of an active spirit. The pilot (for he can shift identity by turning inward) hears again the crackling of snailshells and coral sticks as he walks toward the airplane for his night flight. Each sound and sight is charged with emotion summoned from his excited anticipation of danger. The dreamer's eerie landscape prepares us for the reverie that follows, in which an act uniting man and the most radiant presences in the universe is consummated.

To say as much is to place Dickey's poem in the Romantic tradition of the nineteenth-century, as opposed to that of Saint-Exupéry whose loyalty to the happiness of the earthbound is satirized here even as his sense of wonder at natural forces is imitated. The opening stanza, with many others, constitutes one of those spots of time, as Wordsworth calls them, which come to our aid when

> depressed
> By false opinion and contentious thought,
> Or aught of heavier or more deadly weight,
> In trivial occupations, and the round
> Of ordinary intercourse, our minds
> Are nourished and invisibly repaired;
> A virtue, by which pleasure is enhanced,
> That penetrates, enables us to mount,
> When high, more high, and lifts us up when fallen.
> [*The Prelude*, XII.210–18]

Dickey's description of the flight, beginning at stanza seven, recalls Wordsworth's vision from Mt. Snowdon, the culminating spot of time in *The Prelude*. In both we have, in Dickey's phrase, "the burst straight out / Of the overcast into the moon." (And the phrase recalls the Ancient Mariner: "We were the first that ever burst / Into that silent sea.") To the homeowner, a man confined by earthly possessions, the moon emanates no power of enchantment. Homeowners are not moonstruck Endymions, but susceptible only to the most banal luminary stimuli:

> eating figs in the pantry
> Blinded by each and all
> Of the eye-catching cans that have gladly caught my wife's
> eye.

The last line deliberately recalls, as a contrast, the palm trees which "willingly leap" into retrospective vision; here the wry adverb is a mockery of animism. Man and wife are the victims of Wordsworth's "round / Of ordinary intercourse," but he at least can regain a personal relationship with a more exalted light in his memory.

The speaker of "The Firebombing" undertakes his flight once again to measure his consequence, in the sense cited by Dickey above. He wants to discover if he is the Romantic hero of his own story. The speaker is of necessity a poet. He reports in images, he heightens the intensity of his descriptions, he uses myth to make sense of historical events. Is the speaker *the* poet, James Dickey, writing a confession as apparently sincere as *The Prelude*? A reader is likely to back away from identifying poet and speaker, having been trained by the theory and practice of modernist poets and the New Critics to distinguish the creator's mask from his face. Not the least important fact about "The Firebombing" has been that it sponsored a critical reaction against this habitual distinction. Lamenting what he believes to be misreadings of *Buckdancer's Choice* Robert Bly commented, "We can only lay this blindness to one thing: a brainwashing of readers by the New Critics. Their academic jabber about 'personae' has taken root. Instead of thinking about the content they instantly say, 'Oh, that isn't Dickey in the 'Firebombing' poem! That is a persona!' This is supposed to solve everything." David Ignatow in another review does not hesitate to identify pilot and poet: "Dickey finds himself in a permanent hell from which no *mea culpa* can save." Richard Howard refers to the speaker as "he the poet, James Dickey, no other man. ..." Joyce Carol Oates claims that "it is he, Dickey, the homeowner/killer ... who has tried on the strength of vast powers and has not been able to survive them." And Galway Kinnell, though he suspects Dickey of trying to have it both ways (that is, as a detached creator and a protagonist), offers this praise:

I admire James Dickey for exposing the firebomber within himself – particularly since the firebomber does appear to be a central facet of Dickey's makeup. It is a courageous act. Few poets would be as willing to reveal their inner sickness, and we can be sure that many poets seem healthier than Dickey only because they tell us less about themselves.

The consensus among poets, then, whom one would expect to resist arbitrary associations of author and mask, favors a secure identification of Dickey with the narrator.[3]

If this is so, we as readers can see a dual ambition in the composition of "The Firebombing." First, there is James Dickey's attempt to locate in some past event from his own life the consequence he lacks as a civilian. And second, there is the attempt to recapture that sense of consequence in the artful conversion of memory into text. We can best describe the first ambition by noting the allusive framework Dickey creates within the realistic situation, beginning with an epigraph from the Book of Job which cannot be attributed to a persona, only to the author. Though rhetorical heightening by means of heroic or mythic allusion is a conventional, indeed inescapable element of egoistic reverie, as of poetic discourse, it must be said that the war experience compels such analogizing as a means of preserving emotional stability both during and after conflict. Transformed by worldly authority into a warrior, the citizen-soldier accommodates himself to the new role by recourse to sacred history, and whenever possible he collapses the two authorities into one, as if the prophetic and poetic traditions had conscripted him.

Dickey's poem establishes this kind of referential structure beginning with the epigraph from Job: "Or hast thou an arm like God?" The answer of man to that question is presumably NO. But under certain circumstances in the Bible man does strike with the arm of God, as an agent of the divine wrath which punishes the enemies of the chosen people: "The Lord is a man of war. ... Thy right hand, O Lord, is become glorious in power: thy right hand, O Lord, hath dashed in pieces the enemy" (Exodus 15:3,6). A "deranged, Old Testament light" underlies the firebombing because the pilot takes for granted the rightness of his violent actions against strangers. He refers to "Enemy rivers and trees," "the enemy-colored skin of families," "Oriental fish," and so forth. While in night flight the pilot cannot see terrestrial objects; he must rely upon his conception of them, and that conception is colored by his crusading purpose. In the act of sending down mass destruction upon a monstrous foe the pilot achieves a momentary and mystical union with the divine purpose, as did the Hebrew warriors who slew the alien

Canaanites. "There's a God-like feeling about fighting on our planet," Dickey has remarked. "It's useless to deny it."[4]

The epigraph prepares the reader for the most discomfiting aspect of the implied comparison of pilot and God throughout the poem: that consequence must be tested by the suffering and death of the innocent. The homeowner's deliverance from spiritual decay in the suburbs depends upon the death of his victims – that is the painful fact he is condemned to bring constantly to consciousness, as the Ancient Mariner must expiate the murder of the albatross by repeatedly narrativizing it. It cannot be otherwise. As T. S. Eliot writes of redemption by fire in "Little Gidding":

> Whatever we inherit from the fortunate
> We have taken from the defeated
> What they had to leave us – a symbol:
> A symbol perfected in death

The dove descending in Eliot's poem is both the German bomber and the Word; it brings agony and destruction to the Job-like figures below, "The intolerable shirt of flame / Which human power cannot remove." No explanation will finally satisfy the innocent or justify the guilty, and yet neither punisher nor victim can live without some reason for the horror dealt from the skies. In Western culture that reason is a belief in Providence and millennial peace; that, in Eliot's words, "All shall be well, and / All manner of thing shall be well."[5] Every historical act must be interpreted as part of *some* design or plan consecrated as an inheritable covenant.

Another way of saying this is that every violent act must be transformed by the imagination into a text as sublime as the sacred texts the culture looks to for justification of violence. The agony of Job and the massacres recorded in the Old Testament are the primary points of reference to which "The Firebombing" directs us. But in making the connection between Dickey's sense of consequence as a pilot and his later retrieval of the godlike feeling as a poet, we must take a route through another figure that bonds together flying and textuality. A poem from a wartime anthology will give us the needed cue. "Skyward: A Ballad of the Bomber," by Robert Cromwell, begins:

I am the bomber 17 –
Proud machine – sleek and powerful.
Made by man to kill his foe,
Made of steel and wood and metal,
Built to fight and drop destruction,
Built to rise like Pegasus
Fleet of wing and sure of speed –
I am the bomber 17.[6]

Successive stanzas feature the pilot, navigator, gunner, and radio operator, but Cromwell rightly begins with the *prima materia*, the machine that enables all other beings, subordinate in power as they are in poetic structure, to undertake their vital mission. The reference to Pegasus is certainly meant to recall only one of the flying horse's adventures, its conveyance of Bellerophon into battle against the fire-breathing Chimera. That is a type of the heroic crusade comparable to the religious wars already mentioned. And Pegasus, we remember, had the responsibility of bringing thunder and lightning to Jupiter, a servant of the Almighty's wrathful right arm.

But the legends associated with Pegasus have a broader and more pertinent range of implications, one already sketched in the chapter on Lindbergh. Pegasus sprang from the blood of the slain Medusa, and became the horse of the Muses. Its connection with them has this context: when a group of maidens competed in song with the daughter of Pierus, Mt. Helicon became so full of ecstasy hearing their harmony that it rose toward the heavens until Pegasus, commanded by Poseidon, stopped its exaltation with a kick of its hoof. The Hippocrene spring, whose waters inspire music and poetry, resulted. Pegasus thus sustained the opposition of heaven and earth, gods and men, by acting as the retributive arm of a jealous god. This creature, which still adorned the cover of *Poetry* when "The Firebombing" was published, made poetry possible to man by destruction dealt from the skies.

Now the governing metaphor of flight in "The Firebombing" is horsemanship. The pilot rides out to a land of "grainfields," "grassy mountains," and "ploughlands," his canteen by his side, annoyed by a mosquito while the body under him "shakes   bucks" (and again, "we buck   leap over something") during the night journey. Finally there is the last command: "Say 'down,' and it is done."

As the next lines remind us, "down" is the direction of "different-grassed streets" than those he left behind. Pegasus as flying machine delivers him to the suburbs, to a death-in-life of debased technology: the glad cans in the supermarket, golf carts, grocery baskets, and "jolly garden tools" In the historical arena, divinity belongs to Pegasus, not to its falling rider, which is why in the poetry of firebombing it is so often Pegasus who makes vatic or prophetic utterances: "I am the bomber 17," or, in a Great War lyric already quoted,

> Lord of the gales am I,
> Terror of Kings am I,
> I am the Zeppelin!

Pegasus is the poet's figure of praxis, ready to rise from its imaginative, i.e., textual source and transform the world, perhaps even annihilate it. The chief temptation of the Romantic poet was the "drunken boat" which carried the imagination into timeless states of consciousness. But in the modern world it is the flying machine which dreamers like the homeowner wish to ride in order to achieve specifically historical being.

Dickey's own interest in poetry began when he served in the 418th Night Fighter Squadron during World War II, and he seems to have associated the two occupations ever since. I refer not just to the ubiquitous imagery of flight in his work but to his insistence that poetry has imperial powers akin to those of flying machines, and that composition yields the same kind of sovereign pleasure as piloting. "What a *weapon* poetry is!" he exclaims in his journals, significantly titled *Sorties*. "If you are immersed in it long enough, you know damn near everything. And if you like, you can use it as you wish, for whatever purpose."[7] In an interview he remarks, "I conceive the poetic process as quite a private matter between the poet, his hand, and the blazing white island of paper which he is trying to populate or eliminate."[8] The comparison evokes the firebomber imposing his will on the island of Japan. Dickey has often depicted the blank piece of paper as a kind of enemy, and since paper cannot easily fight back, the act of creation permits a feeling of absolute mastery. "The province of a poem is the poet's, and in it he is God," Dickey commented in another interview.[9]

Dickey has tried to convey what he considers the real language of war, the lyrical excitement of it which stirs multitudes in every age – no matter what their official justifications. "The Firebombing" marks a shift in Dickey's poetic style toward a mode of greater presentational immediacy, a more direct expression of unconscious responses to vivid experience. The form and content are as correspondent as Dickey can make them. He divides the line into units of perception or thought, and registers in typographical layout the movement of the plane as well as the movement of mind (in reverie these two cannot be separated). He tries to give the reader the genuine sensation of flight, "the greatest sense of power in one's life." He clearly rejects the plain style that enfeebled so much writing on flight in the 1930s, though he admits that his first draft made abundant use of data:

> When I was writing "The Firebombing" I got out my old *P61 Tech. Manual* and was going to have a long section of different procedures, because flying, especially military flying, is almost all procedure. It was going to be a section right out of the manual about tolerance in the cylinder heads, speeds at which the wheels and flaps were let down, the way the radar equipment worked – all that sort of thing.[10]

Transcription of this kind would give Pegasus more than half the credit, and Dickey wisely replaced it with the impressionistic lyricism that distinguishes not only pilot from machine but pilot from homeowner. Lyricism expresses the internal or felt language of the crusader, he who proclaims, as Wordsworth did of the French Revolution, "Bliss was it in that dawn to be alive," no matter how many regrets cling to his remembrance of bloody events he once sanctioned.

Dickey also rejects what might be called the language of moral condemnation, as in Randall Jarrell's poems about aerial bombardment in World War II. The chief relationship in Jarrell's poems is not between man and compelling natural presences and sublime historical events, but between man and the cities he is pledged to destroy. In this sense his poems derive from Great War narratives such as Paul Bewsher's "The Bombing of

Bruges," which tried to communicate the unprecedented horror of aerial bombardment. "In bombers named for girls, we burned / The cities we had learned about in school." These celebrated lines from "Losses" give way to an elegiac turn typical of Jarrell's sensibility: "Till our lives wore out; our bodies lay among / The people we had killed and never seen." Jarrell felt intensely the shock of bombing the European origins of his moral and intellectual being. His language is polemical, judgmental; he would think it barbarous to enthuse about aesthetic detachment. In his own favorite war poem, "Eighth Air Force," he figures that kind of detachment in the drunk sergeant who whistles the aria, "O Paradiso," between sorties. Jarrell's poems have extraordinary value as documents of a sensitive writer contemporary with the event; "The Death of the Ball Turret Gunner," especially, deserves its status as the classic epitaph of the wasted draftee. But the poems fall short of a full apprehension of what they witness. Like the portraits of aging women he drew in later life these pitying and self-pitying snapshots of dead soldiers finally rely overmuch on sentimental formulas that subdue their subjects to unrelieved sameness.

The speaker of Dickey's poem describes his former self as one who "sails artistically over" the lands he is bombing. On one level this refers to mastery of aerial procedure, but the adverb belongs especially to the artist who has felt the pleasure of absolute control in the field of the blank page. This control, as Dickey has pointed out, is fiendish as well as godlike, or say that the poet exercises the divine fiendishness we see in works like Numbers and Job. When Richard Eberhart watched the fury of aerial bombardment, in his poem with that title, he was moved to ask, "Is God by definition indifferent, beyond us all?"[11] Dickey's answer is both more comforting and more disturbing, as his poem is greater in moral complexity than Eberhart's: God cares so much that He enters history to impose His destructive will upon human destiny. The *deus ex machina* brings no happy resolution. It may be that we need protection from such a God, but only those who understand the power He offers will have the art to warn us against it. Dickey's poem, in its ecstatic vision of "the greatest sense of power in one's life," seems to perpetuate the Futurist enthusiasm for irresistible aerial instruments, but the retrospective structure of "The Firebombing" ultimately turns the reader's attention back to the earthbound. The quest for consequence ends by confronting and honoring the efforts of men to understand the horror they have inflicted and endured. And that is a triumph of poetry over the other Pegasus, the one who speaks only with tongues of fire.

THE MODERN APOCALYPSE

By means of its credible narrator "The Firebombing" perpetuated the Romantic myth of the individual in a period when aerial strategy increasingly depersonalized the act of bombardment so as to further anesthetize the participants. The evolution of the airplane and the outbreak of World War II led to a monolithic ideology called Air Power, which called for a well-funded and autonomous Air Force, a military–industrial complex geared toward the creation of a vast and irresistible bombing fleet, and, not least, a public policy of strategic (rather than tactical or support) bombing of enemy territory. Air Power revaluated the flying machine by reverting to the abstract conception of war as a combat between the winged hosts of light and of darkness. "The bomber *is* the saver of civilisation," argued J. M. Spaight in *Bombing Vindicated* (1944). "Civilisation ... would have been destroyed if there had been no bombing in this war. It was the bomber aircraft which, more than any other instrument of war, prevented the forces of evil from prevailing."[12] In such a claim, repeated in multitudinous publications as World War II closed in upon the world, the flying machine achieved its most characteristic identity as a modern symbol.

It has been a commonplace of critical discourse, at least since Carlyle's energetic arguments in *Sartor Resartus* and *Heroes and Hero-Worship*, that symbols of the Godlike have a life-cycle akin to organic beings, that each historical period proposes a *Zeitbild* or Time-figure that manifests the divine to the entire community. We have seen how landmarks of flight such as Lindbergh's crossing strengthened the public identification of the airplane as the unique modern symbol of the holy Spirit. But only during World War II could the claim be made that the flying machine had reached the topmost level in the hierarchy of cultural symbols. "Aviation must be apprehended by the whole American people as the essential expression of the present-day world," proclaimed Alexander P. de Seversky in *Victory Through Air Power*

(1942).[13] Just as every Roman was a soldier in his heart, so every American – or member of *any* national group that hoped to survive – must take on the airmindedness previously reserved for the elect few.

The supreme irony in the rise of Air Power to its mythic position is that its chief enemy should be Charles A. Lindbergh, individualist and elect soul, who opposed the internationalist implications of Air Power by urging in articles and radio speeches that America not engage the fascist powers in Europe and Asia but retreat into a fortress position of isolation. The advocates of Air Power found it necessary to demolish the personalist myth that hero-worship had fabricated in 1927 in order to emphasize the communal technocracy required to achieve victory over the fascists. Of Lindbergh's critics Seversky was the most effective. I shall concentrate on his *American Mercury* article of May 1941, "Why Lindbergh Is Wrong," as a paradigm of the shift in symbology.

Seversky approaches Lindbergh's reputation gingerly, for he is aware that his readers will not take lightly to the severe iconoclasm to come:

> All aviation people share, in some measure, the glory that is Colonel Lindbergh's. The laurels on his brow, we know, represent a tribute to all men and women who have given their years to the advancement of American aeronautics.

But the word "advancement" allows him the opening to disagree absolutely with Lindbergh's reading of the world situation. Seversky portrays Lindbergh as fixated on the events of 1927, a victim of "an old-fashioned respect for oceans" because of his harrowing thirty-three hour journey across the Atlantic. Forever enthralled by his epoch-making achievement, Lindbergh "remains impressed with the 'frozen' tactical thinking of the past. It has for him the fascination of novelty. He has not caught up with the fact that the orthodox assumptions have been invalidated by Air Power and the lessons of this war." Seversky transforms Lindbergh into one of those backward-looking types whom Lindbergh himself mocked in 1927 because they would not acknowledge the airplane as an irreversible new fact of life. The final paragraph remarks that "the Lindbergh of the popular imagination is a graven image, a sort of deity of aviation, which the American people have carved for themselves. We should not blame the real Lindbergh, therefore, if that deity does not, on demand, perform miracles of political, economic, and strategic insight."

The metamorphosis of the flying machine from peaceful *Spirit* to warlike bomber is part of Seversky's reversion to the Wellsian or apocalyptic mode. Lindbergh's unprogressive view must be jettisoned in favor of one that assumes the imminent and likely use of bombing raids as part of a fascist strategy for world domination. Seversky's 1941 article is clearly a prelude to his alarmist book *Victory Through Air Power* the following year, in which he seeks to frighten the naive and nostalgic reader into support for an enhanced Air Force capability. The bombing of Pearl Harbor in December of 1941 insured that his message would be heeded. Seversky cleverly appeals in the first chapter to the chronic apprehensiveness of the child in every adult reader. Because of "the process of shrinkage of our planet" (p. 20), a governing metaphor derived most likely from *Alice in Wonderland*, every sector has become susceptible to irrational acts of terror inflicted by frightening aliens. As the nation sleeps, "the invading aerial giants strike at the nerve centers and jugular veins of a great nation" (p. 8). Here the vampire myth is not so discreetly combined with the fantasy of the giant to render the helplessness of the victim. "[The naval force] can now do nothing, literally nothing, against the locust swarms of giant airplanes" (p. 10), Seversky continues. The apocalyptic fantasy, so reminiscent of Leonardo's scenario of the ogre that threatens mankind with destruction (see page 37), reaches a crescendo of horror:

The destruction is now systematic, scientific – the planned wrecking of a great nation. It becomes clear even through the panic and the rising tides of death that the enemy's purpose is not merely to force us to surrender. It is to break our strength, destroy our civilization, lay low our cities, dominate our population, and leave us to dig out of the debris slowly and painfully. [p. 11]

Leonardo had remarked that "the human species in such a plight has need to envy every other race of creatures ... but for us wretched mortals there avails not any flight." Seversky's prescription, of course, is to foil the monstrous assault by putting on those godlike wings that Leonardo's favored city-states lacked. Not to escape the horror, but engage with it in an Armageddon – that is what Seversky presents as the legitimate heroic fantasy of the species.

As Leonardo dramatized in the figure of Leda, however, humankind was capable of welcoming aerial violation as well as resisting it. If Seversky read the English poetry responding to the Nazi bombardments during and after 1940 he would have been surprised at how the authors find in the burning streets sacrificial figures of the longed-for consummation of history. Louis MacNeice's "Brother Fire," for example, begins on a jocular note by comparing the fire leaping about to a dog with cans tied to its tail, but within a few lines this dog becomes an all-devouring Beast which is nothing less than the "Will / That wills the natural world but wills us dead." MacNeice's allusion to Lent earlier in the poem deliberately gives his reference to Will a Christian meaning; this is God's will enacted in history by the agency of the bombers. Knowing this the poet can identify the raging fire as "enemy and image of ourselves," that is, of Everyman's will to violate and be violated:

> Did we not on those mornings after the All Clear,
> When you were looting shops in elemental joy
> And singing as you swarmed up city block and spire,
> Echo your thought in ours? "Destroy! Destroy!"[14]

Similarly, Dylan Thomas in "Ceremony After an Air Raid" observes a child burned to death, imagines her as the first child of Adam and Eve – a figure for all mankind – and thus takes her death to be a promise of the totality of deaths that will occur when divine fire burns up the sea and all souls enter in glory "the sundering ultimate kingdom of genesis' thunder." The London bombings offered an opportunity, as Christian myth offered the terminology, to draw abstracts of the pattern of death and resurrection. To mourn the death of a child in the bombing, he insists in another poem, would be to "blaspheme ... the mankind of her going" by partial vision of the whole providential process.[15]

Less consolatory are the poems which adopt the scriptural figure of the crucifixion for the bombings. To do so asserts that history has done nothing but circle back perpetually to the fundamental crime against the Life recounted in the Gospels. Edith Sitwell's "Still Falls the Rain," for example, imagines the air raids of 1940 as a tormenting crucifixion. Another example is Stephen Spender's "Air Raid across the Bay at Plymouth," the best of his poems on the raids. As in Paul Bewsher's "The Bombing of Bruges," this poem establishes a mutuality of malignant action by the imagery of searchlights. The British send their lights up hoping to catch the flying machine and shoot it down:

> Triangles, parallels, parallelograms,
> Experiment with hypotheses
> On the blackboard sky,
> Seeking that X
> Where the raider is met.
>
> Two beams cross
> To chalk his cross.

Like "the swords of light" in the next stanza, the crossed beams contribute toward the concluding observation that "Man hammers nails in Man / Upon his crucifix." This is so because these Jacob's ladders of light, as Spender calls them, "slant / Up to the god of war / Who, from his heaven-high car, / Unloads upon a star / A destroying star."[16] In wartime God is a god of war; there is no way out of this association. If history is to have a typological meaning informed by the Scriptures, then the bombers – theirs and ours – must all be seen as enacting the same absolute will.

Spender's dolor is made more poignant if we contrast this poem to his earlier, hopeful poems about the flying machine. "Landscape Near an Aerodrome" (1933) had praised the airliner as being "More beautiful and soft than any moth" as it glides quietly down to a "landscape of hysteria." All images of menace and horror are reserved for the city toward which the idealized flying machine makes its fragile descent. "He will watch the hawk with an indifferent eye," the first of his *Collected Poems*, glamorizes the doomed pilot in the manner of Yeats's poem on the Irish airman: "This aristocrat, superb of all instinct" who "With death close linked / Had paced the enormous cloud."[17] But as the 1930s progressed, Spender's romanticism vanished.

The Spanish Civil War, which he witnessed firsthand, offered shocking prefigurations of the horrors to come. Pablo Picasso's mural *Guernica*, André Malraux's *Man's Hope*, and Ernest Hemingway's *For Whom the Bell Tolls* are the memorializing masterpieces of aerial outrages that Spender and his contemporaries imagined to be their unavoidable destiny. Bernard Bergonzi has shown in *Reading the Thirties* how English novelists took care to place bombers in the air as signs of the constraints suffered by their characters. If Virginia Woolf, Graham Greene and George Orwell, to name the most distinguished, construed modern England as a kind of hunting commons, how much more so would poets like Spender conceive their native land as a death camp and themselves as prisoners betrayed by the birdlike figure that once had promised a resurrection of the spirit. Spender remarks of the wartime atmosphere in his memoirs:

> Although the raids stopped, or happened only at rare intervals, this picture of the aeroplane over the huge plain with the people concealed in crevices, can be enlarged to a vision of the new phase of domination and threat by machine-power politics, which the world had now entered and which did not end with the peace. The aeroplane filled ever-widening circles in the minds of people beneath it; but the pilot and even the officers who commanded him at bases, their masters in governments and the vanquished and victors of the war, were diminished, until it seemed that they no longer had wills of their own, but were automata controlled by the mechanism of war.[18]

That Air Power would accomplish its historical imperative none had doubted, but Spender's suspicion of the engineers of this "new phase of domination" sounds a note of increasingly common apprehension, soon to become paranoia.

One wartime book which examines this condition is Rex Warner's novel of 1941, *The Aerodrome*. It opens as the Rector of an English village is "accidentally" shot to death by a flight lieutenant stationed at the nearby aerodrome. At the funeral service the Air Vice-Marshal announces that his unit is taking over most of the buildings and land, including the church lands. The lieutenant becomes the "padre" of the aerodrome, and gradually comes to occupy the Rector's place in the community. The Air Vice-Marshal represents the ideal of Airman-as-Fascist, and in one long speech delivered in the "chapel" he looks forward to a new priesthood of the air that will renounce women and family ties in favor of the glorified civil religion of flight. The speech concludes:

> Let me remind you finally of the pseudo-suchians, reptiles of an exceedingly remote period, whose clumsy efforts resulted in the course of ages in that incredibly finely organized and adjusted thing, the first flyers, the race of birds. Science will show you that in our species the period of physical evolution is over. There remains the evolution, or rather the transformation of consciousness and will, the escape from time, the mastery of the self, a task which has in fact been attempted with some success by individuals at various periods, but which is now to be attempted by us all.[19]

The Air Vice-Marshal's devaluation of human relationships, beginning with the disowning of his two illegitimate children (one is the lieutenant), makes him an unfit model for the village or for the civilization, though it is clear that both require some kind of new religion to replace the hypocrisy and stagnation of the past. Warner draws the line at schemes which argue from Darwinism the necessity of transfiguration in the species. Especially in 1941 the Air Vice-Marshal does not speak the language of a savior, but that of the debased Nietzschean against whom airmen of good will were fighting for survival.

John Hersey's postwar novel, *The War Lover* (1959) offers another model of rabid militance. The title refers to the pilot Buzz Marrow whom the co-pilot and narrator Boman worships as a latter-day Lindbergh, an artist of flight. Marrow enjoys flying and he enjoys the special kind of flying for which he seems perfectly equipped by his apparent courage and mastery of technique: air raids. He accepts the code of the airman enunciated by Yeats's "An Irish Airman foresees his Death," which is recited over the public announcement system to the pilots. They do not recognize the poem but they do recognize the sentiments it proclaims. The achievement of the novel is to expose the "lonely impulse of delight" as an appetite for life-threatening situations which gradually harrows and empties the soul of loyalty

to those people and places that make "courage" meaningful.
The course of the novel is an increasing demystification of
the pilot-hero. The alienation and narcissism that Yeats
anatomized – the submission to impulse that masquerades as a
devotion to technique, the loveless rush to battle that is revealed
to be a vampirish clinging to images of death – compel Boman
to see that the once bright Lucifer of his envying gaze is a Satanic
figure:

> Marrow was my enemy, just as surely as the Nazis were. One
> contest was a matter of life and death; the other, against
> Marrow, whose life was bound with mine to our common
> ship, was one of inner tensions, of all those personal values
> the survival or loss of which would make the rest of life, if life
> remained, worth or not worth living. ... [Marrow] was a
> destroyer. He was in love with war. I could have no peace –
> the world could have none – if men like him were indulged in
> their passion.[20]

In revulsion, Boman vows to do nothing in the plane that would
contribute to the death of any person. He does, however, take
the controls when Marrow, finally eaten clean of his resources,
undergoes a paralysis of fear during flight. Boman becomes the
achieved hero of his own fantasies by rescuing ship and crew
together.

Though less savage in its unmasking of the airman's mystique
than *The Aerodrome*, or, to look forward into the 1960s, *Catch-22*,
The War Lover shares their impatience with the myth of the
flier as hero. Better than Warner or Heller, however, Hersey
understands the dead-end of the aerial technician's vision, and
how his emasculation is speeded by his fear of the claims of
human companionship and human happiness that pull him
earthward. If Dickey's confession in "The Firebombing" is the
truth about the American obsession with power and the American
fear of Icarian descent into the domestic and suburban, then
Hersey's novel, like Saint-Exupéry's memoirs, affirms the sanity
of demobilization as a corrective ideal. An alternative to Air
Power as a dominant cultural myth begins to emerge from such
humanistic texts.

John Hersey is also the author of *Hiroshima*. It is improbable
but true that his brief, semi-sociological account is still the major

work in English on an event universally acknowledged to be the chief determinant of modern consciousness. This is so not because *Hiroshima* is so great a work, but because the events of August 1945 seem to have struck most writers dumb. More than any other modern happening, it usurped language almost entirely, except for the kind of transcription of data one finds in Hersey's book or Thomas Merton's *Original Child Bomb*. The creative imagination seemed to be paralyzed by the uniqueness of the bombing, unable to find either a primal text or a credible analogy by which to articulate its sublimity. It is arguable, however, that all postwar literary works on the subject of firebombing are commentaries on Hiroshima. The ethical and aesthetic force of *The War Lover* and "The Firebombing," in particular, derives from their insistence that the enemy of posterity is not technology per se but the pathology of heroic consequence that seems to come with the territory when men achieve aerial control over the destiny of multitudes and nations. The humbling devaluation of eminence or elevated position, then, becomes a primary motif in the antiwar literature that looks backward upon the Bomb as the monstrous second nativity after Kitty Hawk.

A good example is Hermann Hagedorn's pamphlet-poem *The Bomb that fell on America* (1946), which went through a dozen editions in a few months. Hagedorn has no doubt that this culminating expression of Air Power strategy announces the Apocalypse:

> In a splendor beyond any that man has known, the new age
>   we have claimed came to birth.
> The brightness of its dawning was the fierce shining of three
>   suns together at noonday, shedding, for golden seconds,
>   such beauty over the earth as poets, painters, philosophers
>   and saints have imagined and striven in vain to reveal to
>   man in symbols and parables.
> And we used it to 'destroy a hundred thousand men, women
>   and children!
> God have mercy on our own children!
> God have mercy on America![21]

The new age that begins with "Trinity" – the code name for the Los Alamos Project – will be distinct from all other ages by having no assured future. The future can only be insured,

Hagedorn is told by God in a vision, if each person in America imitates Christ on the cross: "The world is sick ... for dearth of crucifixions" (p. 43). By thus humbling themselves and becoming by suffering and sacrifice the image of the humanity slain in Hiroshima, Americans can exorcize the demon of power and consequence that has possessed them from their Puritan origins.

The Enola Gay is the break point in the sacred history of the flying machine, the dark image that even the most ardent disciples cannot stare at without despair. Even those who had managed to assimilate Air Power to their imaginative prospect of the future could not deny that what Howard Nemerov called "the burnt Phoenix' nest" of Hiroshima resisted the images of resurrection upon which all myth-histories depend.[22] The atomic bomb diminished the pietistic writing about the airplane and its Christic possibilities. The glamor of aerial combat in the Great Crusade, the heroism of the night flight for the sake of mail or personal glory, the transcendent ecstasy of solo ascent – all of these would be succeeded in popularity by a literature of social criticism, of mockery and paranoid expressions of outrage against the airplane, and later the missile, as an instrument of genocide. Just as *Dr. Strangelove* (1963) would parody the conventions of wartime films about the glory of Air Power, so would novels like *The Martian Chronicles, Catch-22, Fail-Safe, On the Beach, Slaughterhouse Five,* and *Gravity's Rainbow* anathematize war lovers and warbirds alike.

And yet, in a paradoxical way, the more apocalyptic the forecast, the more urgent, even desperate, became the sacred history, as if all artworks on the subject of firebombing unwittingly served the masterful closure plotted by the original creator of the flying machine.

10. Spaceflight: Three Versions of Manifest Destiny

ROBERT FROST'S "KITTY HAWK"

Having lost the western frontier in the 1890s after centuries of pioneering under the banner of Manifest Destiny, the American people confronted another vast tract of open space in the postwar world. Like the continent they had settled, outer space offered an exhilarating sense of sublime beauty, as well as opportunities for commercial and political exploitation. Unlike the land, however, access to this new world required a form of as yet undeveloped technology, one that existed plentifully in the literary imagination of the race but had no working physical model. While engineers set their minds to the technical problems of rocketry, some intellectuals, uneasy with the costs and results of the first cycle of expansionism, posed moral questions as well. Not could a space-ship be invented, but *should* it be invented? Wasn't it time to put by the desire to occupy open space as an embarrassment to the human spirit?

If there is such a thing as a representative American answer to that question, Robert Frost's lines in "Kitty Hawk" (1953) qualify better than most:

> Pulpiteers will censure
> Our instinctive venture
> Into what they call
> The material
> When we took that fall
> From the apple tree.
> But God's own descent
> Into flesh was meant

As a demonstration
That the supreme merit
Lay in risking spirit
In substantiation.
Westerners inherit
A design for living
Deeper into matter –
Not without due patter
Of a great misgiving.
All the science zest
To materialize
By on-penetration
Into earth and skies
(Don't forget the latter
Is but further matter)
Has been West-Northwest.[1]

Frost considered "Kitty Hawk" the most important of his later poems, and on speaking engagements around the country often cited this passage as a culminating statement of his natural philosophy. It is a buoyant endorsement of Whitman's progressive ideal, though Frost's clipped verse line discourages comparison with the bard of the pioneers.

The passage seems to proceed from Frost's fascination with desert places. In "Neither Out Far nor In Deep" he comments on people who gaze at the sea and crave the Truth residing in and under that other world. The watchers "turn their back on the land" because land is known, domesticated. In other poems, outer space casts the same spell on the earthbound. Frost credits a book called *Our Place Among the Infinities* as an early influence on his love of astronomy.[2] He uses the book's title in his poem "The Star-Splitter," which tells how a neighbor of the speaker burned down his house for the fire insurance, "And spent the proceeds on a telescope / To satisfy a lifelong curiosity / About our place among the infinities." Like that compelled neighbor, Frost turns the reader's eyes in poem after poem toward the mysteries of the skies. He believes that so long as any place exists which has not been completed by the human spirit, the spirit itself remains incomplete. "The great enterprise of life, of the world, the great enterprise of our race," Frost emphasized in a talk, "is our penetration into matter, deeper and deeper; carrying the spirit deeper into matter. ... And that is our destiny – that is why science is our greatness."³

The expansion of the human spirit, in Frost's view, can be charted geographically, West-Northwest, from the cradle of civilization in the Middle East, through Greece and Italy to Western Europe and then to North America. Christ's descent into matter, "risking spirit / In substantiation," necessarily became the central myth of a restless, wandering people who looked upon external nature as essentially dead until infused with human presence and purpose. In lines immediately following those quoted above, Frost contrasts the Western movement with the "long stagnation / In mere meditation" of the East. Frost's chief metaphor throughout "Kitty Hawk" is the footrace; here the East hurries "to catch up with us" in the enjoyment of material advantages which Western science, "our greatness," has fashioned in its acceleration.

There are many complaints one might lodge against this cracker-barrel history, not least the moral lapse in obliquely congratulating the East upon its reawakened desire to "Trespass and encroach / On successive spheres" in imitation of the West. When Japan invaded China and Southeast Asia in the late 1930s it justified its act by reference to the higher destiny of the technologically advanced. Both World War II and the Cold War should have made Frost more careful in his praise of expansionist impulses, from whatever hemisphere. Instead, Frost overleaps some fifty years of modern history embarrassing to his confident views and selects the Wright brothers' success at Kitty Hawk as a moral demonstration of his West-Northwest thesis. The progress of spirit cannot go further West – it would then sink into the East – so it must advance vertically, toward the open sky and empty planets. Even before President Kennedy proclaimed the moon landing a high priority of his New Frontier administration, Frost had pleaded, in "Kitty Hawk," for no waste of time. "Matter mustn't curd, / Separate and settle," he warned. "Action is the word."

Frost realized that Kitty Hawk could only be made recognizable to a postwar generation if it were approached from the nineteenth-century's vantage. He himself (born 1875) incarnated the previous century's pride in the new birth, and felt the goadings of parental responsibility for its defense. The events of 1903 seemed to need defending a half-century later.

Commenting on the ritual celebrations of the airplane's nativity at Kitty Hawk, Joseph J. Corn remarks, "Gone forever was the purer and more idealistic spirit of earlier anniversaries. December 17th was now a time to parade airforce equipment and demonstrate American air power. The ceremonies at Kitty Hawk in 1949 illustrate the changed spirit. Hundreds of airplanes participated in the rituals that day, but every one of them belonged to the military. In fact, the U.S. Air Force Association handled the planning for the event."[4] In an artwork like Theodore J. Roszak's sculpture, *Spectre of Kitty Hawk* (1946–7), a monster of steel, bronze and brass meant to suggest the predatory pterodactyl, we see a characteristic reflection of – and protest against – this militant interpretation of the meaning of Kitty Hawk. If some poets, as we have seen, likewise sighted Kitty Hawk through the blood-colored filter of World War I and World War II, Frost would remind them that the flying machine contains the enduring promise of numinous life. Despite the seizure of the flying machine by the advocates of Air Power, Kitty Hawk remained for Frost a place of covenant that the congregation of believers could revisit in order to renew their faith. Frost had wanted to compose a long poem on the Wright brothers during the 1930s, but achieved only an epigram, "The Wrights' Biplane." In the late 1940s, however, the astonishing development of rocket technology impressed him as such a perfect analogy for the inventions in the first decade of the century that the Matter of Kitty Hawk seemed more pertinent than ever.

In the poem's opening Frost tells us that the name Kitty Hawk intrigued him before the great flight was even thought of. On his first visit to Kitty Hawk in 1894 he had considered an "Emblematic ditty" in which the baffling personality of his eventual wife, Elinor White, would have been the subject of his song. At that time Frost supposed that a rival had stolen Elinor from him, and he traveled south to brood on his misfortune. Looking back after sixty years, Frost must have perceived a fruitful contrast between his adolescent journey to Cape Hatteras and the carefully calculated experiments of the Wright brothers in the same place. The structure of "Kitty Hawk" preserves this contrast. The first part of the poem is egocentric, determinedly autobiographical, and then, in a typical Frostian turn, the poet is overcome by an intense awareness of some truth beyond his limited point of view. At the line, "Then I saw it all" the poem opens upon the philosophical discourse already quoted, elevating and widening the subject so that the emblematic name achieves the broadest possible reference.

In Part One Frost recalls how sixty years before he had wandered, "a young Alastor," over the same field which the Wright brothers would use a decade later as a runway. In this walk of 1894 the lovelorn Frost was disabled from launching "a flight of words" from a location he recognized as latent with unachieved greatness:

> It was on my tongue
> To have up and sung
> The initial flight
> I can see now might –
> Should have been – my own
> Into the unknown,
> Into the sublime
> Off these sands of time.

That is a poet's responsibility to society, to outrace the practical inventor and set rules for him. But Frost did not and could not sing the initial flight. He returns again and again to his failure, his "might have sung." "Little I imagined," he confesses in the opening of Part Two, "Men would treat this sky / Someday to a pageant / Like a thousand birds."

In 1958 Frost remarked to Louis Mertins, "Anybody who knows even a kindergarten course in my poetry knows that I've been interested in flying ever since Kitty Hawk gave us success under the Wright brothers." He was proud of recognizing the importance of aerial flight, but throughout his life he worried that he had not foreseen, not been a prophet. His anger with himself he projected on others, blaming newspaper editors for not sending reporters to cover the flight at Kitty Hawk and encyclopedias that withheld credit from the Wrights for flying the first heavier-than-air-machine. "When all this thing is written," he told Mertins in 1932, "that about Lindbergh and all, there will still remain only the Wright boys, the Columbuses of the air."[5] Columbus, of course, is a type of the man of action who secures new territories for an imperial power. Bishop Wright had congratulated his son Wilbur in 1908, after successful exhibitions in France, by remarking, "Indeed they treat you in France as if you were a resurrected Columbus; and the people gaze as if you had fallen down from Jupiter ..."[6] Hart Crane, as we have seen, resisted such heroic associations; in the "Cape Hatteras" section of *The Bridge* he gives the honorific title "Great Navigator" not to Wilbur or Orville Wright but to Walt Whitman. Frost might have earned such a title had he possessed sufficient vision on his first visit to North Carolina. He reports in "Kitty Hawk" that he playfully claimed one day to the "Master," his close friend Orville Wright, "Just supposing I – / I had beat him to it." Wright, secure in his glory, laughed at Frost's presumptuous jest.

When we ask an obvious question – Who then had beaten the Wright brothers to it? – we confront the Romantic authors, English and American, of the nineteenth century. Frost's subtitle for his commemorative poem, "A skylark ... in three-beat phrases," directs our attention particularly to Shelley, as does the allusion to "Alastor" in Part One. Frost's presumption that he was actually first at Kitty Hawk represents his lingering devotion to the Romantic tradition, just as his rueful admission that he was second attests to his – and his profession's – diminished vision. To adopt a popular nineteenth-century distinction, Frost awards the palm to the Understanding rather than to the Imagination. "The province of the imagination is principally visionary, the unknown and undefined," William Hazlitt wrote, "the understanding restores things to their natural boundaries, and strips them of their fanciful pretensions."[7] In "Kitty Hawk" Frost exchanges the spatial metaphors. The poet is depicted as egocentric, skeptical, more often setting boundaries than transcending them. Metrical and rhyming patterns are examples of formal limitations he gladly imposes on himself, and though these are, in a sense, risks of spirit in substantiation, they contrast to the risks of the Understanding as it constructs mechanical wings for longer journeys deeper into the undefined.

"Kitty Hawk" is a belated penance that Frost offers to share with his reading public. Poet and audience alike lack the true or prophetic understanding of historical events because both have been insufficiently trained in the quotidian coping ("Action is the word") of a frontier people. In Frederick Jackson Turner's classic definition the "composite nationality" is a "practical, inventive turn of mind, quick to find expedients ... a masterful grasp of material things, lacking in artistic but powerful to effect great ends."[8] Meditative it is not (Frost delights in the rhyme of meditation and stagnation); Americans more often seek to know the spiritual meaning of an event long after it has passed into history. History is an unending process, however, and even the poetic reconsideration remains of practical use. "Kitty Hawk" is also a warning to the nation that stands in 1953 upon the brink of penetration into the infinities. Frost endorses the aims of the space program:

> Ours was to reclaim
> What had long been faced
> As a fact of waste
> And was waste in name.

And that continues to be the American destiny. Frost is too familiar with astronomy to make occupation of planetary bodies an explicit motive for action. But his notion of reclamation, linking all voyages into the unknown, assumes the necessity of outposts and stations for new Columbuses of the air. His model of course is the acts of settlement on the continent which he memorializes in his poem "The Gift Outright":

> Such as we were we gave ourselves outright
> (The deed of gift was many deeds of war)
> To the land vaguely realizing westward . . .

We *will* become contracted to the infinite reaches of space, as we became the land's in due time. Each leap to a new resting-place refreshes the spirit with inspiration. New frontiers must constantly be located and settled.

As if John F. Kennedy had taken "Kitty Hawk" to heart, and perhaps he did, one theme of his election campaign became the necessity of occupying outer space. The conjunction of Frost and Kennedy on Inauguration Day 1961 seemed to endorse the notion of American destiny as Frost had defined it in that poem. Frost's panegyric to the nation's new leader, "For John F. Kennedy His Inauguration" cannily brings further pressure upon his patron to realize his promises. Frost once again cites the Wright brothers as models of excellence, and calls upon Kennedy for a kindred spirit of high endeavor:

It makes the prophet in us all presage
The glory of a next Augustan age
Of a power leading from its strength and pride,
Of young ambition eager to be tried,
Firm in our free beliefs without dismay,
In any game the nations want to play.

It should have come as no surprise, then, that on 25 May 1961 Kennedy, departing from the custom of addressing Congress only once a year, convened an extraordinary session to present a proposal for, his phrase, "mastery of space." The President reminded Congress that the Russians had taken the lead in space technology. He asked that the American program be accelerated, and made the specific recommendation that the nation commit itself to the goal of landing a man on the moon before the end of the decade. Since NASA had not yet put a man in space (Alan Shepard would take a sub-orbital hop the next month), the notion of a moon landing seemed even to poets a vainglorious effort doomed to failure. And yet it happened, though neither Frost nor Kennedy would live to see it. On 20 July 1969 Neil Armstrong, who carried with him a piece of the original linen wing fabric from the *Flyer* of 1903, helped Edwin Aldrin unfurl the Stars and Stripes on the lunar surface.

Writing "Kitty Hawk" at the end of his career, Frost, his nation's unofficial Poet Laureate, aligned his vision with the orthodox American view of civil millennialism. Poets remain earthbound, yearning to penetrate out far and in deep. But science, our greatness, can best play the heroic role which fate has given to the superior in spirit. "Some people worry because science doesn't know where it's going," Frost said in an interview of 1961. "It doesn't need to know. It's none of its business. I like anything that penetrates the mysteries. And if it penetrates straight to hell, then that's all right, too."[9] In "Kitty Hawk" Frost bows to the machine, his vanquisher. "God of the machine," he prays at the conclusion, "Thanks to you and thanks / To the brothers Wright." Those aptly-named mechanics on Kill Devil Hill did win a race against the poet, and, in a larger sense, against poetry itself, but by saying so in 1953 Frost at least outran the astronauts, planting the Imagination's soiled flag in advance.

THOMAS PYNCHON'S *GRAVITY'S RAINBOW*

Frost's nostalgic connection of the Wright brothers and space travel reflects across half a century the conjunction of H. G. Wells's *The First Men in the Moon* (1901) and the flight at Kitty Hawk. As Marjorie Hope Nicolson points out in her standard account, *Voyages to the Moon*, the lunar exploit was such an obsessive topos in the fantasy literature of the West that it can be given substantial credit for inspiring practical invention from ancient times to the present day. Literary texts, in this view of historical evolution, are not merely *responses* to events but *events* in their own right. In the modern period one can chart a succession of transactions between authors who imagined spaceflight and the scientists who contributed to its realization. One example is Robert H. Goddard, who wrote H. G. Wells in 1932, while working on a space vehicle, that his interest in high-altitude research as a means of reaching the moon by rocketship began when he read Wells's work at age sixteen.[10] Goddard pursued his projectile studies throughout World War I, when he developed a form of the bazooka and other ballistic machines, and during the 1920s when he laid the groundwork for much of his future achievement in rocket design. The first flight of a liquid-propellant rocket in Auburn, Massachusetts, on 16 March 1926, is often cited as "The Kitty Hawk of Rocketry." Likewise Wernher von Braun recalled in 1972 that "When I was growing up, my ideas about the world of the future were influenced by ... the inspired imaginings of such gifted science fiction writers as Jules Verne and H. G. Wells."[11] These early pioneers transformed science fiction into modern fact, which in turn engendered more fiction, what we call science fiction – the genre that has responded most actively to the formerly unimagined.

A "science fiction" like *Gravity's Rainbow* suggests another example to place beside Goddard's and von Braun's real-life imitation of Wells's scientific romances. In 1929 the first feature-length film about rocketry and spaceflight appeared, Fritz Lang's *Frau im Mond* (Woman in the Moon). It was inspired in part by the research of Hermann Oberth, a Rumanian professor of mathematics who published in 1923 a monograph, *The Rocket into Interplanetary Space*, and in 1929 his major text, *The Way to Space Travel*. Oberth and Willy Ley were leading members of the Society for Space Travel (*Verein für Raumsschiftfahrt*), and after

Lang approached them for technical advice they helped the director develop models of rocketry anticipatory of those Oberth and others constructed at Peenemünde for the Nazis. Indeed, Hitler later destroyed all the original rocketship models and withdrew *Frau im Mond* from distribution because of the putative similarity between cinematic and actual rockets. In Pynchon's novel the young rocket engineers, including the fictive Franz Pökler with his wife Leni, attend the movie:

> They saw *Die* [sic] *Frau im Mond.* Franz was amused, condescending. He picked at technical points. He knew some of the people who'd worked on the special effects. Leni saw a dream of flight. One of many possible. Real flight and dreams of flight go together. Both are part of the same movement. Not A before B, but all together. . . .[12]

These last sentences testify to the closing gap between fantasies of power and transactions of power in the twentieth century. In Lang's fable of aggression, the first rocket to the moon is financed by a ruthless corporation that plans to rule the world by means of gold extracted from the lunar surface.

It is a fact, though Pynchon does not make use of it, that a rocket successfully fired at Peenemünde on 3 October 1942 had the emblem of a woman sitting in a crescent moon painted on its fuselage.[13] The V-1 and V-2 rockets are a realization of erotic fantasies, "the pornographies of flight," as Pynchon calls them (p. 567), that have the chaste moon goddess as an object but which have a wider target, the whole earth. The destruction at Hiroshima is summoned at the end of *Gravity's Rainbow* as an implied V-3 in which the United States seizes from Germany's "master fantasists" (p. 410) the phallic emblem of a master race's Great Crusade:

> In one of these streets, in the morning fog, plastered over two slippery cobblestones, is a scrap of newspaper headline, with a wirephoto of a giant white cock, dangling in the sky straight downward out of a white pubic bush. The letters
>
> MB DRO
> ROSHI
>
> appear above the logo of some occupation newspaper, a grinning glamour girl riding astraddle the cannon of a tank,

steel penis with slotted serpent head, 3rd Armored treads 'n' triangle on a sweater rippling her tits. The white image has the same coherence, the hey-lookit-me smugness, as the Cross does. It is not only a sudden white genital onset in the sky – it is also, perhaps, a Tree. ...

At the instant it happened, the pale Virgin was rising in the east, head, shoulders, breasts, 17°36' down to her maidenhead at the horizon. A few doomed Japanese knew of her as some Western deity. She loomed in the eastern sky gazing down at the city about to be sacrificed. The sun was in Leo. The fireburst came roaring and sovereign. ... [pp. 693–4]

The moon has always been a taunting symbol of whatever human beings covet in this life. The Romantic poets had imagined the union or reunion of earth and moon as an erotic dream – in Keats's *Endymion* and Shelley's *Prometheus Unbound* especially – and later writers like Verne and Wells had imagined a moon landing as a technological triumph ordained by the manifest destiny of the Western powers. Here Pynchon brings these two fantasies into conjunction. In the Bomb, as in the rocket, he finds the perfect metaphor to hold together the grossest corporeal fantasies with the most exalted spiritual aspirations, a mixture of sensualism and idealism perfectly expressed by the mirrored ideologies of American Puritanism and German Nazism central to the novel. Pynchon takes constant pains to engineer correspondences between his American and German characters – who, for example construct competing rockets – and American and German films which reveal a similar grasping for a climactic apocalypse.

One film relevant to our purposes, as to Pynchon's, is *King Kong*. Whatever its intentions, this fantasy of a "black scapeape we cast down like Lucifer from the tallest erection in the world" (p. 275) is the perfect anatomy of precisely that abject state of victimization shared by the entire world-audience caught in the master-race fantasies of a mad director. The condition and fate of King Kong (he is shot down from the Empire State Building by airplanes) collapses at novel's end into the fate of all doomed native populations annihilated by superior firepower visited upon them by colonizing invaders. The effect is as if the ape were mankind imagined as a single creature, like Hobbes's

Leviathan or Blake's Albion, subject to the depredations of an advanced aerial civilization.

The closure into a single figure of the predacious and the aerial is one we have traced throughout this book. In *Gravity's Rainbow* the archaeology of our contemporary sky-paranoia is established as firmly as in Wells's works or Verne's. Traditional myths or narrative practice tend to place the "monstrous" in some terrestrial place, such as the wilds of Africa, but the effect of modern fantasies beginning with *Master of the World* and *The War of the Worlds* is to place in the upper air what Verne calls "a mighty bird of prey, some monster of the skies" like the flying machine he names *The Terror*.[14] Violations from above become the actual and universal obsession of an age shaped by Goddard at Auburn, Oberth and von Braun at Peenemünde, and finally by the engineers of "Trinity" at Los Alamos. Pynchon's main character, Tyrone Slothrop, is a Puritan, and like his co-religionists has a "peculiar sensitivity to what is revealed in the sky" (p. 26). Puritans came to the New World in hopes of actualizing the fantasy of apocalypse set out in their primal text, but none of them until World War II had reason to think that man could make himself into the monstrous simulacrum of an omnipotent heavenly force. As the American heir to all those Mediterranean fantasies moving West-Northwest, Slothrop and his compatriots represent the hope, and peril, of a postwar world dominated by an intercontinental balance of terror.

Whether *Gravity's Rainbow* is a nihilistic or in some sense a positive work depends on whether the reader's own religion of heaven points to a realm "Beyond the Zero" – to cite the title of the novel's first section. The V-2 firing which opens the novel impacts at Greenwich 000° longitude, as if to indicate that the war and its weapons have inaugurated a new and ambiguous historical era.[15] The rocket cannot have one meaning in a heterodox universe:

> ... The Rocket has to be many things, it must answer to a number of different shapes in the dreams of those who touch it – in combat, in tunnel, on paper – it must survive heresies shining, unconfoundable.... and heretics there will be: Gnostics who have been taken in a rush of wind and fire to chambers of the Rocket-throne ... Kabbalists who study the Rocket as Torah, letter by letter – rivets, burner cup and brass

rose, its text is theirs to permute and combine into new revelations, always unfolding ... Manicheans who see two Rockets, good and evil, who speak together in the sacred idolalia of the Primal Twins ... of a good Rocket to take us to the stars, an evil Rocket for the World's suicide, the two perpetually in struggle. [p. 727]

Is the arc of the Rocket, gravity's rainbow, an emblem of sexual and cultural defeat, the growth and death cycle of individuals and societies, which rise to peak moments of maturity and then die into an Icarian fall? Or is there a regenerative movement beyond the zero point of impact, invisible to our eyes but not to our faith? (An epigraph from Wernher von Braun preceding Part One expresses such a belief.) Pynchon entertains both possibilities.

The utmost point of nihilism, however, is the notion that the "Primal Twins" lead to the same destiny. Regeneration, that is, may only be the beginning of the same cycle extinguished at the end of the rocket's historical trajectory. Or, as Pynchon frames the question in the above quotation, perhaps the good rocket that takes us to the stars is the same as the evil rocket which aims at our destruction. Pynchon is permitted this ambiguity by the fact, which required a quarter-century of "real" time to take form, that Wernher von Braun was responsible both for the V-2 rockets and for the American space program. The novel ends with von Braun and his staff surrendering to American authorities, complete with blueprints and plans for bigger and better rockets. Indeed, one of his associates says, "I couldn't go with von Braun ... not to the Americans, it would only just keep on the same way. ... I want it to really be over, that's all" (p. 456). The migration of von Braun introduces the infection of Nazi fantasies into a country already obsessed with Empire and leading signs in the sky. Blicero's analysis at novel's end sounds like an authorial commentary:

... the impulse to empire, the mission to propagate death, the structure of it, kept on. Now we are in the last phase. American Death has come to occupy Europe. It has learned empire from its old metropolis.

Is the cycle over now, and a new one ready to begin? Will

our new Edge, our new Deathkingdom, be the Moon? [pp. 722–3]

There is no easy answer. Mankind's best hope is that the innocent fantasy prevail: the good Rocket over the evil Rocket. And yet von Braun's migration coincides with Blicero's order to fire the fictive 00000 Rocket in the last pages of the novel, a completion of the fantasy of power Fritz Lang had engineered in his films about the master criminal Dr. Mabuse and the first moon landing. Pynchon's retrospective scenario of 1972, then, unavoidably influences our reading of the more familiar brand of science fiction produced just after World War II. The popularity of that genre can be related to the public's need for an escape from the bleak prospect offered in Blicero's defeatest remarks, derived as they are from the first use of atomic power in 1945. Pynchon's novel reminds us that however much the Rocket of our hopes "rises on a promise, a prophecy, of Escape" it will ultimately be "betrayed to Gravity" (p. 758). No literary work of our time so comprehensively, indeed encyclopedically, explodes the perennial illusion of alternatives to terrestrial limits as *Gravity's Rainbow*. Pynchon cannot be credited with out-sophisticating his immediate predecessors, however. The best science-fiction writers had realistically anatomized the "new Edge" taking shape between the zero hours of 1945 and 1969.

ROBERT A. HEINLEIN'S *THE MAN WHO SOLD THE MOON*

By the 1950s rocket technology put the event of a moon landing into the realm of possibility, earlier than any writer had predicted. Even Robert A. Heinlein, commonly called "The Dean of Science Fiction" placed the event optimistically in 1978 in the chart of "Future History" he devised in the early 1940s. Heinlein's work more than any other responded to the scientific developments beginning with Goddard's experiments, and to the science fiction his generation read so avidly. In Heinlein's short story, "Requiem" (1940), he undoubtedly put into the mouth of his aged businessman D. D. Harriman, financier of the first moon landing, his own aspirations to enter the promised land of the lunar surface:

... it's the one thing I've really wanted to do all my life – ever since I was a young boy. I don't know whether I can explain it to you, or not. You young fellows have grown up to rocket travel the way I grew up to aviation. ... When I was a kid practically nobody believed that men would ever reach the moon. You've seen rockets all your lives, and the first to reach the moon got there before you were a young boy. When I was a boy they laughed at the idea.

But I believed – I believed. I read Verne, and Wells, and [E. E.] Smith, and I believed that we could do it – that we *would* do it. I set my heart on being one of the men to walk the surface of the moon, to see her other side, and to look back on the face of the Earth, hanging in the sky.[16]

Harriman, like Robert Frost, has lived long enough to be an almanac of the whole history of aviation; he bequeaths to the new generation his memory of the psychic yearning that unites the Wright brothers with the makers of spaceships. And Harriman shrinks even less than Frost from the implications for American destiny of an aggressive space program, an "on-penetration / Into earth and skies" that reprises the native doctrine of manifest destiny.

"Requiem" found its way into a collection of stories Heinlein published in 1950, *The Man Who Sold the Moon*, devoted to the life and times of Delos David Harriman and his epoch-making venture, variously called Spaceways Incorporated, Harriman's Lunar Corporation, and Harriman's Lunar Exploitations. No work of the early 1950s offers quite so candid and complex a vision of the space program which succeeded aviation as the object of fantasies of ascent. By casting as his main character an entrepreneur of unlimited cynicism, for whom the moonflight is attractive in part because it offers the promise of incredible profits in real estate, Heinlein anticipates and disarms criticism that the space program had already earned from a growing group of technophobes in American intellectual life. On the other hand, as the above quotation makes clear, Harriman's pleasure in gain is inextricably mingled with the authentic need for a meaningful goal that will redeem his (and his country's) sordid history. Harriman, named for a nineteenth-century railroad magnate who sponsored scientific explorations, possesses all the rich complications of American capitalism, which had more than one reason to win the postwar space race with an alien empire.

Prewar science fiction usually featured a stalwart pilot as hero, a Lindbergh figure whose forceful actions overcame the predations of the Enemy. The commanding officer of the spaceship in Heinlein's short story, "Destination Moon" (also 1950, also about the first moon landing), derives from the older model. *The Man Who Sold the Moon*, however, eschews this figure for a managerial type because Heinlein recognized that changes in rocket technology call for an organizational effort. It is one thing to write a "juvenile" like *Rocket Ship Galileo* (1947) showing three eager youngsters and an adult scientist building and flying a rocket to the moon all by themselves. But Heinlein, who worked as a civilian engineer at the Philadelphia Navy Yard during the war, knew that only a team effort sustained by billions of dollars could make such a venture feasible. In *The Man Who Sold the Moon* a private corporation raises the money by merging stocks from its many other profitable holdings; in later works Heinlein will acknowledge that only the federal government could finance such a scheme, and that given the threat to national security posed by the Soviet entry into space, the more input by the military the better.

Heinlein's faith in the moonflight as an imminent possibility was solidified by the Manhattan Project, his constant referent in the fiction of this period. The Project offers a supreme example of a team of experts solving a complex problem in a short period of time, and constructing a technological product that bore the proof of their conclusions. Specifically, the space age is said to begin in Heinlein's work when an "X" or atomic fuel is invented to propel rockets out of the atmosphere. In one of his earliest short stories, "Blowups Happen" (1940), he imagines a space satellite as the repository of an atomic breeder or "Big Bomb." Space shuttles ferry synthetic radioactive fuel bred from this "Bomb" back to earth for various purposes; Harriman's scheme is to use some of it for a lunar rocket. But cosmic radiation apparently ignites one shuttle-ship's payload, which in turn triggers an explosion of the satellite. When Heinlein revised the story for publication in *The Man Who Sold the Moon* he conveyed the magnitude of such an explosion by comparing it to "a thousand Hiroshimas" (p. 106). The flammability of the atomic energy which led to the primal catastrophe in Heinlein's fiction (the satellite's explosion/Hiroshima) is clearly a metaphor of the dangerous stuff mankind will carry in its flying machine to the moon: the will to power. Thinking of the military implications of his lunar voyage, Harriman remarks to his underlings, "This is the biggest thing for the human race since the discovery of fire. Handled right, it can mean a new and braver world. Handle it wrong and it's a one-way ticket to Armageddon" (p. 190).

Which one shall it be? The method of science is to examine the available empirical evidence, and in shaping a future historiography the best evidence is of course the national past. The lunar voyage is compared constantly in Heinlein's early work (as in most science fiction and popular journalism) to Columbus's landing in the new world. Because the new world was settled and populated by so many people with Harriman's own exploitative motives – mixed with genuine awe at the beauty and fecundity of the continent – it had become a mirror image of the old world's predacious materialism. Harriman and his associates plan to sell the moon in every possible way from franchises and utility rights to contracts for land and resources. "This is the greatest real estate venture since the Pope carved up the New World," Harriman exclaims (p. 173). The analogy is perfectly apt. In this skewed version of ecclesiastical history the voracious entrepreneurs who exploit the moon take as their model the corrupt form of the Church, which exercised worldly power by dispossessing natives in favor of imperial forces.

As H. Bruce Franklin has shown in his study of Heinlein, the Cold War that succeeded World War II provoked fantasies of American hegemony over the planet similar to the expansionist models of imperial Britain and Nazi Germany. Franklin cites one early Heinlein story, "Solution Unsatisfactory" (1941), in which an Army colonel comes into possession of a weapon linked to atomic research, radioactive dust. He now has the power to enforce a Pax Americana, and does so by means of an aerial Peace Patrol. His rationale is the following: "The United States was having power thrust on it willy-nilly. We had to accept it and enforce a world-wide peace, ruthlessly and drastically, or it would be seized by some other nation."[17] What is true of the earth is also true of the moon. There will always be an enemy vying for rights to the lunar property, and so the kind of violence needed to preserve and extend a world peace will be necessary to maintain control of the moon.

The historical vision of Heinlein's books is pessimistic, but the tone of *The Man Who Sold the Moon* is exuberant, humorous, and optimistic. In "Requiem" the aged Harriman says, "This has been a wonderful, romantic century, for all its bad points. And it's grown more wonderful and more exciting every year." We might be tempted to take this as ironic, a satire on the gospel of positive thinking. And yet Heinlein utters the same sentiment in his preface to the book: "It's a great and wonderful age, the most wonderful this giddy planet has yet seen." The rhetorical effect is precisely that of Frost's poem, to sweep aside the detritus and horror of the modern century in favor of a wider prospect, a renewable future. And like the conclusion of "Kitty Hawk," Heinlein's language tends toward the commercial, as if to acknowledge that a bit of huckstering is essential to make the idea of progress palatable. It is not sacred history but business history that governs the obligatory comparison of the moonflight to Kitty Hawk, for example:

> "You ask me to show figures on a brand-new type of enterprise knowing I can't. It's like asking the Wright brothers at Kitty Hawk to estimate how much money Curtiss-Wright Corporation would someday make out of building airplanes." [p. 162]

Harriman summons Lindbergh to make a similar point. He can find a historical example to sell any product, and nothing is sacred for his purposes. His partners are in awe of his wheeling and dealing; they compare him to Moses; they remark on his Messiah complex; they try to find some scriptural model that will suit Harriman's zeal to found the New Jerusalem he has called "Luna City" since his childhood.

And yet the book is not really about the moonflight. The lunar trip is given very few pages, and the pilot, Les Le Croix, is the most colorless figure in the narrative. Compared to the extensive attention to the preparations for flight, during which Harriman heroically beats down every obstacle, the flight is treated with condescension and humor. In short stories of the same period collected in *The Green Hills of Earth* (1951), Heinlein also demystifies the act of spaceflight. In "Space Jockey," the pilot, who works the earth-moon shuttle for Harriman Lunar Exploitations, meditates ruefully on the tedious monotony of his job. Heinlein is extrapolating from the commercial pilot's experience, but his point has a predictive truth to it. The astronaut depends almost entirely upon machines to do the work automatically for him. It is an inescapable technological rule that the more ambitious the flight the more controlled by computers. In *Rocket Ship Galileo*, it is Joe the Robot who takes over operations once the ship is aloft. The situation lends itself to fantasies of usurpation, as in HAL's murderous takeover of the spaceship in the film *2001*. By metaphorical extension the space vehicle comes to resemble the enclosed and oppressive character of terrestrial life itself. The rocket may be no true escape from the big machine of an imperial government, only its unromantic microcosm or tool.

Harriman's multinational corporation is a reasonable stand-in for the national government, and in later works the world federation, which controls and patrols its empire by irresistible aerial force. It is at least a neat coincidence that Harriman's first name, Delos, refers to the birthplace of Apollo. (His middle name, David, recalls the founder of the Israelite empire.) In his last novel before the Apollo 11 moon landing, *The Moon Is a Harsh Mistress*, Heinlein shows the moon tyrannized by a Lunar Authority delegated from a militaristic federation on earth. The semi-anarchist population of Luna rebels against this authority, in an act compared to the American Revolution. The novel ends with an aerial bombardment of the earth by "Loonies" in which rocks are hurled upon vulnerable targets. It is a fate bound into Harriman's Columbus-like landing upon the moon, and his later dispatching of the rocket *Mayflower* to found the first lunar settlement. By "The Logic of Empire," to cite the title of one Heinlein story, the moon will in time establish colonies of her own, and send out starship troopers to suppress the strivings for independence. Even Heinlein's more benign scenarios suggest that ascent into the heavens will not gratify human desire, as the nineteenth century had dreamed, but will succeed instead in making the moon nothing more than the enemy and image of ourselves.

11. The Moon Landing and Modern Literature

On the fourth of July, 1969, *Life* magazine published a special issue, "Off to the Moon," beginning with a color photo of Neil Armstrong and ending with "A Message from Charles Lindbergh" in which the aviator compared his flight of 1927 to the forthcoming launch of Apollo 11. As we have seen, poets applauded Lindbergh's transatlantic crossing as an epic achievement, not least because the boundary-breaking event seemed a prelude to the long-imagined era of spaceflight. But the Apollo 11 crew would receive less gracious treatment from poets than Lindbergh, as James Dickey's ambivalent poem "The Moon Ground," published in that issue of *Life*, foreshadowed. "What Comedy's this Epic," Allen Ginsberg would soon complain in verse, as he summoned the context of starving millions in Biafra and the bloodletting in Vietnam.[1] And when Robert Vas Dias edited the one anthology of that year to commemorate the event, he noted that most of the poems about Apollo 11 expressed doubts about the value of the mission. Poets did not rejoice in the adventure so much as worry about technological spinoffs that might further bind them in mechanical systems beyond their comprehension and control. In this they echoed Lindbergh's own conclusions about the destructive impact of modern inventions in his equivocal "Message."

A convenient measurement of the radical change in response is two poems by Babette Deutsch, the only poet to appear in the 1927 and 1969 anthologies. In the former she praised Lindbergh for "Showing to the mean heart and cruel mind / Provinces undiscovered, rich beyond imagination."[2] By contrast, in her address "To the Moon, 1969" she describes a diminishment of imagination caused by the success of Apollo 11:

There is no lament for you – who are silent
   as the dead always are.
You have left the mythologies, the old ones, our own.
But, for a few, what has happened is the death of a divine
   Person,
is a betrayal, is a piece of
The cruelty that the Universe is witness to
       while displaying its glories.[3]

The moon is "simply a planet that men have, / almost casually, cheapened." Like others in the anthology the poem is an elegiac curse upon the astronauts for their act of deicide.

From all accounts the negative response of poets to the moon landing took supporters of the space program by complete surprise. If there was one ally in the public they had counted on it was the visionary poets, who had generated for millennia the myths and texts which inspired engineers to construct machines that flew. Poetry and science had been joined in mutual wonder against drab bourgeois misgivings about spending priorities. Hardly a book exists about space travel that does not quote Tennyson's "Ulysses" on the need to seek a newer world, "To sail beyond the sunset, and the baths / Of all the western stars." Or the conclusion of T. S. Eliot's "Little Gidding": "We shall not cease from exploration / And the end of all our exploring / Will be to arrive where we started / And know the place for the first time."

If poets once felt this way, why no longer? The moonflight was deliberately designed as a sacred event, as the culminating modern type of "magical flight" into the heavens. It was undertaken not principally as a source of practical benefits but as a symbolic expression of humanity's continuing quest for self-definition and spiritual renewal. If the event did irrevocably alter the psychic relation of every person to the cosmos, who could speak with more authority about its impact than artists trained to discern and articulate the invisible links of attraction between the individual mind or soul and the external world? The resentment of poets toward Apollo 11 suggests both a wound in the public psyche and a violation of privileged beliefs within the literary tradition. For the purpose of analysis, there can be no separation of event and archetype.

Historical incidents rarely have the power to denature enduring symbols, but, as Babette Deutsch's poem indicates, the moon suddenly became vulnerable in the summer of 1969 to a radical transformation of value because of human technics. Her reference to the departed moon goddess encompasses a figure who in Greek and Roman mythology had various names: Artemis, Cynthia, Diana, Luna, Phoebe, Selene. From prehistoric times the gradual appearance and disappearance of the moon in the heavens had been connected to the biological process of generation, decay, and regeneration identified with the Feminine. The moon was creator, preserver, and destroyer, and thus shared an affinity with the masculine God that supplanted (but did not extinguish) her in Western myth. She continued to compel by her chastity, inaccessible as the unrealized potential of the human soul she came to symbolize.

The moon goddess reigned as a rival of the scientific perception of lunar being. It was not so much the moon's appearance which inspired poets as its astronomical position as a luminous consort of earth. Centuries after Galileo pointed his telescope at the moon and pronounced her "uneven, rough, replete with cavities, and packed with protruding eminences," poets celebrated her as the consummate image of beauty. The Romantic art of the nineteenth century, especially, sustained the exalted vision bequeathed by the classical period. The emphasis, whether in Blake's or Shelley's or Keats's conception of the moon goddess, is devoutly personalist. The poet treated the moon as an anima figure worthy of affectionate worship. Keats's Endymion, for example, in the imaginary flight of the poem's first book, embraces "that completed form of all completeness ... that high perfection of all sweetness" (I.606–7). But *Endymion* was the last great expression of the lunar myth. Generations of poets after Keats narrowed the myth to dramatize self-pity and loveless yearning, as in Longfellow's "Moonlight," Matthew Arnold's "Isolation: To Marguerite" and Ernest Dowson's verse play "Pierrot of the Minute." Cynthia descended no more to men. While anthropologists and psychologists anatomized lunar mythology exhaustively, removing some of its mysteries in the process, poets increasingly surrounded the subject with a fashionable irony as part of their reaction against Romanticism. What was myth became hard image in the new century as modernist poets adopted a descriptive mode reminiscent of Galileo. T. E. Hulme compared the moon to a red-faced farmer and a child's balloon; E. E. Cummings saw it as a "fragment of angry candy"; T. S. Eliot lamented that a senile moon "has lost her memory" and that "A washed-out smallpox cracks her face."[4]

"There's no moon goddess now," James Dickey has remarked, adding that the twentieth century moon is "simply a dead stone, a great ruined stone in the sky."[5] Dickey, who has written more, and more favorably, about the space program than any important American poet, undertook the task of restoring Cynthia to her former status. As a neoromantic Dickey welcomed the infusion of new life which he believed the Apollo program could give to a nearly exploded mythology. In an uncollected poem he wrote for *Life* in 1968, "The Triumph of Apollo 7," Dickey effaced himself in honor of the technicians who could, better than he, forge a new public consciousness of a diminished thing. "In a sense they [the astronauts] are all poets," he wrote. "Because of them, / the death-cold and blazing craters of the moon will / think with us, and the waterless oceans of Mars; / the glowing fogs of Venus will say what they are." By penetrating deeper into space the astronauts will give the cosmic landscape a voice, and necessarily alter man's conception of himself and his destiny. The astronauts "return / to tell us what we will be."[6]

Dickey confidently assured readers of *Life* that the astronauts would find the language to describe the sensations of outer space. But *Life* discovered differently when it signed the astronauts of Apollo 11 to exclusive contracts and requested colorful prose articulating their innermost thoughts and feelings. "This is what *Life* paid to find out, and what the others pried to find out without paying, and in truth, neither unearthed very much," Michael Collins confessed in his autobiography. "I suppose this was mainly because, as technical people, as test pilots whose bread and butter was the cold, dispassionate analysis of complicated facts, we were frankly embarrassed by the shifting focus. It didn't seem right somehow for the press to have this morbid, unhealthy, persistent, prodding, probing, preoccupation with the frills, when the silly bastards didn't even understand how the machines operated or what they had accomplished."[7] Because the astronauts had to master an immensely complex mechanical system they seemed obsessed with data, addicted to the language of "NASA-ese." If the public wanted information, they could have it in abundance; if they wanted the language of epics or Scripture, they would have to hire James Dickey or

Norman Mailer. The astronauts' language of flight would not soar, it would probe and itemize; it would report on procedure. (By the time Dickey came to write his second poem on the Apollo missions, "For the First Manned Moon Orbit," he would understand that the astronauts "float on nothing / But procedure alone."[8]) They would not launch a flight of words, they would triumph by the art of silence, by photography.

   When the first astronauts uttered words they relied cautiously on an uncontroversial vocabulary of stock phrases. They catalogued data, or, when describing an object, relied on downward comparisons. James Lovell on the lunar surface: "Looks like plaster of paris or grayish beach sand." William Anders concurred: "a dirty beach." Mission Control favored the comparison to gray paint. Dickey, leaping into the rhetorical vacuum, attempted to capture what the astronauts might have seen if they *were* poets. His poem on the first manned moon orbit is a failure, however, because its inflated diction is devoid of clarity. For example, the image of the suspended earth, reproduced on so many wall posters afterward, receives this phrasing:

> And behold
> The blue planet steeped in its dream
> Of reality, its calculated vision shaking with
> The only love.

This is lazy writing, unworthy of the poet who composed the intricate spots of time in "The Firebombing." Unless presented through precisely detailed tableaux such terms as "dream," "reality," "vision" and "love" are hollow and bombastic. And to describe earth's "calculated vision," whatever that is, as "shaking" seems nothing more than the poetic sensibility faking emotion by imposing a febrile excitement. "The dim ritual / Random stones of oblivion" may be more sonorous than "plaster of paris or grayish beach sand" but it is not better poetry.

   Dickey's failure arises from trying to impose the language of narrative upon deidentified relationships. The whole function and effect of the space program was the annihilation of persistent archetypes which had, since the days of Galileo, slowed the development of tools for the exploration of the cosmos. Dickey, having understood that the astronauts would bring back a *new* language because of their experience, proceeded to write about their missions as if Endymion and Cynthia were still available figures. In fact, reference by space technicians to the old personal mythology tended to be derisive. On the morning of Armstrong's and Aldrin's descent to the lunar surface in their module, Mission Control reported to the astronauts:

> An ancient legend says that a beautiful Chinese girl called Chango has been living there for four thousand years. It seems she was banished to the moon because she stole the pill of immortality from her husband. You might also look for her companion, a large Chinese rabbit, who is easy to spot since he is always standing on his hind feet in the shade of a cinnamon tree.

Michael Collins responded, "Okay, we'll keep a close eye for the bunny girl."[9] What is this story, this bit of comic relief, but an exorcism of myth itself? It treats parodically the traditional elements of lunar mythology, the beautiful moon maiden and the promise of immortality. The large rabbit reminds one of the theatrical Harvey; they occupy the same universe of blithe nonsense that Reason rolls back in its quest for quantifiable data. The meaning of the exchange is: we have by this act outgrown the make-believe of our childhood; we declare our independence from archetypes.

The cultural meaning of an event is determined by its relation to the set of pre-existing beliefs of the community. If it can be assimilated into the constellation of myths by which the community understands its nature and destiny then the event will be celebrated as enthusiastically as was Lindbergh's flight of 1927. If it challenges and disorders the arrangement of beliefs, the shock waves are registered first by artists trained to discern disturbances in the public imagination. Though the myth of Endymion and Cynthia was often summoned as a scenario of lunar enchantment, and therefore as a legitimate model for the Apollo missions, poets realized that this myth – which had always been *their* myth – had been decreated by the events of July 1969. As Robert Lowell put it in "Moon Landings" Cynthia would be rendered a "disenchantress" by Apollo, and worse:

> chassis orbiting about the earth,

grin of heatwave, spasm of stainless steel,
gadabout with heart of chalk, unnamable
void and cold thing in the universe...[10]

Rather, the informing myth behind lunar exploration seemed to
be John F. Kennedy's New Frontier, a version of the territorial
imperative which some anthropologists had begun to describe
as universal to the species. (Robert Ardrey's bombshell, *African
Genesis*, was published the same year as Kennedy's
recommendation to Congress that a man be landed on the moon
within the decade.) These two myths are irreconcilable: Cynthia
is forever chaste, inviolable; dominion over her is fatal.

The desire to settle new plantations in a foreign place, so
firmly associated with the "Augustan Age" of the Roman and
British empires, has usually been criticized by poets, though
there are famous exceptions. Colonization involves the stamping
of the parent image on new territory, the extinction of native or
aboriginal life in favor of the overmastering civilization that
duplicates itself in name and nature (*New* England, *New* York,
New Jersey). Technology, the practical application of scientific
research, figured in many literary works as a means by which
the imperial state could overrun not only lands and peoples, but
even the moon. Or so Thomas Gray playfully imagined in his
Latin verse exercise, "Luna habitabilis" (1737). The poem begins
as Gray asks his muse for wings to fly toward the beckoning
moon, and is told that with the aid of a small tube he can see
Phoebe herself. As he gazes at the bare landscape his fancy
begins to work; he imagines an inhabited moon, the mirror
image of his own civilization. He conceives a lunar tyrant in his
palace who looks toward earth and plans its conquest. However,
Gray concludes with a vision of England's "dominion over the
conquered air."[11] This is whimsy and not a political tract, but it
emerges from a set of cultural assumptions that enforced the
claims of imperial policy.

Though writers like Keats strove to bring back the erotic
goddess of classical mythology, by the end of the nineteenth
century the imperial myth, which favors masculine domination
over feminine desire, had regained its sway. The turn of the
century is full of poetry and fiction that imagines men on the
moon. In H. G. Wells's *The First Men in the Moon* the Leonardo-
like inventor Cavor, and his fellow-astronaut Bedford, do not

shirk their imperial responsibilities. The narrator Bedford remarks: "Suddenly I saw as in a vision the whole solar system threaded with Cavorite liners and spheres *de luxe*. 'Rights of pre-emption,' came floating into my head – planetary rights of pre-emption. I recalled the old Spanish monopoly in American gold." Later he declares, "We must annex this moon."[12] Likewise in Jules Verne's satire, *From the Earth to the Moon* (1865), Impey Barbicane, President of the Gun Club of Baltimore, promises in a speech to his colleagues that he will make the moon the thirty-sixth state of the Union. President Kennedy's speech to Congress, of which Barbicane's is a parodic forerunner, culminated a long history of lunar attraction. The basic question remained: did the space program's stated desire to eliminate boundaries ("We came in peace for all mankind" the plaque read) disguise a naked desire for imperial possession as old as the arboreal apes?

To the dissenting counterculture of 1969 this new pioneering effort, this conquest of space, resembled an errand into the wilderness less than the Caesarism or hunger for power over peoples which had turned even Christian doctrine to its purposes. It did not escape the notice of writers, in this regard, that the presiding genius of the Apollo program was Wernher von Braun, who had developed the V-1 and V-2 rockets for Nazi Germany before joining the Allied cause after the war. Von Braun is the perfect example of the amoral technological intelligence, welcoming any opportunity that advances research, no matter what its human cost. He told Oriana Fallaci:

> ... we've been taken far by the discovery of new seas, of new continents, by the settling of new lands. And nobody can tell in advance whether it will bring good or ill. Until now man has done nothing but bring a heap of trouble; but it has been through these very troubles that man has advanced and new civilizations have been built to replace those which have been destroyed. So I do not think that we are doing anything ill. Men must always travel farther and farther afield, they must always widen their horizons and their interests: this is the will of God. If God didn't want it to be so, He wouldn't have given us the ability and the possibility to make progress and to change. If God didn't want it, He would stop us.[13]

This speech could be placed in the mouth of "Wernher von

Braun" in *Gravity's Rainbow*, except that it would strain credibility. It is a fervent summoning of sacred history that recalls the enthusiasm about the nature and destiny of the flying machine before World War II dampened public optimism by offering a competing and apocalyptic scenario. Von Braun recalls Cabal, the technocrat-father of the first astronaut to fly to the moon in *Things to Come*, the 1936 film adaptation of Wells's *The Shape of Things to Come*. He also recalls the Leonardo-like villain Weston of C. S. Lewis's Perelandra trilogy written in response to the prospace propaganda of that film and the ethos of space colonization that nourished it.

Von Braun became the space program's spokesman because he articulated America's manifest destiny in the twentieth century: to climb the chain of being by sending spaceships further and further into the cosmos. At each stage humanity would collect more data which would enlarge its understanding, until the whole species became a kind of *Übermensch*. Von Braun remarked on the evening before the launch of Apollo 11 that "what we will have attained when Neil Armstrong steps down upon the moon is a completely new step in the evolution of man."[14] Yet the next stage of evolution, as the space technicians defined it, seemed to be not a human figure like Armstrong but the computers that enabled Apollo 11 to rise and return to earth. In the moon shot there was no question of Lindbergh's "WE," the equality of man and his plane. Machines dominated the space voyages; they were the beginning and in a sense the end of the program. Hardware, as it was always called, had reduced the erstwhile "birdman" to a robot-like twister of dials. The machines created an epic event, but Allen Ginsberg's question, "What Comedy's this Epic," returned to haunt the human passengers. Norman Mailer compared the first men on the moon to "Laurel and Hardy in space suits" and *Lovecraft's Follies*, James Schevill's popular play of 1970, depicted them jumping maniacally on pogo sticks over the lunar surface.

The most significant convert to the technophobic point of view in 1969 was James Dickey. In his journals he pondered the matter at length:

All the revolutions and the revolutionary activities of the past ten or fifteen years have been protests of the increasing trivialization of life. One thrashes around like a creature caught in a wire net to escape the enormous emphasis on trivia, on the inconsequential. This is why the journeys to the moon are important: for once, we all say, or feel, here is something, at last, that is not trivial. But what must be seen is that this enormous and impressive "step for mankind" is a *triumph* of the trivial. We all want to think large thoughts. But the question that hangs before us no matter which way we turn is this: what is *not* trivial?[15]

For the Apollo 11 mission several thousand spacecraft systems existed, involving more than one and a half million working parts overseen by a network of computers. These computers could talk to each other at the rate of 51,200 bits per second, providing some five hundred pages worth of data to Mission Control for every second of the flight. "Enormous and impressive," but is this different in *kind* or only in number and novelty from the trivial artifacts which diminish the suburban homeowner in Dickey's poem of the firebombing? When Dickey asks what is not trivial, what assists man in his enterprise as a conscious and consequential being, he is hinting again at the preeminence of ancient myth and Scripture as a way of "knowing."

And so when Dickey came to write the third and last of his poems on the Apollo flights he adjusted his praise to fit his increasing skepticism about the space program. In "The Moon Ground" rhetorical questions fill the poem, along with affirmations – if that's what they are – that the meaning of this adventure will emerge somehow from the data processed by computers. It will not be discovered by poets, or by the astronauts either. Dickey acknowledges that the astronauts are servants and not masters of the enterprise: "We are here to do one / Thing only, and that is rock by rock to carry the moon to take it / Back." The rocks have the "secret of Time" and though an older culture relied on artists to unravel this secret, now the machines will establish its true, quantifiable nature. From this data, and data collected on voyages deeper and deeper into space, the machines will tell us, because only they have the appropriate language, what we will be. Dickey's poem ends with the line, "We bend, we pick up stones." This is the definitive image of Natural Man in the space age, the image used in the film *2001* to depict cavemen engaged in the brute warfare coded into the species. If it is not Laurel and Hardy, neither is it an image of heroic consequence. Dickey had looked to the space program as deliverance from the trivial; after Apollo 11 he would look to wilderness as deliverance from the mechanistic life of which the moon landing came to seem the apotheosis.

Poised between a Romantic enthusiasm for space which he realized would lead him into the machine-worship of Wernher von Braun, and devotion to terracentric values, Dickey in 1969 embodied the whole set of ambivalent feelings about the moon landing that stirred unspoken in the American public. Because it expresses these divided loyalties so clearly, "The Moon Ground" is the most significant poem about the moon landing yet written, the most worthy of study, the most likely to illuminate for future generations the mixed emotions of a majority of onlookers.

For all its exclamatory tone "The Moon Ground" is an elegiac poem about human entrapment in time. Its central question is "What hope is there at home / In the azure of breath, or here with the stone / Dead secret?" The ancient moon goddess had the power to redeem time, to grant immortality. But the astronaut-speaker of Dickey's poem reports that as he walks the lunar surface Thomas Gray's "Elegy Written in a Country Churchyard" comes "helplessly" from his heart. The astronaut repeats from memory the elegy's evocation of twilight, leaving unstated the famous and pertinent conclusion:

> The boast of heraldry, the pomp of power,
> And all that beauty, all that wealth e'er gave,
> Awaits alike th'inevitable hour.
> The paths of glory lead but to the grave.

Here is the ironic fulfillment of Dickey's earlier claim that the astronauts will return to tell us what we will be. After the giddy experience of weightlessness they testify to the weight of human mortality. Having traveled further in space than anyone, they return to tell us that all the space a man needs is six feet underground. Dickey must have appreciated the remarks of Edwin Aldrin in a pre-splashdown interview: "Personally, in reflecting the events of the past several days, a verse from Psalms comes to mind to me: 'When I consider the heavens, the work of Thy fingers, the moon and the stars which Thou hast ordained, what is man that Thou art mindful of him?' "[16]

Dickey, with a poet's brilliant tact, had concluded his poem with a biblical allusion even more appropriate. The astronauts bending and picking up stones recall the most mournful of all poems on the human condition, Ecclesiastes: "[There is] A time to cast away stones, and a time to gather stones together.... For that which befalleth the sons of men befalleth beasts; even one thing befalleth them: as the one dieth, so dieth the other; yea, they have all one breath; so that a man hath no preeminence above a beast: for all is vanity" (3:5,19). As Thomas Gray had adjusted his vision downward from his verse exercise recommending conquest of the moon, "Luna habitabilis," to the country churchyard, so Dickey surrenders the aspirations of his early prophecies in order to establish the vanity of Apollo 11's glorious achievement. That vanity *and* glory are both present in the poem distinguishes it from almost every other verse on the subject. Other poets proclaim, as Dickey does, "We have brought the gods." But Dickey sees too that the astronauts have brought death to what Aldrin called the "magnificent desolation" of the moon. The return journey to earth, then, would have the symbolic force of a resurrection, though Dickey does not dramatize splashdown in the poem. The earth is present throughout the poem as an image reflected to the speaker by his companion's face mask. In this "dead new world" only the parent world displays life and lures the astronauts toward a fortunate fall back into the creatureliness they cannot disown. It is no accident that Dickey's most brilliant poem before "The Moon Ground" is a long narrative about the fall of a stewardess from an airliner toward her death, a "brief goddess" who finds a grave in the flowering harvests of Kansas.

Dickey's spoiling of the object certainly derives in part from his former envy of these latter-day knights of the air. His retreat before the awesome linguistic power of advanced communications networks and toward a reliable tradition of moral utterance, however, represents a farewell to the possibility of a new poetics invigorated by the vocabulary and perspectives of the astronauts. If there was to be such a poetics it must, somehow, account for the plenitude of experience which computer science has revealed in such detail without abandoning the hard-won language that synthesizes thought and feeling into a uniquely human mode of knowledge. This expansion of vision, rather than the "data overkill" which even scientists began to complain of during the Apollo missions, would most surely guide the public toward the community of wonder that humanists enjoyed before the division of wisdom into the "two cultures."

THE TESTIMONY OF MAILER AND BELLOW

Not many texts in the period just after the moon landing attempted to reconcile the two cultures, but Norman Mailer's *Of A Fire on the Moon* is an honorable exception. Having studied engineering in college, Mailer possessed the competence to see the spaceflight as more than (in W. H. Auden's phrase) "so huge a phallic triumph," though of course he cherished it for that reason as well. Mailer must have known that the odds against producing an interesting text on the subject were formidable. He would have to negotiate through at least three languages in which no literary masterpiece had ever been composed: the scientific, the bureaucratic (in which a favorite word of Mailer's like "shit" is translated into "post-nutritive disposal substance"), and the language of hype. There was no question of ignoring these languages; he must incorporate them without losing his own characteristic style in the process. Mailer does so by making his struggle with words the manifest content of his book. He becomes an open-eared Everyman bringing to bear upon an extraordinary event all the encyclopedic resources of his civilization, and listening to himself make meaning at the same time. The self-consciousness is not offered as a perfect solution but a tentative one until modern technology offers the storyteller a privileged place in its system. By the end of his quest, when he stands before a moon rock, Mailer feels thankful for the sufficient inspiration:

> that rock ... gave him certitude enough to know he would write his book and in some part applaud the feat and honor the astronauts because the expedition to the moon was finally a venture which might help to disclose the nature of the Lord and the Lucifer who warred for us; certainly, the hour of happiness would be here when men who spoke like Shakespeare rode the ships: how many eons was that away! [p. 471]

A colon barely disguises Mailer's ambition to put his book in competition with Shakespeare. If Shakespeare's eloquence is a mixture of the golden and common languages, so Mailer will yoke together elements of a capacious vocabulary to reveal a world of which his readers are presumably ignorant.

The whole book is constructed from oppositions, paradoxes, dual meanings, symbolic crossings. First, there is the fundamental question: "Was our venture into space noble or insane, was it part of a search for the good, or the agent of diabolisms yet unglimpsed?" (p. 140). The identity of the flying machine depends on the answer. Apollo-Saturn might be the angelic agent of the Divine Will, as he hypothesizes in many places, or "a child of the Devil" (p. 103). Similarly NASA has the ambiguity of Harriman's Lunar Corporation in Heinlein's fiction: NASA is "a new church, it had been born as a high church," and yet the communion it offers seems more often risible than solemn. It announces that a new order begins with the first American footprint on the lunar surface, but the annunciation is in the German accent of Wernher von Braun, and the climactic first footstep is finally judged to be a boring event.

How is one to make sense of all these contradictions and role changes? As we have seen, poets by and large kept their distance from the event; they seized upon the gap between intention and appearance as an opportunity for ironic commentary. If Mailer remains sceptical about the astronauts, he does not join the raillery of the poets either. The reason is that Mailer never loses his invidious feelings toward the astronauts: "It was simple masculine envy. He too wanted to go up in the bird" (p. 97). Envy in this case permits Mailer to assume both positive as well as negative postures toward each aspect of the launch and landing. The desire for emulation promotes a sympathetic attitude toward the astronauts and their vehicle, an identification so close that he can for a period enact his dream of being a Shakespeare aboard the great ship. The equal and opposite emotion, a resentment at not going up in the bird, makes him acutely aware of the abundant absurdities of the mission. Mailer cannot conceal his pleasure in wounding the rocket and its crew by his poison-tipped rhetoric – a common sport of his technophobic generation.

Neil Armstrong and the rocket form a composite being so far as Mailer is concerned, just as he will describe Michael Collins's lonely orbit of the moon in the Command Module as an experience of the "legitimate narcissism of the pilot who lives in a machine which is an exquisite extension of his will" (p. 241). We can trace the continuity by examining a sample passage, Mailer's description of the blastoff from Cape Kennedy:

> ... the lift-off itself seemed to partake more of a miracle than a mechanical phenomenon, as if all of huge Saturn itself had begun silently to levitate, and was then pursued by flames ...
> No, it was more dramatic than that. For the flames were enormous. No one could be prepared for that. Flames flew in cataract against the cusp of the flame shield, and then sluiced along the paved ground down two opposite channels in the concrete, two underground rivers of flame which poured into the air on either side a hundred feet away, then flew a hundred feet further. Two mighty torches of flame like the wings of a yellow bird of fire flew over a field, covered a field with brilliant yellow bloomings of flame, and in the midst of it, white as a ghost, white as the white of Melville's Moby Dick, white as the shrine of the Madonna in half the churches of the world, this slim angelic mysterious ship of stages rose without sound out of its incarnation of flame and began to ascend slowly into the sky, slow as Melville's Leviathan might swim, slowly as we might swim upward in a dream looking for the air. [pp. 99–100]

The opening and closing of the quotation establish the first connection between pilot and ship. The illusion of levitation associates the rocket with a boyhood dream of Neil Armstrong's first reported by Dora Jean Hamblin in a profile for *Life*, that he could, by holding his breath, hover over the ground. Mailer calls the dream "awesome, prophetic, profound, mysterious, and appropriate" (p. 46). The dream of levitation evokes a spiritual force frozen in lonely, intransitive, and narcissistic self-completeness. It is this self-sufficiency that links the Saturn rocket with Armstrong. Far from being an interchangeable part of the great machine that is NASA, Armstrong embodies the magical will which forms the motive power of the enterprise; it is his dream that all of NASA, and the rocket itself, came into being in order to realize. A case might have been made for Wernher von Braun, whom Mailer calls "the *deus ex machina* of the big boosters" (p. 64), but he disappears into the background of the book after a single early appearance. Armstrong as the captain remains the central character, the soul of the action. And as captain he unavoidably recalls Captain Ahab; Mailer remarks that Armstrong "might need some of the monomania of Captain Ahab" (p. 331) to perform his task.[17]

Armstrong's monomania shows up first as an addiction to the depersonalized language appropriate to his profession. He refuses to speak as if he were emotionally subject to concerns beyond that of his mission. "The heart of astronaut talk, like the heart of all bureaucratic talk," Mailer writes, "was a jargon which could be easily converted to computer programming, a language like Fortran or Cobol or Algol" (p. 25). And yet later in the book Mailer acknowledges that the computer is a means of striking through the mask of phenomenal appearances in order to realize the dream of unitive and comprehensive knowledge. The computerized rocket, then, is a figure not only for the *Pequod*, the floating factory that seeks to capture and destroy the energy of nature, but for the whale-god which has its own powers of annihilation. The whiteness of the rocket is a sign of the invisible force that threatens to swallow the world in fire, as once in water.

In the passage describing liftoff we see that the rocket's whiteness links it not only with the whale but to the Madonna. It is a subtle association, made no doubt with Henry Adams in mind, but pertinent also to Leonardo da Vinci, artist of the Annunciation. The Madonna is a carnal being whose conception enables her to deliver forth into the created world a force that can and will dissolve that world in favor of a new order. Armstrong and Aldrin are sent to the heavens to found this new order on mankind's behalf. To the extent that Mailer is the angel who brings the tidings of this event, he legitimizes his place in the hierarchy; not just as Shakespeare or Melville (whose model was Shakespeare), but as a Gabriel-like figure. In his book he will tell Rocket, crew, NASA, and the public what each *is* and *will be* in the sacred history illuminated by his scriptural sources.

Mailer glories in his envy-inspired rivalry with Armstrong for control of the "rocket-ship." He notes that NASA wanted as their representative "a man like Lindbergh" (p. 327) to ensure public interest in the space program. Armstrong conforms to the Lindbergh model, not only in his bravery and technical expertise – he is a superb pilot – but in his demeanor. By contrast to Armstrong's tight-lipped sense of privacy, Mailer informs the reader about his own life in lurid detail. He is determined to be more *interesting* than any of the astronauts. And yet he wants to beat them on their own ground, too. He includes an encyclopedic survey of the engineering principles underlying the moon launch, on the model of the chapters of cetology in *Moby-Dick*. This data has not endeared the book to most readers, but it is an essential part of Mailer's rescue of the event from the grip of ironists and single-minded statisticians alike. Like Saint-Exupéry, Mailer seeks a language faithful to fact as well as feeling. If the danger in rocket technology is that "the real had become more fantastic than the imagined" (p. 141), that technology has swallowed up the furthest reach of the common man's imaginative thrust, then the sons and daughters of Shakespeare must absorb enough data to keep the imagination from being overwhelmed by unassimilated fact. If the imagination can keep ahead of technology, then machines may follow some imperative besides their own blind accelerated trajectory.

It takes Mailer the whole book to find an alternative to the Futurist fantasy of force and speed that is the Saturn–Apollo rocket. In the last two pages he fixes upon a moon rock as the terminus of his quest. The rock is small and helpless as a baby but imaginable (as least by Mailer; this has not been one of his most admired passages) as a mistress as well, the body of Cynthia brought to earth as poets like Keats had dreamed. As opposed to the "nightmare of sound" (p. 100) that is the rocket, the rock is silent, and Mailer even imagines he can smell it behind double glass partitions. The moon becomes real to him in a way it never could when televised. As he glimpsed the moon from time to time by remote transmission, Mailer had the recurrent and paranoid thought, shared by many around the world, that the whole event had been shot in a TV studio. (A successful film, *Capricorn One*, would later exploit this suspicion.) No longer an envious secret sharer of someone else's propinquity with a new world, Mailer undergoes a seizure of genuine belief. He has still not answered his book's central question – whether the rocket is God's work or the Devil's – but he has made a virtue of irresolution by affirming that earth is the best place for love, even love of the moon. Mailer's ambivalent text becomes another one of those autobiographical statements, like "The Firebombing," that later writers must absorb and annotate in their meditations on the tradition of magical flight – for example, Thomas Pynchon, who uses *Of a Fire on the Moon* as Mailer uses *Moby-Dick*.

Seeing Mailer's book by means of Pynchon's gloss, we can read his piety and affection toward the moon rock in a different way. Now that the rock is entirely confined within protective glass, placed on exhibit like King Kong, an alien creature conquered by the phallic mastery of the WASP, it has been displaced into earth's entropic historical process. To "humanize" it, as Mailer does, may be to degrade and demythify it in precisely the way NASA and the astronauts denude the cosmos of emotional depth by treating it as an object of conquest rather than profound mystery. The capture of the fire on the moon may end by confining the imagination further, leading to further claustrophobia as humanity sees nothing in space that is not itself. The blind thrashing about for liberation would come to resemble a perpetuation of the death agony Mailer observes in contemporary America, and which some of his chapter titles – "A Burial by the Sea," "The Hanging of the Highwayman" – relate to *The Waste Land*. The moon rock may have the effect on the populace that the moonstone did in Wilkie Collins's Victorian novel. It was stolen from the forehead of an icon in a Buddhist temple by English marauders, and its degradation from an object of worship to a piece of loot brings death to the community that possesses it. A curse always comes with stolen property which has once been a portion of the sacred. Every text on the thief of fire, from the first narrative of Prometheus to *Gravity's Rainbow*, knows that much.

Saul Bellow's novel *Mr. Sammler's Planet* (1970) assesses the relation of crime to the moon landing almost as if it were responding to Mailer's claims at the end of *Of a Fire on the Moon*. Artur Sammler, a seventy-year old Polish refugee, broods upon the dark romanticism of the urban outlaw, a figure Mailer has praised in many places as an existential hero. Sammler has been the near-victim of one fantasy of liberation, the Third Reich, which annihilated much of his family. Having been compelled to dig his own grave at a concentration camp and having crawled out of it alive, he is a ghostly, post-apocalyptic intelligence wandering through a metropolis collecting (as his German name suggests) ciphers and portents for an indictment of a doomed culture. His days in New York are dominated by figures who act their will, most strikingly a Negro pickpocket whom Sammler stalks daily when the noble savage boards the bus at Columbus Circle. And while he laments the explosion of libidinous desire in the century, an Apollo mission is in process, raising the question of whether the space program is just one more mad dream inherited by the twentieth century from Verne and Wells, or whether it is a transcendent act that offers escape from labyrinthine cities like New York.

Sammler has not made up his mind, and proves willing to listen to both sides. From his nephew Wallace, who like most of his family enacts a fantasy of liberation – his greatest pleasure is taking voyeurist photos from a low-flying Cessna – Sammler hears news of the moon's popularity as a resort attraction. Wallace is number 512 on the Pan American Airways reservation list for a lunar excursion. A more serious argument for going to the moon is offered by V. Govinda Lal, an Indian scholar who has written a manuscript, *The Future of the Moon*, stolen by Sammler's daughter because she thinks her father can use it for a projected memoir of H. G. Wells. Lal, as his palindromic name suggests, is a Janus figure who looks backward to a rich native culture and forward to a millennium of space colonization that will extend the fruits of world civilization into the cosmos. Lal impresses Sammler with his utopian visions of an ascetic lunar community liberated from the pull of earthly gravity. His extrapolations recall Robert A. Heinlein's happier views of Luna City in his Future History. Though one part of Sammler despises the notion of such a technocracy, the part that because of the Holocaust cannot abide a religion of "rationality and calculation, machinery, planning, technics,"[18] the other part responds favorably to the appeal of an invitation to voyage through space.

Sammler recognizes the scheme of lunar colonization as one that H. G. Wells championed, and in fact discussed with Sammler in the 1930s when they had been companions in Bloomsbury. Though Sammler is not overly fond of Wells's fiction, he grants the author of *The War of the Worlds* truly prophetic powers appropriate to the century. Sammler returns frequently to Wells's satyriasis, so much like the obsessed philandering of his less than angelic niece Angela. Perhaps it is prolonged experience of the demands of the flesh which engender utopian fantasies like The Puritan Tyranny or The Air Dictatorship of *The Shape of Things to Come*, or interstellar colonies more humane and disciplined than earth's. Sammler is at least willing to consider the possibility that Wells's nightmares can direct mankind to some refuge from the instinct for destruction he anatomized in his scientific romances. The trick is to fight fantasy with fantasy, black magic with white magic. If the great crime of the century is the product of a conspiratorial tyranny which fused rational calculation with depraved instinct for destruction, the escape from its memory and its historical imperative may be an equal and opposite fusion of the efficient and fantastic, as promoted by scientist-mystics like Dr. Lal. As for Wells, so for Sammler and Lal, the options in the atomic age are limited. If man is indeed the slave of his curiosity and his passion for technological reproduction, as Freud argued in his study of Leonardo, then safe sublimations represent his only salvation. "Kingdom Come is directly over us and waiting to receive the fragments of a final explosion," Sammler thinks. "Much better the moon" (p. 200).

Bellow has never concealed his distaste for Mailer's style of apocalyptic speech, which he (Bellow) commonly puts into the mouths of his less attractive characters. It is the *rationality* of Sammler and Lal, the elevation of their discourse, rather than any Faustian craving for necromantic powers, that reveals the godlike possibilities of the human intelligence. John Jacob Clayton observes that "the *tone* of the novel is Sammler's real spaceship. I mean simply that the abstract contemplation, the resigned disdain for this turbulent, rebellious world, lift Sammler off, away from the planet."[19] Similarly, Lal presents a human face for NASA which formerly employed him. He is sensitive to the show business aspects of the moonshot and to the crass commercialism represented by Pan American Airways' eagerness to sell the moon. But in the central scene of the novel, the long conversation between the two men after Lal comes to recover his stolen manuscript, Lal argues persuasively that the space flight has a meaning beyond its obvious appeal as a public spectacle. He senses that Sammler is receptive to his ideas, and his ability to overcome the misgivings of one who has so many reasons to suspect the ingenuity of modern technics seems to fuel Lal's eloquence. His discourse expresses the official credo of the space program:

As far as the organizers and engineers are concerned, it is a vast opportunity, but that is not of high theoretical value. Still, at the same time something serious happens within. The soul most certainly feels the grandeur of this achievement. Not to go where one can go may be stunting. I believe the soul feels it, and therefore it is a necessity. It may introduce new sobriety. Naturally the technology will impress minds more than the personalities. The astronauts may not seem so very heroic. More like superchimpanzees. Especially if they do not express themselves beautifully. But after all, this is the function of poets. If any. [pp. 217–8]

If any. As we have seen, Lal's pessimism is well-founded. The engineers have accomplished their appointed task in realizing the archaic fantasy of humankind, but both Sammler and Lal feel the inconclusiveness of the Apollo program for the imagination. Like Rilke's statue of Apollo which articulates the single message, *You must change your life*, it challenges the rising generation to effect some radical change of being.

The cultured Sammler is too old and old-worldly to change. When he looks at a TV image of the astronauts he sees mainly his own ruined face reflected back at him, and remembers that the lobby in which he stands is the one where the black pickpocket exposed his penis to Sammler as a sign of superior potency and a savagery that would not be victimized by the keepers of civilization. So the response must come from the poets, whom Sammler blames for creating the anarchy of modern times. If the moon is indeed a "new Eden" (p. 125), Sammler's most extravagant hope, other sammlers will have to celebrate it, as Renaissance poets did the discovery of the Americas. Columbus restored dreams of Eden by locating primitive cultures – but dreams, Eden, and the primitive cultures alike disappeared in the rapacious onslaught that followed his first footsteps on the virgin land. By confirming that other worlds in our solar system are essentially stone dead, the space voyages have unexpectedly turned greater attention toward spaceship earth. For the time being, earth remains the measure of all things, the end of all our exploring. It is a remarkable paradox in the sacred history of flight that after the most nearly incredible of all ascents, earth, and not the upper air, should be revealed as the nearest paradise.

12. Conclusion: Some Texts of the 1970s

> Deftly they opened the brain of a child,
> And it was full of flying dreams.
> —Stanley Kunitz[1]

THE DESCENT

This book began by citing Mircea Eliade's claim that from its very beginnings *Homo sapiens* defined its distinction from the rest of the Creation in terms of flight. Ascent was not a technical possibility for most of its existence on the planet but a metaphor of self-transcendent acts in the realm of the spirit or imagination. As we have seen, the desire to realize these acts in the body by means of technics nourished a dialectical myth of progress which found its triumphant aeronautical symbol in the first moon landing. No more astonishing event had been seriously imagined until this century than a voyage to the moon; it should have been received by writers with the kind of sublime rhetoric that accompanies a fulfillment of archaic fantasy.

It was skepticism that greeted the first footsteps on the lunar surface, however, for reasons traced throughout this study. Critics of the sacred myth of flight have deplored for centuries the desire to transcend (that is, escape) a condition characterized by stable space-time relationships, ecological cycles, and historicity in the form of inheritable laws, customs, beliefs, and artistic traditions. The effect of transcendence, they have warned, can only be a strengthening of the militant ego, which, free from its former limitations, would constrain nature and humanity alike by means of superior technology. Such was Leonardo da Vinci's prescient warning in his tale of the necromancer. Such was H. G. Wells's vision of the new age in his seminal fiction

The War in the Air. Though the advocates of flight have produced polemics of equal cogency that try to reconcile the evolution of the flying machine with the frailty of planet Earth, the technophobes still hear in their siren voices Frank Ernest Hill's oracular announcement, "Earth is our yesterday. ... Air is today."

Inevitably, Americans have conceived the alternatives in terms of competing frontiers. The traditional form of the frontier is the natural wilderness which began to shape national identity as soon as European colonists proclaimed a manifest destiny for "God's New Israel." The Romantic form of nature-worship succeeding the Puritan model provided writers with persuasive rhetorical figures for resisting the powerful attraction of new machinery. Even Charles A. Lindbergh, by the time of the first moon landing, had reverted to the classic interpretation of the American experience. In his "Message" to *Life* magazine on the fourth of July 1969 he wrote:

I have turned my attention from technological progress to life, from the civilized to the wild. In wildness there is a lens to the past, to the present and to the future, offered to us for the looking – a direction, a successful selection, an awareness of values that confronts us with the need for and the means of our salvation.[2]

The other locus of "salvation" is the high frontier, as Gerard K. O'Neill has memorably named it in his 1977 book of that title. As in Robert Frost's "Kitty Hawk," aviation history is offered as a prelude to a renewed form of the Puritan mission to new worlds beyond the cosmic oceans. The only guarantee of safeguarding the Garden, argue the advocates of space colonization, is an escape from the endangered Garden to which humanity is presently confined.

At least since James Fenimore Cooper's *The Pioneers* (1823), American writers have evaluated the progressivist claims of a technologically-advanced civilization by confronting machine power with wilderness frontier. In the 1970s, a period of ecological consciousness sponsored in part by achievements in space, the same rhetorical strategy has prevailed. Norman Mailer sets his novel of 1967, *Why Are We in Vietnam?*, in the ultimate Western frontier as a means of reviving Cooper's forebodings about man's stewardship over the lower creation. He uses the pursuit of Alaskan bears by hunters in helicopters as a paradigm of the overkill practiced in modern warfare. The weaponry carried by the hunters, catalogued at immense and loving length by the crazed narrator D. J., serves the same purpose:

> Maybe a professional hunter takes pride in dropping an animal by picking him off in a vital spot – but I like the feeling that if I miss a vital area I still can count on the big impact, shock! it's like aerial bombardment in the last Big War.[3]

The helicopter is wrenched into association with ballistic monstrosities and acts of firebombing. The bear serves Mailer as King Kong does Pynchon in *Gravity's Rainbow*, as a creaturely figure of the eternal victim, crucified by an all-powerful and all-predatory imperial air power. Readers of Mailer's novel better understood the imagery of helicopters and bombers on the nightly news after 1967, for he had imagined the reality Vietnam became. In turn, Mailer's critique of the Apollo mission in *Of a Fire on the Moon* derives from his war-related suspicions about the possession of fire/power by a nation that had recently chosen Lyndon Johnson and Richard Nixon as its supreme leaders.

Repeated views of aerial bombardment in Vietnam darkened the collective psyche, and therefore the literary imagination, because they recalled from deep mental sources the horrific imagery of World War II, and especially of the atomic bombings upon other Oriental targets. All figures of ascent are liable to take on a demonic quality given such models, even the bird. In English poet Ted Hughes's volume of 1970, *Crow*, the bird of bad omen is inflated into a cruel, even apocalyptic type of the modern. In "The Black Beast," for example, Crow flies through the world destroying living things in his quest for the Satanic entity he calls "the black beast." As in the story of King Kong, the quester proves to be the real beast; his persistent Crusade to annihilate the Other, and his power to do so by virtue of his wings, is unceasing. The final effect can be seen in another poem, "King of Carrion," in which Crow rules over a world he has emptied of life.[4] As in Robinson Jeffers's poem "Shiva," already discussed, Crow becomes a figure of Man-as-Mass-Murdering-Bird. Similarly, Robert Bly's *The Teeth Mother Naked at Last*, a long poem about the bombings in Vietnam, begins with these lines:

Massive engines lift beautifully from the deck.
Wings appear over the trees, wings with eight hundred rivets.

Engines burning a thousand gallons a minute sweep over the
huts with dirt floors.

The chickens feel the new fear deep in the pits of their beaks.[5]

What causes human beings to mimic among themselves the
interspecific predation of birdlife? In an essay that follows Bly's
poem in the volume *Sleepers Joining Hands* (1973), he argues that
a figure for destructive impulses in the unconscious, variously
called The Death Mother, The Stone Mother, and The Teeth
Mother, rules the psyches of Western males. Unlike the Good
Mother, who encourages "those parts in us that are linked with
music, solitude, water, and trees," The Death Mother sponsors
malignant ambition, envy, and lust for power – the qualities of
mind and soul that make humans aspire beyond their natural
element of earth. Thus the concluding lines of the poem balance
the desire to ascend with the historical necessity of mortifying
that desire by a sacrificial gesture: "Let us drive cars / up / the
light beams / to the stars ... // And return to earth crouched
inside the drop of sweat / that falls / from the chin of the
Protestant tied in the fire."

The opposition of air and earth, rendered as an Oedipal
struggle of generations, is dramatized in another important book
of the 1970s, Kenneth Brower's *The Starship and the Canoe* (1978),
which describes the contrary destinies of Freeman Dyson, an
astrophysicist obsessed with space colonization, and his son
George, who explores the Pacific Northwest with considerably
more natural piety than Mailer's maniacal hunters. Opposite in
most ways, father and son are linked by their fascination for
large engineering projects. Freeman Dyson, as he chronicles in
his autobiography *Disturbing the Universe* (1979), had worked with
J. Robert Oppenheimer after the war at The Institute for
Advanced Study at Princeton, in the light (or shadow) of the
century's most ambitious engineering project. In revulsion at
the Bomb, and at his own participation in the (British) Bomber
Command during World War II, Dyson began work on the Orion
Project in the 1950s. For this early and finally unsuccessful entry

in the American space program, some architects of the hydrogen bomb joined with other scientists to test the feasibility of sending a giant spaceship to the asteroids between Mars and Jupiter, where life could be sustained because of the presence of water. The ship would be propelled not by liquid fuel but by the timed explosions of hydrogen bombs contained in its rear – an idea that Robert A. Heinlein and other science-fiction writers had used in their search for some credible means of providing enough thrust to send a manned ship into and beyond the solar system in a reasonable period of time. As in Heinlein's fiction, so in real life the project had its expiatory dimension. By Daedalean manufacture, the weapon that most endangered human survival would now preserve the race, when "Malthusian pressures" or nuclear war made the earth unlivable. Brower quotes from one of Dyson's scientific papers of the period:

> The emigration into distant parts of the solar system of a substantial number of people would make our species as a whole invulnerable. A nuclear holocaust on Earth would still be an unspeakable tragedy, and might still wipe out ninety-nine percent of our numbers. But the one percent who had dispersed themselves could not be wiped out simultaneously by any man-made catastrophe, and they would remain to carry on the promise of our destiny.[6]

The promise of our destiny. Once again, the flying machine is proposed as the means toward preserving an elect few from the destruction incurred by the Caesars who abuse their power. Dyson's figure for the spaceship, needless to say, is Noah's Ark.

An ark of a different kind is being constructed by George Dyson, and Brower moves from one story to another throughout the book to reveal significant correspondences between the two inventions. George is building the largest kayak ever made, for exploration of the Northwest. In imitation of native American methods but using modern materials, George proposes to undertake his errand into the wilderness as another kind of life-saving maneuver. It is the human spirit, the specifically nature-nurtured spirit, that he wants to enlarge by participation with a biosphere of which his father's imagined artificial environment will only be a meager simulacrum. On his test journeys north he encounters experiences that reflect those his father believes to be uniquely celestial. Even the harmonious music of the spheres is echoed on earth during an evening when George is moved to rapture by the eerie howling of wolves and what seems the answering song of offshore whales. If the father seeks to harness the full energy of the Creation to shoot himself away from the earth, George locates the richest source of energy by penetrating further into the mysteries of the far western Garden.

In these and many other works of the 1970s the memory of aerial bombardment seems to valorize an imagery of containment and descent. "Continue to walk in the world. Yes, love it!" is the message of Robert Penn Warren's long poem *Audubon: A Vision* (1970), which proposes the nineteenth-century artist–naturalist as a cultural model superior to contemporary figures who walk on the moon.[7] Though Audubon murdered birds in great numbers, he did so in order to preserve them in the imagination by his realistic art. Writers of the 1970s reenact this sacrificial rite, canonizing as new Scripture those texts which seek to defend the Leda-like world's body from aerial violation.

THE ASCENT

The paradox of the literature of flight, as we have seen, is that the predictable response to fears of aerial violation is almost always a compensatory wish-fantasy of flight. C. G. Jung notes in his analysis of the UFO phenomenon that large numbers of people began spotting flying saucers at the same time nuclear missiles became household words and that public opinion seemed to be divided as to whether the aliens intended to save mankind from itself or annihilate it in a latter-day war of the worlds.[8] The increasing sophistication of nuclear weapons in our own time and the proliferation of scenarios about war in space have exposed the UFOs for the allegorical figures they clearly were all along. The fact is that space, once the realm of promise for Renaissance visionaries, is a frontier destined to be settled by machines. The number of recent recommendations for the military use of space suggests that it may become more of a battlefield for future generations than a safe passageway out of battle. If flight is to be redeemed, then, if the *transcendent* mode is to seize its prerogative from the mode of *engagement*, alternative structures of ascent must be located and popularized.

The reader who has proceeded this far will not be surprised to hear that the model for recent appreciations of ascent is Romantic myth. Nostalgia for the origins of the flying machine is an important mode in such works, and acts to strengthen the positive connection between the speaker and the upper air. Dick Allen brings into conjunction his poetic impulse and the early days of aviation:

> I am
> the first pilot from Boston.
> Seeing a boy in a field,
> I wave from the cockpit,
> dip low my wings.
> *Aeroplanes.*
>   They called them
> crosses in the sky.[9]

And in "The Poem of Flight," the first poem in the volume *One for the Rose* (1981), Philip Levine returns in fancy to Kitty Hawk as a preparation for the flights of imagination to be performed later in the volume:

> I would be
> the original pilot, thirty-one, bare-headed,
> my curly brown hair cut short and tinged
> with blood from a wounded left hand
> that must be attended to. Only an hour
> before it was a usual summer morning,
> warm and calm, in North Carolina,
> and the two hectic brothers had laid aside
> their bicycles and were busily assembling
> the struts, wires, strings, and cranking
> over the tiny engine. I faced the wind,
> a cigarette in one hand, a map of creation
> in the other. Silently, I watch my hand
> disappear into the white gauze the lady
> turns and turns. I am the first to fly.[10]

I am the first; that is the passionate cry of both poets as they turn back longingly to the Edenic time when God made his energies visible by means of sportive signs in the sky. By recovering hopeful images of ascent from the ceremonial "firsts" of aviation history, the nostalgic mode recreates an American Adam appropriate to the twentieth century.

A daring and sophisticated use of the retrospective mode is Tom Wolfe's best-selling chronicle of 1979, *The Right Stuff*. Wolfe's rhetorical strategy is the use of sacred history to construe the Mercury astronauts as heirs of the romance tradition. Throughout the book he compares them to the single champions a nation put forward to fight the champions of the enemy. Wolfe's chief analogy is David and Goliath, and when John Glenn emerges as the first among equals he is constantly compared to David as the savior of the new Israel. (Glenn's political ambitions serve Wolfe considerably, as when he portrays Glenn's courtship of John Kennedy by reference to David's wooing of Saul.) Glenn is "The Presbyterian Pilot," one of "the elect and the anointed" who, unlike the other Mercury astronauts – addicted as they are to the mentality of "Flying and Drinking, Drinking and Driving" – maintains himself as a pure image of the uncorrupted knight of the air. Glenn possesses the manly courage and sense of honor Wolfe attributes to Saint-Exupéry. Furthermore, Glenn constantly identified himself with his charismatic predecessors. He spoke of the Wright brothers at his first press conference; he meditated in *We Seven* on the similarities and differences between himself and Lindbergh. If the other astronauts seemed to savor most their celebrity status, Glenn, who was also the most successful war pilot, seemed to appreciate the historical and cultural significance of his role most keenly.

Wolfe acknowledges that Glenn's piety and sense of mission struck a responsive chord in the American psyche. "People came up to him as if they knew him personally and loved him. *He is my protector. He risked his life and challenged the Russians in the heavens for me.* They adored him so much it would have been hard for him to brush past them, even had he been that sort of disposition."[11] If such obvious comparisons to Jesus seem mock-Scriptural playfulness, Wolfe is also quite serious about establishing the mood of the time as a pre-apocalyptic one. Sputnik and the Vostok sequence heralded, according to Speaker of the House John McCormack, the possibility of "national extinction." Glenn and the other six champions were the latest incarnations of the knights who would protect the holy land – call it Camelot or Canaan – from violation.

The chief irony of Wolfe's book is the immense gap between this superhuman, indeed Christic sense of mission, and the ludicrous impotence of the astronauts once they enter the flying machine itself. Strapped into their tiny capsules, they have no more use for their talents than the chimpanzees who test fly the same spacecraft. "Spam in a can" is their own derisive term for their role in the Mercury flights. Moreover, what little they can do while in orbit has been so thoroughly practiced in "desensitizing" training sessions that the real flight has no more reality than the simulation. The astronauts gradually come to resemble the "zombies" or non-pilots whom they originally ridiculed. By contrast, Wolfe's subplot tells of the development of the supersonic jets at Edwards Air Force Base, where the pilots do indeed fly their own machines, obeying the traditional rules and enjoying the traditional pride of the pilot's craft. Chuck Yeager, the first man to break the sound barrier, emerges as the authentic hero of Wolfe's account; he is a man who takes greater risks for considerably less publicity, who harbors no professional ambitions except to fly a faster and better jet. On him, not on media-created celebrities like Glenn and (by implication) Armstrong, falls the mantle of glory worn by great solo pilots of the past. Like them he is privileged to experience viscerally the ecstasy of ascent.

Another work of 1979, J. G. Ballard's novel *The Unlimited Dream Company*, may provide the most useful paradigm for the diverse traditions studied in this book. Set in England, it tells of a would-be aviator, significantly named Blake, who is obsessed by Leonardo's dream of man-powered flight. Constantly tortured into dementia and "compulsive role-playing" by inward urgings toward the infinite, he dresses as a pilot and fantasizes a messianic place for himself in the sacred history of aeronautics: "Already I was planning the world's first circumnavigation, and saw myself as the Lindbergh and Saint-Exupéry of man-powered flight."[12] Blake steals a Cessna and flies toward Shepperton, site of the film studios, where he sees a World War I aviation film being made. It is a cunning allusion. On the ground, Art is going about its mimetic business, reiterating history's violent failures for the titillation of the masses. Blake comes to release those sleepers in Plato's cave from their nostalgia for a debased aerial spectacle.

He crash-lands in a river, and somehow pulls himself from the submerged plane – though we learn later that it is his spirit-self that exited, leaving his physical self behind. (The obvious source is the two John Miltons, mortal and immortal, in William Blake's *Milton*.) He becomes the favorite of a representative group in the community, including the beautiful Miriam St. Cloud. In the world of Shepperton he becomes a Pan figure offering salvation from the role-playing each person undergoes in the false and fallen world of appearances. Especially Father Wingate, the local curate, responds to Blake's presence: "Now I was the returning prodigal, the young flying priest, not only his son fallen from the sky but his successor" (pp. 75–76). The major part of the narrative follows Blake as he gradually takes on the identity of all living things in preparation for a final consummation of desire in the form of a great ascent. Sexuality is the metaphor for his prolific union with bird, beast, flower, and person. There is nothing immediately attractive about Blake's efforts; in fact Ballard reveals them as apparently sadistic, outrageous and violent. Ballard is clearly relying on works by modern authors who recommend a shocking union of heaven and hell. Yeats's monstrous Swan certainly presides in Blake's fevered imagination: "Like a great bird, I had mated and fed myself on the wing. Could I feed on the people of this town, use their eyes and tongues, their minds and sexes, to construct a flying machine that would carry me away? I was almost sure now that my powers were limitless, that I was capable of anything I wished to imagine" (p. 159). He introjects living things into his body, enabling his ascent, until he meets a nemesis named Stark, a hunter who despoils the dream by shooting Blake in the local church. (Stark, we remember, is the plume hunter who desecrates the bird spirit Ornis in Percy Mackaye's masque, *Sanctuary*.) Stark represents the eternal Ancient Mariner, whose vindictive envy for the flying life causes him to shoot down the Christic bird. Blake is then buried in a tomb, where he gathers strength from the willing sacrifice of small creatures. He awakens like his avatars the vegetation gods of myth, and rises with the townspeople of Shepperton, "an immense aerial congregation." In the process he "takes" Stark into his body, a symbolic dissolution of the pathology of envy which has prevented imaginative flight by erecting hostile rivalries between the earthbound and the aerial. In "wedding" Blake each living thing rejoins "the great bird of which we were all part" (p. 237). Blake dresses Miriam, his Jerusalem, or Asia figure, with the wings of an albatross, to signify the ultimate redemption of the holy Other which fallen man has always feared and plundered. The novel ends with a vision of Parousia like that of the Book of Revelation:

> Already I saw us rising into the air – fathers, mothers, and their children – our ascending flights swaying across the surface of the earth, benign tornados hanging from the canopy of the universe, celebrating the last marriage of the animate and inanimate, of the living and the dead. [pp. 237–8]

The reader is free to think that such a vision is the product of mental derangement, and that Ballard has satirized the impulse to transfigure the Creation into the Romantic Image of a flying machine. My own reading is that Ballard, unlike the American authors who became suspicious of the apocalyptic mode, offers his paradigm of the "unlimited dream" in the spirit of (William) Blake himself.

What equivalent act of apotheosis is history likely to offer, now that Ballard and other fantasists have so entirely telescoped the technology of this century into the primitive/Christian dream of universal resurrection? Freeman Dyson hypothesizes that after the achievements of aviation and space technology, "the third romantic age will see little model sailboats spreading their wings to the sun in space."[13] These "heliogyros" are (once again!) attempts to mimic the flight of birds on the model of Leonardo's earliest designs. One-person airplanes like the pedal-driven *Gossamer Albatross* or the smaller-scale "ultralight" have revived archaic fantasies of the *volo strumentale*. Unlike the gigantism of the technological sublime, these modest artifacts evoke a sense of birdlike play and vivifying participation with the circumambient universe. William Wharton's novel *Birdy* (1978) and James Dickey's long poem "Reincarnation (II)" (1967) are certainly the literary masterpieces of this mode, and Richard Bach's novel *Jonathan Livingston Seagull* (1970) its most popular rendering to date.

The other line of force is what Dyson calls "the greening of the galaxy." Devotees of space colonization in the generation bred on science fiction and on film romances like *Star Wars, Close Encounters of the Third Kind, Star Trek, Superman*, and *E.T.* are likely to have less trouble imagining a superplanetary destiny than those (like myself) who reached maturity in the period bounded by Hiroshima and the first landing at Tranquility Base. For them the sacred history of aviation is not finished, nor can it be entirely displaced into the realm of literature. This is a generation born after the 1962 launching of Telstar, the first artificial communication satellite. First proposed in a technical paper of 1945 by Arthur C. Clarke and subsequently featured in innumerable science fictions as a means of achieving the psychic proximity required for a planetary or species identity, this form of the flying machine, like its predecessors and such later inventions as the Space Shuttle and the Hubble Space Telescope promise the possibility of global co-operation in advancing human destiny further into the cosmos. Treatises on space colonization like Gerard K. O'Neill's *The High Frontier* and *2081: A Hopeful View of the Human Future* are typical of the scenarios that will nourish not only the imaginative literature but the actual history of the 21st century.

Flight is an area of human interest, or obsession, in which the two cultures are bonded together like Siamese twins. The dialectical interaction of art and science in the field of aerial technology is the social dynamics from which human destiny will take its ultimate form. In the first century of flight the making of complex and military hardware has thrived at the expense of playful and peaceful designs. If there is an antidote to this dangerous situation it lies in the wonder and optimism that welcomed the flying machine in earlier centuries and in the first decades of this century, and which has survived every shock of aerial outrage. Writers unhappy with existing forms of air- and space-crafts need to conceive ideal machines that reconcile the claims of earth and air. In turn, engineers will go on articulating the wings placed in their imagination, and what they accomplish will provoke new scripture to inspire and restrain them. In this sense, the seemingly opposed epigraphs of this book, from Shelley and Pynchon, shade into a common vision that compels assent.

Notes

1. INTRODUCTION

1. See *The Complete Works of Ralph Waldo Emerson* (Boston and New York: Houghton, Mifflin, 1887), IX (*Poems*), p. 283.
2. Mircea Eliade, *Myths, Dreams and Mysteries*, tr. Philip Mairet (New York: Harper Torchbooks, 1967), p. 106.
3. Alberto Santos-Dumont, *My Airships: The Story of My Life* (London: Grant Richards, 1904), p. 328.
4. *The Chanute-Mouillard Correspondence, April 16, 1890 to May 20, 1897*, tr. Eugene Moritz and M. Louise Kraus; ed. Juliette Bevo-Higgins (Lancaster, PA: Privately printed, 1962), pp. 34, 75, 228.
5. *The Papers of Wilbur and Orville Wright*, ed. Marvin W. McFarland (New York: McGraw-Hill Book Co., 1953), II, 1168–9. Italics added.
6. From his poem, "To a Locomotive in Winter."
7. See the discussion of this work in H. G. Schenk, *The Mind of the European Romantics: An Essay in Cultural History* (London: Constable, 1966), pp. 201–2.
8. Lynn White, Jr., *Machina ex Deo: Essays in the Dynamism of Western Culture* (Cambridge, Mass: MIT Press, 1968), p. 50.
9. Jean-Jacques Rousseau, *Le Nouveau Dédale* (Pasadena: The Institute of Aeronautical History, 1950), p. 6 of French text.
10. Andrew Lang, *The Mark of Cain* (Bristol: J. W. Arrowsmith, 1886), p. 159.
11. *The Papers of Wilbur and Orville Wright*, II, 1042, 979, 1019. Italics mine.
12. Northrop Frye, *The Great Code: The Bible and Literature* (New York: Harcourt Brace Jovanovich, 1982), p. 106.
13. Norman Mailer, *Of a Fire on the Moon* (Boston: Little, Brown, 1970), p. 141.
14. Cecil Lewis, *Sagittarius Rising* (London: Peter Davies, 1936), p. 57.
15. Robert Beum, "Literature and *Machinisme*," *The Sewanee Review*, LXXXVI: 2 (Spring 1978), p. 231.

2. LEONARDO DA VINCI AND THE MODERN CENTURY

1. Rachel Annand Taylor, *Leonardo the Florentine: A Study in Personality* (New York and London: Harper and Brothers, 1928), p. 34.
2. Elbert Hubbard, *Leonardo*, in the series *Little Journeys to the Homes of Eminent Artists* (East Aurora, N.Y.: The Roycrofters, 1902), p. 30.

3. Emil Ludwig, *Genius and Character*, tr. Kenneth Burke (New York: Harcourt, Brace, 1927), p. 152.

4. Paul Valéry, *Leonardo, Poe, Mallarmé*, Volume 8 of *The Collected Works of Paul Valéry* (Princeton: Princeton University Press, 1972), p. 135. An excellent comparison of Valéry's and Freud's approaches to Leonardo is Roger Shattuck, "The Tortoise and the Hare: A Study of Valéry, Freud, and Leonardo da Vinci," *Leonardo da Vinci: Aspects of the Renaissance Genius*, ed. Morris Philipson (New York: George Braziller, 1966). It is almost certainly Valéry's early essay that inspired T. S. Eliot to praise Leonardo as the type of the classicist: "He lived in no fairyland, but his mind went out and became a part of things." See *The Sacred Wood* (1920; London: Methuen and Co., 1928), p. 27.

5. Edward MacCurdy, *The Mind of Leonardo da Vinci* (1928; New York: Dodd, Mead & Co., 1940), p. 279.

6. *The Notebooks of Leonardo da Vinci*, ed. Edward MacCurdy (New York: George Braziller, 1955), p. 67. MacCurdy's translation is "Our body is subject to heaven, and heaven is subject to the spirit," but I have used the more common and commonsensical rendering of this sentence.

7. Ernst Cassirer, *The Individual and the Cosmos in Renaissance Philosophy* (1927; New York: Harper Torchbooks, 1964), p. 168.

8. Karl Jaspers, *Leonardo, Descartes, Max Weber* (1953; London: Routledge & Kegan Paul, 1965), p. 14.

9. Leonardo da Vinci, *Treatise on Painting*, tr. A. Philip McMahon (Princeton: Princeton University Press, 1956), I, 113.

10. Raymond S. Stites, *The Sublimations of Leonardo da Vinci* (City of Washington: Smithsonian Institution Press, 1970), p. 61.

11. *Marinetti: Selected Writings*, ed. R. W. Flint (New York: Farrar, Straus and Giroux, 1972), pp. 67, 41.

12. Clive Hart, *The Dream of Flight: Aeronautics from Classical Times to the Renaissance* (New York: Winchester Press, 1972), pp. 52–9.

13. Niccolò Machiavelli, *The Prince* and *The Discourses* (New York: The Modern Library, 1940), p. 53.

14. *Selected Writings of Francis Bacon*, ed. Hugh G. Dick (New York: The Modern Library, 1955), p. 581.

15. Carlo Pedretti, *Leonardo: A Study in Chronology and Style* (Berkeley and Los Angeles: University of California Press, 1973), p. 87.

16. Ritchie Calder, *Leonardo and the Age of the Eye* (New York: Simon and Schuster, 1970), p. 222. Calder's work is the best study of the relation between aerial perspective in painting, a significant subject in Leonardo's *Treatise*, and Leonardo's obsession with flight.

17. A fragment from a proposed treatise on war, cited in *Leonardo da Vinci*, memorial edition of the Leonardo Exposition in Milan, 1938 (New York: Reynal and Co., 1956), p. 283.

18. Baldassare Castiglione, *The Book of the Courtier* (London: J. M. Dent & Sons, 1956), p. 113.

19. Kenneth Clark, *Leonardo da Vinci: An Account of His Development as an Artist* (Cambridge: The University Press, 1939), p. 123.

20. *The Works of Théophile Gautier*, ed. E. C. de Sumichrast (Boston and New York: C. T. Brainard Publishing Co., 1901), V, 270. Perhaps Goethe has Leonardo's work in mind when Homunculus describes Faust's dream of Leda,

"composed and terror-free … with proud and womanly delight" (tr. Bayard Taylor). See *Faust*, Part II, Act II, 6903–20. A good contrast in Romantic (graphic) art is the dejected Leda of Blake's *Jerusalem*, Plate 71.

21. J. B. S. Haldane, *Daedalus, or Science and the Future* (New York: E. P. Dutton and Co., 1924), p. 87.

22. H. G. Wells, *The Shape of Things to Come* (1933; New York: The Macmillan Co., 1936), p. 362.

23. W. B. Yeats, *A Vision* (New York: The Macmillan Co., 1956), pp. 293, 52–3.

24. Paul Valéry, *History and Politics*, Volume 10 of *The Collected Works of Paul Valéry*, p. 29.

3. BIRDS WITH A HUMAN FACE

1. Louis Blériot, "Atlantic Monoplanes of Tomorrow," *The Graphic*, 3 September 1927, p. 347.

2. From "Ode to the Cuckoo," *The Works of Michael Bruce*, ed. Alexander B. Grosart (Edinburgh: William Oliphant and Co., 1865), p. 124.

3. From the essay "Circles." *The Complete Works of Ralph Waldo Emerson* (Boston: Houghton Mifflin Co., 1903), II, 301.

4. *The Dialogues of Plato*, ed. Benjamin Jowett (New York: Random House, 1937), I, 251.

5. Melanie Klein, *Envy and Gratitude: A Study of Unconscious Sources* (London: Tavistock Publications Ltd., 1957), p. 11.

6. *Shelley's Prose*, ed. David Lee Clark (Albuquerque: University of New Mexico Press, 1954), pp. 291–2.

7. From Cayley's essay of 1809, "On Aerial Navigation," reprinted in J. Laurence Pritchard, *Sir George Cayley* (London: Max Parrish, 1961), pp. 226, 240–1.

8. William Paley, *Natural Theology, or Evidences and Attributes of the Deity collected from the Appearances of Nature* (New York: 1843), p. 205.

9. Robert Paltock, *The Life and Adventures of Peter Wilkins*, ed. Christopher Bentley (London: Oxford University Press, 1973), p. 107.

10. Marshall McLuhan, *The Mechanical Bride: Folklore of Industrial Man* (New York: The Vanguard Press, 1951), p. 22.

11. Martin Farquhar Tupper, "A Flight Upon Flying," *Ainsworth's Magazine* (London: Hugh Cunningham, 1842), I, 19.

12. William Wordsworth, *Home at Grasmere*, ed. Beth Darlington (Ithaca: Cornell University Press, 1977), p. 55.

13. *The Poetical Works of Howitt, Milman, and Keats* (Philadelphia: Crissy and Markley, n.d.), p. 124.

14. James Grahame, *The Birds of Scotland, with Other Poems* (Edinburgh: William Blackwood, 1806), p. 3.

15. William John Courthope, *The Paradise of Birds* (1870; London: Macmillan and Co., 1896), pp. 80, 84–5.

16. From "A Drama of Exile" (1844), *The Complete Poetical Works of Elizabeth Barrett Browning* (Boston: Houghton Mifflin, 1900), p. 72.

17. The phrases derive respectively from poems by James Thomson, Charles Mackay, Robert Burns, and Felicia Hemans. A useful compendium of such quotations is Phil Robinson, *The Poets' Birds* (London: Chatto and Windus, 1883).

18. *The Poetical Works of Howitt, Milman, and Keats*, p. 136.

19. Percy Mackaye, *Sanctuary: A Bird Masque* (New York: Frederick A. Stokes Co., 1914), p. 56.

4. WELLS AND *THE WAR IN THE AIR*

1. *The Works of H. G. Wells*, Atlantic Edition (London: T. Fisher Unwin, 1926), XX, 416. All quotations from Wells are taken from this edition.

2. See *La Conquête De L'Air, vue par l'Image (1496–1909)*, ed. John Grand-Carteret and Leo Delteil (Paris: Librarie des Annales, 1911), p. 32.

3. Norman and Jeanne Mackenzie, *H. G. Wells* (New York: Simon and Schuster, 1973), p. 24.

4. *Works of Jules Verne*, ed. Charles F. Horne (New York: Vincent Parke and Co., 1911), XIV, 200. For other possible sources, see Chapter 4, "From Jules Verne to H. G. Wells," of I. F. Clarke, *The Pattern of Expectation 1644–2001* (New York: Basic Books, 1979), and the whole of W. Warren Wager, *Terminal Visions* (Bloomington: Indiana University Press, 1982).

5. Cited in I. F. Clarke, *Voices Prophesying War, 1763–1984* (New York: Oxford University Press, 1966), p. 87. Italics added.

6. Cited in Captain Joseph Morris, *The German Air Raids on Great Britain 1914–1918* (London: Sampson Low, Marston and Co., n.d.), p. 11.

7. *War Verse*, ed. Frank Foxcroft (New York: Thomas Y. Crowell Co., 1918), p. 109. See also Laurence Binyon, "The Zeppelin," *The Cause: Poems of the War* (London: Elkin Mathews, 1918), p. 83; and Maurice Baring's parody of Blake beginning "Zeppelin, Zeppelin, burning bright" in *Flying Corps Headquarters* (1920; rpt. London: William Heinemann, 1930), pp. 148–9. Baring quotes the poem from a diary he kept during wartime.

8. *The Collected Letters of D. H. Lawrence*, ed. Harry T. Moore (New York: The Viking Press, 1962), I, 366. Ironically, Wells himself came to ridicule the airship during World War I, apparently because it proved so vulnerable to attack by airplanes. See H. G. Wells, *Italy, France and Britain at War* (New York: Macmillan, 1917), pp. 175–6.

9. V. Sackville-West, *Grand Canyon* (New York: Doubleday, Doran and Co., 1942), p. 292.

10. William Rose Benét, *With Wings as Eagles: Poems and Ballads of the Air* (New York: Dodd, Mead & Co., 1940), pp. 7, 10.

5. "TUMULT IN THE CLOUDS": THE FLYING MACHINE AND THE GREAT CRUSADE

1. *The Education of Henry Adams* (Boston: Houghton Mifflin, 1961), p. 496.

2. W. H. Berry, *Aircraft in War and Commerce* (New York: George Doran, 1918), pp. 228–30, 271.

3. *The Journal of Arnold Bennett* (New York: Garden City Publishing Co., 1933), p. 636 (entry of 10 October 1917). Wells warned that if the world did not organize for peace after the war, "We shall get air offensives . . . that will drive people mad by the thousand." See *In the Fourth Year* (New York: Macmillan, 1918), pp. 108–9.

4. Arnold Bennett, *The Pretty Lady* (New York: George Doran Co., 1918), pp. 230–1. As one might expect from a novel being written during the events it describes, many of the scenes of air raids are based on Bennett's own experiences. See for example the descriptions in his *Journal* on pp. 568 (15 Sept. 1915), 572 (18 Oct. 1915), 585 (1 April 1916), and 641 (19 Dec. 1917).

5. *Rudyard Kipling's Verse*, Definitive Edition (New York: Doubleday, 1943), p. 387.

6. Lt. Col. William A. Bishop, *Winged Warfare*, ed. Stanley M. Ulanoff (New York: Doubleday, 1967), p. 21. In William Faulkner's short story, "Ad Astra," the captured German aviator says, "Then it iss 1916. I see by the paper how the cadet iss killed by your Bishop . . . that good man." *Collected Stories of William Faulkner* (New York: Random House, 1950), p. 419. That Bishop continues to interest a modern audience is suggested by the success of a recent musical biography, *Billy Bishop Goes to War*, by John Gray and Eric Peterson. A film of the play has been shown repeatedly on Canadian television.

7. Paul Bewsher, *The Bombing of Bruges* (London: Hodder and Stoughton, 1918).

8. Paul Bewsher, *'Green Balls': The Adventures of a Night Bomber* (Edinburgh: William Blackwood and Sons, 1919), pp. 78–9.

9. *The Education of Henry Adams*, p. 476.

10. David Lloyd George, *The Great Crusade: Extracts from Speeches Delivered During the War* (New York: George H. Doran, 1918), p. 212.

11. W. H. Auden, *Forewords and Afterwords* (New York: Random House, 1973), p. 16. See also the classicizing of wartime pilots in Walter Raleigh, *The War in the Air: Being the Story of the Part Played in the Great War by the Royal Air Force* (Oxford: The Clarendon Press, 1922), I, 14.

12. Cecil Lewis, *Sagittarius Rising* (London: Peter Davies, 1936), p. 45.

13. *The Poems of W. B. Yeats*, edited by Richard J. Finneran (New York: Macmillan, 1983), p. 142.

14. Sir Gordon Taylor, *Sopwith Scout 7309* (London: Cassell, 1968), p. 57.

15. The poem is available in *The Variorum Edition of the Poems of W. B. Yeats*, ed. Peter Alt and Russell K. Anspach (New York: Macmillan, 1957), p. 71.

6. LINDBERGH IN 1927: THE RESPONSE OF POETS TO THE POEM OF FACT

1. Richard J. Beamish, *The Boy's Story of Lindbergh* (Philadelphia: John C. Winston, 1928), p. 22.

2. Cited in Charles A. Lindbergh, *"WE"* (New York: G. P. Putnam's Sons, 1927), p. 311. In the introduction to *"WE"* Myron T. Herrick, then Ambassador to France, remarks, "I feel in every fibre of my being that Lindbergh's landing

here marks one of the supreme moments in the history of America and France, and the faith we have had in the deciding power of spiritual things is strengthened by every circumstance of his journey, by all his acts after landing, and by the electrical effect which ran like some religious emotion through a whole vast population. The 'Spirit of St. Louis' was to the French people another sign come out of the sky – a sign which bore the promise that all would be well between them and us" (p. 8).

3. James E. West, *The Lone Scout of the Sky* (Philadelphia: Published for the Boy Scouts of America by John C. Winston, 1928), p. 49.

4. *The Short Fiction of Edgar Allan Poe*, ed. Stuart and Susan Levine (Indianapolis: The Bobbs-Merrill Co., 1976), p. 557.

5. I. A. Richards, *Poetries and Sciences* (New York: W. W. Norton, 1970), p. 20.

6. *The Standard Edition of the Complete Psychological Works of Sigmund Freud*, ed. James Strachey (London: The Hogarth Press and The Institute of Psycho-Analysis, 1964), XI, 126.

7. Charles A. Lindbergh, *The Spirit of St. Louis* (New York: Charles Scribner's Sons, 1953), p. 403.

8. Ibid., p. 262.

9. Charles Vale (pseud. for Arthur Hooley), ed., *The Spirit of St. Louis* (New York: Doran, 1927), p. vi.

10. Cited in West, *Lone Scout*, p. 23.

11. Harriet Monroe, *Poets and Their Art* (New York: Macmillan, 1926), pp. 202–7.

12. See George Buchanan Fife, *Lindbergh* (New York: The World Syndicate, 1927), p. 179.

13. Cited by John William Ward, "The Meaning of Lindbergh's Flight," *American Quarterly*, 10:1 (Spring 1958), 13. For poems comparing Lindbergh to Icarus, see *The Spirit of St. Louis*, pp. 22, 25, 152, 172, 204.

14. *The Wartime Journals of Charles A. Lindbergh* (New York: Harcourt, Brace Jovanovich, 1970), p. 450.

15. Anne Morrow Lindbergh gives this capsule definition of the phrase "The Wave of the Future" in *War Within and Without: Diaries and Letters of Anne Morrow Lindbergh, 1939–1944* (New York: Harcourt Brace Jovanovich, 1980), p. 174.

7. ORIGINS: SOME VERSIONS OF KITTY HAWK

1. *Shadows of the Sun: The Diaries of Harry Crosby*, ed. Edward Germain (Santa Barbara: Black Sparrow, 1977), p. 146.

2. Lindsay remarks, "If it is the conviction of serious minds that the mass of men shall never again see pictures out of Heaven except through such mediums as the kinetoscope lens, let all the higher forces of our land courageously lay hold upon this thing that saves us from spiritual blindness." *The Art of the Moving Picture* (2nd ed., 1922; rpt. New York: Liveright, 1970), p. 299. See my discussion in "The American Poet at the Movies: A Life and Times," *The Centennial Review*, XXIV:4 (Fall 1980), pp. 432–52.

3. Geoffrey Wolff, *Black Sun: The Brief Transit and Violent Eclipse of Harry Crosby* (New York: Random House, 1976), p. 261.

4. *Letters of Hart Crane and His Family*, ed. Thomas S. W. Lewis (New York and London: Columbia University Press, 1974), pp. 588–9. Crane was reminded constantly of his rivalry by friends and family, as in this letter from his grandmother: "Cleveland is preparing for a great reception for Myron T. Herrick and Lindenburgh [sic], but this is no special news. They are doing it everywhere. He is famous the world over, these days, but there are others, who, though in a more quiet way, may be as much appreciated along another line in the literary world. Oh my dear boy I would like to express myself and interest in you, but I feel sure you understand me at least" (pp. 586–7).

5. *The Papers of Wilbur and Orville Wright*, ed. Marvin W. MacFarland (New York: McGraw-Hill, 1953), I, 6.

6. *Hart Crane and Yvor Winters: Their Literary Correspondence*, ed. Thomas Parkinson (Berkeley: University of California Press, 1978), p. 89.

7. *The Letters of Hart Crane*, ed. Brom Weber (Berkeley: University of California Press, 1952), p. 347.

8. Lawrence Dembo, "Hart Crane's 'Verticalist' Poem," *American Literature*, XL:1 (March 1968), pp. 77–80.

9. Louise Kertesz, *The Poetic Vision of Muriel Rukeyser* (Baton Rouge: Louisiana State University Press, 1980), pp. 24–5. Commenting, for example, on Crane's lines, "Dream cancels dream in this realm of fact / From which we wake into the dream of act; / Seeing himself an atom in a shroud – / Man hears himself an engine in a cloud!", Kertesz writes, "'Cape Hatteras' is filled with images of technology, for here the poet is at the core of his theme: the birth of the glorious future of America out of 'this new realm of fact.' At this exciting moment in history, 'man hears himself an engine in a cloud!'" Compare this to R. W. B. Lewis's commonsensical reading of the same passage: "In a culture worshipful primarily of scientific fact, the old dreams of human dignity and noble accomplishment are repudiated, and man sees himself as a figure of absolute insignificance, destined only for the grave; by recompense, as a revenge against reality, man has recourse to sheer blind action and imagines himself as a pure machine hurtling through space." *The Poetry of Hart Crane: A Critical Study* (Princeton: Princeton University Press, 1967), pp. 327–8.

10. I use the text in *The Collected Poems of Muriel Rukeyser* (New York: McGraw-Hill, 1978), pp. 21, 38.

11. M. L. Rosenthal, "Muriel Rukeyser: The Longer Poems," *New Directions 14* (New York: New Directions, 1953), p. 205.

12. *The English Auden*, ed. Edward Mendelson (New York: Random House, 1977), p. 81.

13. Gorham B. Munson, *Style and Form in American Prose* (New York: Doubleday, Doran & Co., 1929), p. 304.

14. Barbara Foley, "The Treatment of Time in *The Big Money*: An Examination of Ideology and Literary Form," *Modern Fiction Studies*, 26:3 (Autumn 1980), pp. 460–1.

15. John William Ward, "Lindbergh, Dos Passos and History," *The Carleton Miscellany*, 6:3 (Summer 1965), p. 37. That Dos Passos was interested in Lindbergh's career can be seen in his play *Airways, Inc.* (New York: Macaulay, 1928), about a pilot obviously modeled on Lindbergh.

16. John Williams Andrews, *Prelude to 'Icaros'* (New York: Farrar and Rinehart, 1936), p. 129.

17. Selden Rodman, *The Airmen: A Poem in Four Parts* (New York: Random House, 1941), p. 89.

18. Jacques Ellul, *The Technological Society*, tr. John Wilkinson (New York: Alfred A. Knopf, 1964), p. 143.

8. "THE NEAREST PARADISE": FORMS OF FLIGHT IN THE 1930s

1. F. T. Marinetti, "The Aeropainting of the Italian Future," tr. Samuel Putnam, *New Review*, I (Winter 1931–2), pp. 295–7.

2. Frank Ernest Hill, *Stone Dust* (New York: Longmans, Green, 1928), p. 21.

3. Bruce Gould, *Sky Larking: The Romantic Adventures of Flying* (New York: Liveright, 1929), pp. 126–7.

4. Alexander Key, *The Red Eagle: Being the Adventurous Tale of Two Young Fliers* (New York: The Wise-Parslow Co., 1930), p. 11.

5. *Collected Poems of C. Day Lewis* (London: Jonathan Cape with The Hogarth Press, 1954), p. 142.

6. *Vertical: A Yearbook for Romantic–Mystic Ascensions*, ed. Eugene Jolas (New York: The Gotham Bookmart Press, 1941), pp. 94–5. Wyndham Lewis was one English writer responsive to this association. He praised the technological dynamism of fascism in his journalism collected in *Hitler* (1931), and the following year remarked on Saint-Exupéry's novel *Night Flight*: "A consciousness on the part of these here written about, that on account of the intensity of their experience, they are marked off from other men, is stressed throughout. If all airman felt like this ... we should speedily have an Aristocracy of the Air." *Filibusters in Barbary* (New York: McBride, 1932). As a pilot-superman, Lewis asserted, Saint-Exupéry produced an "air-epic" appropriate to a new age of wonders.

7. Guido Mattioli, *Mussolini Aviator, And His Work for Aviation* (Rome: L'Aviazione, 1935), p. 4.

8. Antoine de Saint-Exupéry, *A Sense of Life*, tr. Adrienne Foulke (New York: Funk & Wagnalls, 1965), pp. 21–2.

9. Cited in Curtis Cate, *Antoine de Saint-Exupéry* (New York: Putnam, 1970), p. 97.

10. Antoine de Saint-Exupéry, *Southern Mail*, tr. Curtis Cate (London: Penguin Books, 1976), pp. 23–4.

11. Antoine de Saint-Exupéry, *Night Flight*, tr. Stuart Gilbert (New York: New American Library, n.d.), p. 112.

12. Antoine de Saint-Exupéry, *Wind, Sand and Stars*, tr. Lewis Galantière (New York: Reynal & Hitchcock, 1939), p. 240.

13. Cited in *The New York Times Magazine*, 8 May 1977, p. 17.

14. Marianne Moore, *Selected Poems* (London: Faber and Faber, 1935), p. 38.

15. Robinson Jeffers, *Roan Stallion, Tamar, and Other Poems* (New York: The Modern Library, 1935), p. 294. A good contemporary comparison would be Robert Penn Warren's poem, "Sunset Scrupulously Observed," *Rumor Verified: Poems 1979–1980* (New York: Random House, 1981), p. 31.

16. *The Selected Poetry of Robinson Jeffers* (New York: Random House, 1938), p. 611.

17. Allen Tate, *Collected Poems 1919–1976* (New York: Farrar, Straus & Giroux, 1977), pp. 29, 107.

18. Archibald MacLeish, *A Time to Speak* (Boston: Houghton Mifflin Co., 1941), p. 105. MacLeish's radio play *Air Raid* (New York: Harcourt, Brace and Co., 1938), had depicted the aerial bombardment of a typical small town. The unwillingness of his fellow intellectuals to protest, as he did, fascist depredations in Spain, Czechoslovakia, Poland, and elsewhere prompted him to write the essay.

19. Cited in Radcliffe Squires, *Allen Tate: A Literary Biography* (New York: Pegasus/Bobbs-Merrill, 1971), p. 162.

9. THE POETRY OF FIREBOMBING

1. I use the text in James Dickey, *Poems 1957–1967* (Middletown, Conn.: Wesleyan University Press, 1967), pp. 181–8.

2. James Dickey, *Self-Interviews* (New York: Doubleday, 1970), p. 138.

3. Robert Bly, "The Collapse of James Dickey," *The Sixties*, No. 9 (Spring 1967), p. 77; David Ignatow, "The Permanent Hell," *The Nation*, 202:25 (20 June 1966), p. 752; Richard Howard, *Alone With America* (New York: Atheneum, 1969), p. 93; Joyce Carol Oates, *New Heaven, New Earth* (New York: Vanguard, 1974), p. 228; Galway Kinnell, "Poetry, Personality, and Death," *A Field Guide to Contemporary Poetry and Poetics*, ed. Stuart Friebert and David Young (New York: Longmans, 1980), p. 207.

4. *Self-Interviews*, p. 137.

5. T. S. Eliot, *Collected Poems 1909–1962* (New York: Harcourt, Brace & World, 1963), pp. 207, 206.

6. *Reveille: War Poems by Members of Our Armed Forces*, ed. Daniel Henderson, John Kieran, and Grantland Rice (New York: A. S. Barnes and Co., 1943), p. 48.

7. James Dickey, *Sorties* (New York: Doubleday, 1971), p. 88.

8. *Writers at Work: The Paris Review Interviews*, Fifth Series, ed. George Plimpton (New York: The Viking Press, 1981), p. 210.

9. *Self-Interviews*, p. 32.

10. *Self-Interviews*, p. 62.

11. Richard Eberhart, *Collected Poems 1930–1976* (New York: Oxford University Press, 1976), p. 90. The following poem, "An Airman Considers His Power," expresses sentiments more similar to Dickey's Firebomber: "... I know in the bomb's release / The truth I felt of the will, / From destruction is peace, / In peace the will to kill." (p. 91).

12. J. M. Spaight, *Bombing Vindicated* (London: Geoffrey Bles, 1944), p. 7. A short list of publications with the same message would include William Bradford Huie, *The Fight for Air Power* (New York: L. B. Fischer, 1942); V. E. R. Blunt, *The Use of Air Power* (Harrisburg: Military Service Publishing Co., 1943); Allan A. Michie, *Keep the Peace Through Air Power* (New York: Henry Holt and Co., 1944); Eugene E. Wilson, *Air Power for Peace* (New York:

McGraw-Hill, 1945); Louis A. Sigaud, *Air Power and Unification* (Harrisburg: Military Service Publishing Co., 1949); Alexander P. de Seversky, *Air Power: Key to Survival* (New York: Simon and Schuster, 1950); Asher Lee, *Air Power* (London: Gerald Duckworth and Co., 1955); and Eugene M. Emme, *The Impact of Air Power* (New York: Van Nostrand, 1959).

13. Alexander P. de Seversky, *Victory Through Air Power* (New York: Simon and Schuster, 1942), p. 6.

14. Louis MacNeice, *The Collected Poems of Louis MacNeice*, ed. E. R. Dodds (New York: Oxford University Press, 1967), p. 196.

15. *The Collected Poems of Dylan Thomas* (New York: New Directions, 1957), pp. 146, 112. See also his poem "Deaths and Entrances."

16. Stephen Spender, *Collected Poems 1928–1953* (New York: Random House, 1955), pp. 117–8.

17. Spender, *Collected Poems*, pp. 41, 3.

18. Stephen Spender, *World Within World* (New York: Harcourt, Brace, and Co., 1951), p. 257. "My own private fantasy was of emerging out of a cellar after the first air raid on London onto a scene which consisted entirely of ruins," Spender recalls of his anxieties during the 1930s in *The Thirties and After* (New York: Random House, 1978), p. 11.

19. Rex Warner, *The Aerodrome* (London: John Lane/The Bodley Head, 1941), pp. 206–7.

20. John Hersey, *The War Lover* (New York: Alfred A. Knopf, 1959), p. 169.

21. Hermann Hagedorn, *The Bomb that fell on America* (Santa Barbara: Pacific Coast Publishing Co., 1946), p. 9.

22. *The Collected Poems of Howard Nemerov* (Chicago: University of Chicago Press, 1977), p. 384.

10. SPACEFLIGHT: THREE VERSIONS OF MANIFEST DESTINY

1. *The Poetry of Robert Frost*, ed. Edward Connery Lathem (New York: Holt, Rinehart and Winston, 1969), pp. 434–5.

2. *Interviews with Robert Frost*, ed. Edward Connery Lathem (New York: Holt, Rinehart and Winston, 1974), p. 231.

3. Reginald Cook, *Robert Frost: A Living Voice* (Amherst: University of Massachusetts Press, 1974), p. 131.

4. Joseph J. Corn, *The Winged Gospel: America's Romance with Aviation* (New York: Oxford University Press, 1983), p. 67. According to Angela Elliott, another expression of postwar disillusionment with the Wright brothers' legacy is Canto 74 of Ezra Pound's *Pisan Cantos* (1948), which links the moment "When Lucifer fell in N. Carolina" to the perversions of fascist ideology. As Hart Crane did in "Cape Hatteras," according to Elliott, Pound identifies Walt Whitman's poetry as the spiritual alternative to the flying machine. See "Pound's Lucifer: A Study in the Imagery of Flight and Light," *Paideuma*, 12:2,3 (Fall/Winter 1983), pp. 237–66.

5. Louis Mertins, *Robert Frost: Life and Talks-Walking* (Norman: University of Oklahoma Press, 1965), pp. 373, 195.

6. Cited in Harry Combs, *Kill Devil Hill: Discovering the Secret of the Wright Brothers* (Boston: Houghton Mifflin, 1979), p. 299.

7. From his essay, "On Poetry in General" in *Lectures on the English Poets. The Collected Works of William Hazlitt*, ed. A. R. Waller and Arnold Glover (London: J. M. Dent & Co., 1902), V, 9.

8. Frederick Jackson Turner, *The Frontier in American History* (New York: Henry Holt and Co., 1920), pp. 22, 37.

9. *Interviews with Robert Frost*, p. 266.

10. Cited in Milton Lehman, *This High Man: The Life of Robert H. Goddard* (New York: Farrar, Straus and Co., 1963), p. 23.

11. Wernher von Braun, "Prospective Space Development," *Astronautics and Aeronautics*, 10:4 (April 1972), p. 27.

12. Thomas Pynchon, *Gravity's Rainbow* (New York: Viking Press, 1973), p. 159.

13. See the photo portfolio section of Ernest Klee and Otto Mark, *The Birth of the Missile* (London: George G. Harrap & Co., 1965). I owe my knowledge of this fact to Thomas Moore's essay, "A Decade of *Gravity's Rainbow*, the Incredible Moving Film," *Michigan Quarterly Review*, XXII:1 (Winter 1983), pp. 78–94.

14. *Works of Jules Verne*, ed. Charles F. Horne (New York: Vincent Parke and Co., 1911), XIV, 152.

15. See the discussion of Pynchon's use of the Zero motif in Douglas Fowler, *A Reader's Guide to* Gravity's Rainbow (Ann Arbor: Ardis, 1980), pp. 50–2.

16. Robert A. Heinlein, *The Man Who Sold the Moon* (Chicago: Shasta Publishers, 1950), p. 273.

17. H. Bruce Franklin, *Robert A. Heinlein: America as Science Fiction* (New York: Oxford University Press, 1980), p. 61.

11. THE MOON LANDING AND MODERN LITERATURE

1. Allen Ginsberg, *The Fall of America* (San Francisco: City Lights, 1972), p. 127.

2. Babette Deutsch, "The Flight," *The Spirit of St. Louis*, ed. Charles Vale (New York: George H. Doran, 1927), p. 85.

3. Babette Deutsch, "To the Moon, 1969," *Inside Outer Space: New Poems of the Space Age*, ed. Robert Vas Dias (New York: Doubleday Anchor, 1970), pp. 61–2.

4. Hulme's poems are reprinted in Ezra Pound, *Personae* (New York: New Directions, n.d.), p. 252; E. E. Cummings, *Poems 1923–1954* (New York: Harcourt, Brace & World, 1954), p. 58; T. S. Eliot, *Collected Poems 1909–1962* (New York: Harcourt, Brace & World, 1963), p. 17.

5. James Dickey, *Self-Interviews* (New York: Doubleday, 1970), p. 67. The image of a "ruined stone in the sky" appears in Dickey's poem "Near Darien."

6. James Dickey, "A Poet Witnesses a Bold Mission," *Life*, 65:18 (1 November 1968), p. 26.

7. Michael Collins, *Carrying the Fire: An Astronaut's Journey* (New York: Farrar, Straus and Giroux, 1974), pp. 53–4.

8. James Dickey, *The Eye-Beaters, Blood, Victory, Madness, Buckhead and Mercy* (New York: Doubleday, 1970), p. 26.

9. *First on the Moon: A Voyage with Neil Armstrong, Michael Collins, Edwin E. Aldrin, Jr.*, written with Gene Farmer and Dora Jean Hamblin (Boston: Little, Brown, 1970), p. 266.

10. Robert Lowell, *History* (New York: Farrar, Straus and Giroux, 1973), p. 185.

11. *The Poems of Thomas Gray, William Collins, Oliver Goldsmith*, ed. Roger Lonsdale (London: Longmans, 1969), p. 303.

12. *The Works of H. G. Wells*, Atlantic Edition (London: T. Fisher Unwin, 1925), VI, 38, 100.

13. Oriana Fallaci, *If the Sun Dies*, tr. Pamela Swinglehurst (New York: Atheneum, 1968), pp. 230–1.

14. Cited in Norman Mailer, *Of a Fire on the Moon* (Boston: Little, Brown, 1970), p. 77.

15. James Dickey, *Sorties* (New York: Doubleday, 1971), pp. 72–3.

16. *First on the Moon*, pp. 402–3.

17. In the one volume of poems published by an astronaut, Apollo 15's Alfred M. Worden, Mailer's comparison is repeated: "A spacewalk / Is like / Being let out / At night / For a swim / By Moby Dick." "Spacewalk," *Greetings from Endeavor* (Los Angeles: Nash Publishing Co., 1974), p. 51.

18. Saul Bellow, *Mr. Sammler's Planet* (New York: The Viking Press, 1970), p. 19.

19. John Jacob Clayton, *Saul Bellow: In Defense of Man*, 2nd Edition (Bloomington: Indiana University Press, 1979), p. 244.

12. CONCLUSION: SOME TEXTS OF THE 1970s

1. Stanley Kunitz, "My Surgeons," *The Poems of Stanley Kunitz 1928–1978* (Boston: Little, Brown, 1979), p. 153.

2. "A Letter from Lindbergh," *Life*, 67:1 (4 July 1969), p. 61.

3. Norman Mailer, *Why Are We in Vietnam* (New York: G. P. Putnam's Sons, 1967), p. 85.

4. Ted Hughes, *Crow* (London: Faber and Faber, 1970), pp. 23, 77.

5. Robert Bly, *Sleepers Joining Hands* (New York: Harper & Row, 1973), p. 18.

6. Kenneth Brower, *The Starship and the Canoe* (New York: Holt, Rinehart and Winston, 1978), p. 51.

7. Robert Penn Warren, *Audubon: A Vision* (New York: Random House, 1970), p. 19.

8. C. G. Jung, "Flying Saucers: A Modern Myth of Things Seen in the Sky," *Collected Works of C. G. Jung*, ed. Herbert Read, Michael Fordham, and Gerhard Adler (New York: The Bollingen Foundation, 1964), 10, pp. 307–433.

9. Dick Allen, *Regions with No Proper Names* (New York: St. Martin's Press, 1975), p. 9.

10. Philip Levine, *One for the Rose* (New York: Atheneum, 1981), p. 3.

11. Tom Wolfe, *The Right Stuff* (New York: Farrar, Straus and Giroux, 1979), p. 387.

12. J. G. Ballard, *The Unlimited Dream Company* (New York: Holt, Rinehart and Winston, 1979), p. 8.

13. Freeman Dyson, *Disturbing the Universe* (New York: Harper & Row, 1979), p. 116.

Supplementary Bibliography

I. BIBLIOGRAPHIES

Barron, Neil. *Anatomy of Wonder: Science Fiction*. New York: Bowker, 1976. An annotated list of more than a thousand works of science fiction from the Renaissance to the present, including secondary materials.

Hallion, Richard P. "A Source Guide to the History of Aeronautics and Astronautics," *American Studies International*, XX:3 (Spring 1982), 3–50. A comprehensive guide to works on the history of the flying machine.

II. ANTHOLOGIES

Anon. *The Romance of Ballooning*. New York: The Viking Press, 1971. A plentifully illustrated documentary history of the balloon in fact and fiction, with a good bibliography.

Collison, Thomas. *This Winged World: An Anthology of Aviation Fiction*. New York: Coward-McCann, 1943. The best of a popular genre, it represents all responses to the airplane.

De la Bère, Rupert. *Icarus: An Anthology of the Poetry of Flight*. London: Macmillan, 1938.

Duke, Neville and Edward Lanchbery. *The Saga of Flight*. New York: The John Day Co., 1961. An invaluable assemblage of non-fiction accounts of flight by inventors, pilots, and reporters.

Gilbert, James. *Skywriting: An Aviation Anthology*. New York: St. Martin's Press, 1978. English fiction on the subject is well represented.

Goldstein, Laurence. "The Moon Landing and Its Aftermath," *Michigan Quarterly Review*, XVIII:2 (Spring 1979). A special issue exploring the significance of the moon landing of 1969. Includes fiction and poetry.

Hallion, Richard P. and Tom D. Crouch. *Apollo: Ten Years Since Tranquility Base*. Washington D.C.: National Air and Space Museum, 1979.

Knowles, Susanne. *Chorus: An Anthology of Bird Poems*. New York: Funk & Wagnalls, 1969. Especially good for recent poems.

Massingham, H. J. *Poems about Birds: From the Middle Ages to the Present Day*. New York: E. P. Dutton, 1923.

Miller, Francis Trevelyan. *The World in the Air: The Story of Flying in Pictures*. Two volumes. New York: G. P. Putnam's Sons, 1930. Indispensable survey of the iconography of flight, from ancient times to the triumphs of Lindbergh and Byrd. Includes a multitude of rare items.

Murray, Stella Wolfe. *The Poetry of Flight*. London: Heath, Cranton, 1925.

Roberts, Joseph B. and Paul L. Briand. *The Sound of Wings: Readings for the Air Age*. New York: Henry Holt and Co., 1957. A valuable collection of fiction and poetry from the Renaissance to the Korean War.

Rodman, Selden. *The Poetry of Flight*. New York: Duell, Sloan and Pearce, 1941.

Skinner, Richard M. and William Leavitt. *Speaking of Space: The Best from Space Digest*. Boston: Little, Brown, 1962. Splendid survey of spacemindedness before the Apollo project.

Wollheim, Donald A. *Men on the Moon*. New York: Ace Publishing, 1969. Collects short fiction on the subject, as well as responses by 28 scifi authors to the moon landing.

III. NON-FICTION PROSE

Ackerman, Diane. *On Extended Wings*. New York: Atheneum, 1985. A fine poet's first-person account of learning to fly, with meditations throughout on the relation of flight to the human imagination.

Adams, Hazard. *Philosophy of the Literary Symbolic*. Gainesville: Florida State University Press, 1983. A historical survey of the theory of symbols from Kant to Cassirer, Langer, Frye, and Eliade.

Armstrong, Edward A. *The Life and Lore of the Bird: In Nature, Art, Myth, and Literature*. New York: Crown Publishers, 1975.

Bachelard, Gaston. *The Poetics of Space*. New York: The Orion Press, 1964. A phenomenological account of "immensity" with significant implications for the literature of flight.

Baker, David. *The Rocket: The History and Development of Rocket and Missile Technology*. New York: Crown Publishers, 1979. Supplements and updates von Braun and Ordway below.

Barthes, Roland. *Mythologies*. New York: Hill and Wang, 1972. See especially the essay on "The Jet-Man."

Becker, Beril. *Dreams and Realities of the Conquest of the Skies*. New York: Atheneum, 1967. Derivative but useful history of aviation.

Bercovitch, Sacvan. *The American Jeremiad*. Madison: University of Wisconsin Press, 1978. Describes the models for modernist typology and ecclesiastical history.

Berget, Alphonse. *The Conquest of the Air*. London: William Heinemann, 1911. The apocalyptic rhetoric of this book excited a whole generation of readers.

Bilstein, Roger. *Flight in America 1900–1983: From the Wright Brothers to the Astronauts*. Baltimore: The Johns Hopkins University Press, 1984. A well-researched chronicle that surveys in familiar terms the landmark events and significant personalities of aviation history.

Bond, Douglas D. *The Love and Fear of Flying*. New York: International Universities Press, 1952. A psychological study of flight.

Burroughs, John. *Birds and Poets*. Boston: Houghton Mifflin, 1894.

Campbell, Joseph. *The Flight of the Wild Gander: Explorations in the Mythological Dimension*. South Bend: Regnery/Gateway, 1979. The chapters on avian myths survey the archaic fantasy of ascent.

Carnochan, W. B. *Confinement and Flight: An Essay on English Literature of the Eighteenth Century.* Berkeley and Los Angeles: University of California Press, 1977. "The dialectic of limit and limitlessness" is studied in sample works like *Rasselas* and *Peter Wilkins*.

Clough, Rosa Trillo. *Futurism: The Story of a Modern Art Movement.* New York: The Greenwood Press, 1969.

Combs, Harry. *Kill Devil Hill: Discovering the Secret of the Wright Brothers.* Boston: Houghton Mifflin, 1978. No recent history approaches the Genesis myth with such enthusiasm and piety. Of special interest is Neil Armstrong's introduction celebrating the Wrights.

Coutts-Smith, Kenneth. *The Dream of Icarus.* New York: George Braziller, 1970. Cultural history of the postwar period with principal reference to the impact of machinery on the arts.

Dillon, Richard Taylor. *The Sound of Wings: Aviation in Twentieth-Century Literature.* Ph.D. dissertation, University of California, Berkeley, 1970. The chapters on Faulkner's aviation fiction persuasively document the influence of minor writers like Elliott White Springs and James Warner Bellah. A full if undiscriminating bibliography.

Edwards, Thomas P. *Imagination and Power: A Study of Poetry on Public Themes.* New York: Oxford University Press, 1971. A judicious discussion of the value and limitations of poetry that responds to historical events and personalities.

Eissler, K. R. *Leonardo da Vinci: Psychoanalytical Notes on the Enigma.* New York: International Universities Press, 1961. A study with significant implications beyond its subject.

Engle, Paul. "Poetry in a Machine Age," *The English Journal*, XXVI:6 (June 1937), 429–39.

Faulkner, William. "Folklore of the Air," *The American Mercury*, XXVI (November 1935), 370–2. This review of Jimmy Collins's *Test Pilot* calls for an innovative literature to describe "this whole new business of speed."

Ferkiss, Victor C. *Technological Man: The Myth and the Reality.* New York: George Braziller, 1969. Classic study of human alternatives in the age of "absolute technology." Includes a comprehensive bibliography.

Fraser, John. *America and the Patterns of Chivalry.* Cambridge: Cambridge University Press, 1982. The chapters on the fantasy life of England and America preceding The Great War illuminate the mythology of the Knights of the Air.

Frye, Northrop. *The Secular Scripture: A Study of the Structure of Romance.* Cambridge, Mass.: Harvard University Press, 1976.

———. *Spiritus Mundi: Essays on Literature, Myth, and Society.* Bloomington: Indiana University Press, 1976. These two books summarize and refine Frye's seminal theories relating literary modes and texts to social and intellectual structures.

Garnett, David. *A Rabbit in the Air.* London: Chatto and Windus, 1932. One of the best in the genre of personal accounts of flight.

Gibbs-Smith, C. H. *Flight Through the Ages.* New York: Thomas Y. Crowell, 1974. An authoritative survey by the dean of aviation historians.

Giedion, Sigfried. *Mechanization Takes Command.* New York: Oxford University Press, 1948. An influential study of the impact of industrial forms on modern art and society.

Gilman, Charlotte Perkins. "When We Fly," *Harper's*, LI (9 November 1907), 1664. An apocalyptic celebration of aerial man, who "cannot think of himself further as a worm of the dust, but ... as butterfly psyche, the risen soul."

Grosser, Morton. *Gossamer Odyssey: The Triumph of Human-Powered Flight*. Boston: Houghton Mifflin, 1981. The realization of Leonardo da Vinci's fantasy is one of the most fascinating stories of recent aviation.

Ginestier, Paul. *The Poet and the Machine*. Chapel Hill: The University of North Carolina Press, 1961. Contains almost nothing on the flying machine but usefully applies Bachelard's methods to modern (mainly French) texts.

Grant, Elliott Manfield. *French Poetry and Modern Industry, 1830–1870*. Cambridge, Mass.: Harvard University Press, 1927. The origins of *machinisme* are explored in a study that has implications far beyond its topic.

Haining, Peter. *The Compleat Birdman: An Illustrated History of Man-Powered Flight*. New York: St. Martin's Press, 1977. The text is unreliable, but the illustrations are worth consulting.

Harrison, Robert. *Aviation Lore in Faulkner*. Philadelphia and Amsterdam: John Benjamins, 1986. Surveys Faulkner's use of aviation material in his novels and stories.

Hastings, Max. *Bomber Command*. New York: The Dial Press, 1979. In this history of the English unit during World War II the author surveys as well the controversy among intellectuals about the practice of bombardment.

Hearne, P. *Airships in Peace*. London: John Lane/The Bodley Head, 1908. Like Wells's *The War in the Air*, published the same year, this book accurately foresees the full range of meanings for the flying machine.

Hewison, Robert. *Under Siege: Literary Life in London 1939–1945*. New York: Oxford University Press, 1977. The psychological impact of the Nazi bombings is skillfully traced in the literature, including letters and diaries of English authors.

Hillary, Richard. *The Last Enemy*. London: Macmillan, 1942. A memoir of the joy and peril of flight that describes a wounded pilot's difficult convalescence.

Hoffmann, Frederick J. *The Twenties*. Rev. Ed., New York: The Free Press, 1965. Especially good on the desire to create a Machine Age literature.

Horne, E. H. *The Significance of Air War*. London and Edinburgh: Marshall, Morgan and Scott, 1939. This symptomatic and eccentric pamphlet argues that aerial bombardment is the sign of the Second Advent promised in the Book of Revelation.

Hynes, Samuel. *The Auden Generation*. New York: Oxford University Press, 1976. Surveys a group of writers who brooded and wrote constantly about the flying machine.

Jablonski, Edward. *The Knighted Skies: A Pictorial History of World War I in the Air*. New York: G. P. Putnam's Sons, 1964. A well-researched history of the aerial warfare, with special attention to the chivalric language and rituals of the fliers.

Jameson, Fredric. *The Political Unconscious: Narrative as a Socially Symbolic Act*. Ithaca: Cornell University Press, 1981. A model study of how political content can be recovered from seemingly unpolitical events, fantasies, and texts.

Josephy [Jr.], Alvin M. *The American Heritage History of Flight*. New York: American Heritage Publishing Co., 1962. Invaluable compendium of materials relating to the history of flight, in addition to an authoritative chronicle.

Kasson, John F. *Civilizing the Machine: Technology and Republican Values in America 1776–1900.* New York: Grossman, 1976. Superb background study of the ambivalent feelings about technology in the century preceding the invention of the flying machine.

Kenner, Hugh. *A Homemade World: The American Modernist Writers.* New York: Alfred A. Knopf, 1975. Like Sypher below, Kenner emphasizes the valorization of technics in the practice of modern literature.

Kermode, Frank. *Romantic Image.* London: Routledge & Kegan Paul, 1957.

Kern, Stephen. *The Culture of Time and Space, 1880–1918.* Cambridge, Mass.: Harvard University Press, 1983. In this important, synchronic study the significant change in European perceptions of proximity, and danger, is attributed in large part to technological inventions like the airplane.

Kernan, Alvin B. *The Imaginary Library: An Essay on Literature and Society.* Princeton: Princeton University Press, 1982. See especially the chapter on Mailer's *Of a Fire on the Moon.*

Ketterer, David. *New Worlds for Old: The Apocalyptic Imagination, Science Fiction, and American Literature.* Bloomington: Indiana University Press, 1974. A superb study relevant in essential ways to the myth of the flying machine.

Lauretis, Teresa de, Andreas Huyssen, and Kathleen Woodward. *The Technological Imagination: Theories and Fictions.* Madison: Coda Press, 1980. Excellent essays illustrating the most current approaches to the subject.

McDougall, Walter A. . . . *the Heavens and the Earth: A Political History of the Space Age.* New York: Basic Books, 1985. A comprehensive account of policymaking in the United States and the Soviet Union related to spaceflight.

Marx, Leo. *The Machine in the Garden: Technology and the Pastoral Ideal in America.* New York: Oxford University Press, 1964. Classic study of the responses of American writers to the machine.

Maxim, Hiram. *Artificial and Natural Flight.* London: Whitaker and Co., 1908. Neglected early work on the ontology of the manmade flying machine.

May, Rollo. *Symbolism in Religion and Literature.* New York: George Braziller, 1960. Essays by different hands explore a subject of obvious relevance to the airplane.

McPhee, John. *The Deltoid Pumpkin Seed.* New York: Farrar, Straus & Giroux, 1973. Reports on one man's attempt to revive the airship as a mode of transportation suitable to modern needs.

Michelet, Jules. *The Bird.* London: Thomas Nelson & Sons, 1876. No work has ever made greater claims for the spirituality of the bird and the ecstasy of ascent.

Mumford, Lewis. The Myth of the Machine. Volume I, *Technics and Human Development* (1967). Volume II, *The Pentagon of Power* (1970). New York: Harcourt Brace Jovanovich. Both magisterial and intensely polemical, this history of technology synthesizes information from a variety of disciplines. Though it gives little attention to aerial technology, it provides a capacious context for discussion of the Air Age.

Murchie Guy. *Song of the Sky.* Boston: Houghton Mifflin, 1954. Practical information about flying is intermixed with lyrical evocations of the heavens.

Nicolson, Marjorie Hope. *Voyages to the Moon.* New York: Macmillan, 1960.

The classic study of its subject and the culmination of many studies by the same author on the esthetics of the sublime.

O'Neill, Gerard K. *The High Frontier: Human Colonies in Space.* New York: Simon and Schuster, 1977. Enormously influential argument for the feasibility of settlement in space.

Rabkin, Eric S. *The Fantastic in Literature.* Princeton: Princeton University Press, 1976. Provides a good background for understanding science fiction and the literature of aviation in general.

Rowland, Beryl. *Birds with Human Souls: A Guide to Bird Symbolism.* Knoxville: University of Tennessee Press, 1978. Well-researched anatomy with implications for literary perspectives on the airplane.

Ruzic, Neil P. *Where the Winds Sleep: Man's Future on the Moon.* New York: Doubleday, 1970. Like Dr. Lal's manuscript in *Mr. Sammler's Planet*, this blueprint for settlement on the high frontier owes much to science fiction of the previous decades.

Salkeld, Robert. *War and Space.* Englewood Cliffs, N.J.: Prentice-Hall 1970. A realistic discussion of what the Mercury and Apollo flights portend in the subsequent decades.

Schoek, Helmut. *Envy: A Theory of Social Behavior.* New York: Harcourt, Brace and World, 1966.

Shroder, Maurice Z. *Icarus: The Image of the Artist in French Romanticism.* Cambridge, Mass.: Harvard University Press, 1961. Examines the imagery of flight in nineteenth-century literature.

Spengler, Oswald. *Man and Technics.* New York: Alfred A. Knopf, 1932. The religion of machinery is caustically surveyed as a pathology of the modern period.

Steinbeck, John. *Bombs Away: The Story of a Bomber Team.* New York: The Viking Press, 1942. Replaces the myth of the heroic pilot with a description of teamwork.

Stovel, Nora Foster. "The Aerial View of Modern Britain," *Ariel*, 15:3 (July 1984). Surveys the use of aerial perspective, for social satire especially, in works by Auden, Waugh, and Drabble.

Sussman, Herbert L. *Victorians and the Machine: The Literary Response to Technology.* Cambridge, Mass.: Harvard University Press, 1968.

Sypher, Wylie. *Literature and Technology: The Alien Vision.* New York: Random House, 1968. Studies the interaction between art, technology, and science in the modern period.

Von Braun, Wernher, and Frederick I. Ordway III. *History of Rocketry and Space Travel.* New York: Thomas Y. Crowell, 1966.

Weber, Ronald. *Seeing Earth: Literary Responses to Space Exploration.* Athens, Ohio: Ohio University Press/Swallow Press, 1985. A useful survey of poetry, fiction, and non-fiction produced in the wake of Sputnik and the Apollo missions. Especially good on the astronauts' memoirs.

Wecter, Dixon. *The Hero in America: A Chronicle of Hero-Worship.* 1941; rpt. Ann Arbor: University of Michigan Press, 1963. A useful discussion for understanding the idolatry of the Wright brothers and Lindbergh in particular.

West, Thomas Reed. *Flesh of Steel: Literature of the Machine in American Culture.* Vanderbilt University Press, 1967. Recreates the debate over the place of the machine in American life, with useful attention to the Jeffersonian stance in modern letters.

IV. FICTION

Barth, John. *Chimera*. New York: Random House, 1972. The "Bellerophoniad" is a profound meditation on myths of flight and heroism.

Bates, H. E. *The Purple Plain*. Boston: Little, Brown, 1947.

Berger, John. *G*. New York: The Viking Press, 1972. The first flight over the Alps, by Georges Chavez, and Chavez's death, are important events.

Cozzens, James Gould. *Guard of Honor*. New York: Harcourt, Brace, 1948.

Davenport, Guy. *Tatlin: Six Stories*. New York: Charles Scribner's Sons, 1974. The title story, especially, is interesting for its recreation of Russian futurism and fascination with the airplane.

Disch, Thomas M. *On Wings of Song*. New York; St. Martin's Press, 1979.

Faulkner, William. *A Fable*. New York: Random House, 1954.

———. *Collected Stories*. New York: Random House, 1950. See especially "Ad Astra," "All the Dead Pilots," and "Turnabout."

———. *Pylon*. New York: Random House, 1935.

Findley, Timothy. *Famous Last Words*. New York: Delacorte Press, 1981. A fiction about aestheticism and fascism in which Lindbergh makes a significant appearance.

Gangemi, Kenneth. *The Interceptor Pilot*. London and Boston: Marion Boyars, 1980. A novel told in the form of a screenplay about an American combat pilot who defects to Russia in order to become a fighter pilot for North Vietnam.

Gann, Ernest K. *In the Company of Eagles*. New York: Simon and Schuster, 1966. About the air aces, real and imaginary, of World War I.

Heller, Joseph. *Catch-22*. New York: Simon and Schuster, 1961.

Hemingway, Ernest. *For Whom the Bell Tolls*. New York: Charles Scribner's Sons, 1942.

Jong, Erica. *Fear of Flying*. New York: New American Library, 1973. For a reading pertinent to this study, see Jane Chance Nitzsche, "Isadora Icarus: The Mythic Unity of Erica Jong's *Fear of Flying*," *Rice University Studies*, 64:1 (Winter 1978), 89–100.

Koch, Kenneth. *The Red Robins*. New York: Vintage, 1975. A nonsense fiction in the modernist manner that features a group of aviators traveling through Asia.

Lewis, Sinclair. *The Trail of the Hawk*. New York: Harper and Brothers, 1915.

Malraux, André. *Man's Hope*. New York: Random House, 1938.

Michener, James A. *The Bridges at Toko-Ri*. New York: Random House, 1953.

Moorcock, Michael. *The Warlord of the Air*. New York: Ace Books, 1971. A futurist fantasy concerning airships in the spirit of Wells.

Phillips, Jayne Anne. *Machine Dreams*. New York: Dutton/Lawrence, 1984. Events in the lives of many characters are interwoven with historical events like the moon landing and the air war in Vietnam.

Pratt, John Clark. *The Laotian Fragments*. New York: The Viking Press, 1974. Experimental novel about Vietnam documents, by means of intelligence summaries, diary entries, news releases, etc. the life of Major William Blake, M.I.A.

Redman, Ben Ray. *Down in Flames*. New York: Paysan and Clarke, 1930.

Shepard, Jim. *Flights*. New York: Alfred A. Knopf, 1983. A boy's fascination with flight, culminating in his theft of an airplane, is powerfully described.

Shute, Nevil. *The Mysterious Aviator*. Boston: Houghton Mifflin, 1928.

———. *Pastoral*. New York: William Morrow, 1944.

Tucker, George. *A Voyage to the Moon*. 1827; rpt. Boston: The Gregg Press, 1978. This is the first American novel to imagine a moon landing.

Updike, John. *Rabbit Redux*. New York: Alfred A. Knopf, 1971. The novel begins on the day of the Apollo 11 moon launch, and among other things is a meditation on the relation of human nature and spaceflight.

Vonnegut, Kurt. *The Sirens of Titan*. 1959; rpt. New York: Delacorte Press, 1971.

———. *Slaughterhouse Five*. New York: Delacorte Press, 1969.

Wylie, Philip. *The Disappearance*. New York: Rinehart, 1951.

Zamyatin, Yevgeny. *We*. Translated by Mirra Ginsburg. New York: The Viking Press, 1972. This futurist novel of 1920 uses the airplane as a central icon of the new society.

V. POETRY

Ackerman, Diane. *Lady Lazarus*. New York: William Morrow, 1983. Contains many first-rate poems on Lindbergh and the Space Shuttle and on her personal experiences as a pilot.

———. *The Planets: A Cosmic Pastoral*. New York: William Morrow, 1976.

Apollinaire, Guillaume. *Alcools*. Translated by Anne Hyde Greet. Berkeley and Los Angeles: University of California Press, 1965.

Black, Macknight. *Machinery*. New York: Horace Liveright, 1929.

Cassity, Turner. "The Airship Boys in Africa," *Poetry*, CXVI:4 (July 1970), 211–55. A sequence of poems recreating the awe of Zeppelins during the Great War.

Ciardi, John. *Other Skies*. Boston: Little, Brown, 1947. A book based on Ciardi's flying experiences in World War II. "Death of a Bomber" is especially interesting for its application of elegiac conventions to an airplane.

Frederick, Brooks. *Rocket to the Moon*. Calcutta: Writer's Workshop, 1973. Perhaps the most impressive single volume to respond to the moon landing of 1969.

Hall, Donald. *The Alligator Bride: Poems New and Selected*. New York: Harper and Row, 1969. See especially "The Idea of Flying," "An Airstrip in Essex," "The Old Pilot," and "The Man in the Dead Machine."

Ingalls, Jeremy. *Tahl*. New York: Alfred A. Knopf, 1945. An epic poem featuring an aviator-hero.

Kinnell, Galway. *The Book of Nightmares*. Boston: Houghton Mifflin, 1971. Occult myths of flight are tested against images of aerial bombardment in Vietnam.

Jarrell, Randall. *The Complete Poems*. New York: Farrar, Straus and Giroux, 1969. See especially Part II.

Pudney, John. *Flight Above Cloud*. New York: Harper and Brothers, 1944.

Trowbridge, John Townsend. *Darius Green and His Flying Machine*. Boston: Houghton Mifflin, 1910.

Vas Dias, Robert. *Speech Acts and Happenings*. Indianapolis: Bobbs-Merrill, 1972.

VI. DRAMA

Auden, W. H. and Christopher Isherwood. *The Ascent of F6*. London: Faber and Faber, 1937. Mountain climbing as an expression of the yearning for elevation above the underpeople. See Freeman Dyson's *Disturbing the Universe* for a comprehensive discussion that makes the connection to flight explicit.

Blackmur, R. P. *Hero*. An unpublished four-act play in the Special Collections of Princeton University Library. A meditation on the career of Lindbergh, this play concerns the aviator Royal Frazer, who flies solo to South America and becomes a national legend. "You are a public idol," his father-in-law warns him, "Whatever you do – wrong or right – will be received as divine revelation."

Brecht, Bertolt. *Der Ozeanflug* (originally *Der Flug der Lindberghs*). Volume II of *Gesammelte Werke*. Frankfurt am Main: Suhrkamp Verlag, 1967. A radio play of 1928–9 celebrating the recent transatlantic flight.

————. *The Good Woman of Setzuan*. Reprinted in *Seven Plays*. Translated by Eric Bentley. New York: Grove Press, 1961. Contains a less enthusiastic view of aviation than the foregoing entry.

Hart, Moss. *Winged Victory*. New York: Random House, 1943.

Rice, Elmer. *Flight to the West*. New York: Coward-McCann, 1941.

Schevill, James. *Lovecraft's Follies*. Chicago: Swallow Press, 1971. Wernher von Braun has a featured role in this burlesque of the first moon landing.

Shaw, George Bernard. *Misalliance, The Dark Lady of the Sonnets, and Fanny's First Play*. New York: Brentano's, 1914. The descent of an airplane and its dynamic passengers into the glass house of an estate in Surrey in *Misalliance* is often cited as a useful metaphor for the inescapable intervention of the flying machine into the new century.

Sweeney, Tom. *Legend of Leonardo: A Drama in Verse*. New York: G. P. Putnam's Sons. 1936.

Index